Planning Reforms in the Soviet Union, 1962-1966

Planning Reforms in the Soviet Union 1962-1966

AN ANALYSIS OF RECENT TRENDS IN ECONOMIC ORGANIZATION AND MANAGEMENT

by Eugène Zaleski

translated by
Marie-Christine MacAndrew and G. Warren Nutter

THE UNIVERSITY OF NORTH CAROLINA PRESS
CHAPEL HILL

Manufactured in the United States of America
Library of Congress Catalog Card Number 67-17035
Printed by The Seeman Printery, Durham, N.C.

THIS BOOK WAS DIGITALLY PRINTED.

Foreword

The basic aim of the Office of Soviet Economic Research, a unit of the Thomas Jefferson Center at the University of Virginia, is to improve the climate of scholarship in the field of Soviet studies by encouraging scholarly interchange. We have chosen as our inaugural effort the translation and publication of Dr. Eugène Zaleski's works on Soviet planning. This book on recent reforms opens a series that we believe will greatly enrich knowledge of the Soviet planning system.

We are grateful to the American Oil Foundation, the Lilly Endowment, the Relm Foundation, and the Scaife Foundation for generous financial support in making this publication possible. We also owe a special debt to Marie-Christine MacAndrew, whose translating and editing skills have contributed so much to the finished product.

G. WARREN NUTTER
Director, Office of Soviet Economic Research

Charlottesville, Virginia
November, 1966

Preface

This report on recent planning reforms in the Soviet Union stems from a larger study of the evolution on the Soviet planning system. The earliest period was covered in *Planification de la croissance et fluctuations économiques en U.R.S.S.*, Volume I: 1918-1932, published in Paris in 1962 and since translated into English for publication by The University of North Carolina Press in the near future. A second volume on planning under Stalin (1933-52) will appear soon in French; and a third volume, on the most recent period, is in preparation. These, too, are scheduled for translation.

The purpose of this book is to present some preliminary findings on the most recent period while they are timely. The core of the book has emerged from a series of three articles: "Les réformes de la planification en U.R.S.S.," *Cahiers de l'Institut de Science Economique Appliquée*, Series G: Planned Economy (June, 1964), pp. 5-104; "Les tendances réformistes dans la planification soviétique," *Il Politico*, No. 4 (1965), pp. 657-89; and "Les réformes d'octobre 1965 et la gestion de l'entreprise en U.R.S.S.," *Cahiers de l'Institut de Science Economique Appliquée*, Series G: Planned Economy (May, 1966), pp. 133-78. The material in those articles has been thoroughly revised and brought up to date as of October, 1966.

The Soviet planning system is today in flux, and a final assessment of the new system must await its general adoption within the next year or so. But a survey of the reforms introduced over the last five years will make it easier to evaluate the final results as they unfold.

My work on recent planning reforms in the Soviet Union was begun while I was at the Thomas Jefferson Center of the University of Virginia during the first semester of 1963. I want to express my gratitude to Professors James M. Buchanan and G. Warren Nutter for their help in facilitating this work. I owe a special debt to Professor Nutter, who was kind enough to arrange for publication of this report and who, together with Marie-Christine MacAndrew, took on the difficult task of translating and editing a manuscript that grew out of the earlier articles. I should also like to thank Professors Henri Chambre, Bruno Leoni, and François Perroux for their advice and their permission to reproduce here many passages which first appeared in those articles.

This work would not have been possible without the constant encouragement that I received from the Centre National de la Recherche Scientifique. I am very grateful to Professor Jean Marchal for his interest and help in my early work on Eastern European economies and to Professor André Piatier for his assistance and advice in my studies of Soviet planning. I would also like to thank very much Professors Maurice Allais, Pierre Dieterlen, and Henri Guitton, who were kind enough to give me continuous support and encouragement.

EUGENE ZALESKI
Maître de Recherche
Centre National de la Recherche Scientifique

Paris, France
November, 1966

Contents

Charts

Planning Reforms in the Soviet Union, 1962-1966

CHAPTER 1. Permanent Features of Soviet Administrative Planning

Administrative planning of the Stalinist type presupposes that virtually all targets for economic units, as well as the means for attaining them, are determined by central authorities. Directives on production, distribution, and investment are transmitted from the center down to lower agencies, following a set hierarchy, by means of administrative dossiers. The plan consists simply in the aggregate of those current administrative dossiers.

Such a system has certain essential corollaries: control by the central Party apparatus and the police, frequent recourse to noneconomic coercion, a high level of investment spending, drafting of plans that are too taut and poorly coordinated, and disproportionate stimulation of growth in the various economic sectors.

THE VAIN SEARCH FOR COHERENT PLANS

The administrative system of planning cannot produce coherent plans for administrative, economic, and technical reasons. The plan is, as stated above, the aggregate of administrative dossiers. In principle, it is the collection of dossiers approved by appropriate agencies. In fact, there is never time to approve them all, so that many are put into operation while still preliminary. The result is a series of uncoordinated decisions.

In the administrative system of planning, the formal aspect—*i.e.*, approval by higher authorities—takes precedence over the real aspect, which is examination of details for coherence. Final approval is given by the supreme authority (the Party Secretariat or the Restricted Committee of the Council of Ministers) after summary examination of a limited number of indexes. Over-all coherence derives essentially from arbitrarily fixed growth rates. Tasks are then distributed to agencies upon which the government imposes both targets and means of attaining them.

The bargaining between those giving orders and those executing them that revolves around price in a market economy is, by definition, impossible in a planned economy of the administrative type, since prices are fixed in advance. Yet that bargaining reappears at another stage, when means are assigned for production. The executors of the plan try to obtain the largest possible investment, manpower, and volume of raw materials for the smallest possible production. But there is nothing to indicate that all this bargaining during the formulation of the plan results in over-all coherence.

The economic causes of lack of coherence are perhaps not inevitable. They stem from preparation of taut plans that stress maximum end results for minimum effort. High growth rates for production, consumption, national income, and productivity are forecast for minimal inputs of labor and investments. The most favorable external conditions are also assumed—good harvests, favorable terms of trade in foreign commerce, and shortening of the investment cycle. The desire for rapid progress as well as for solutions favorable to various social groups also creates inflationary pressures compromising the plan's coherence.

The technical difficulties are just as important. In theory, coherence might be tested by means of input-output tables. In the Soviet Union these tables are based on total production, final demand having been estimated. After the war, the first retrospective input-output table was made for the year 1957; a second one, eighty-three sectors square but also retrospective, was made for 1959. In 1962, the first current planning table (also eighty-three by eighty-three) was drawn up for that year but solely to control plan figures already adopted. The tautness of certain targets was evident and an imbalance between needs and resources appeared in some cases.[1] It is not known to what extent the plan itself was modified to take this work into account. Similar test-

1. See N. I. Kovalev in *Ekonomisty i matematiki za kruglym stolom* [Economists and Mathematicians at a Round Table Discussion], held in Moscow, March 18 and 23, 1964, Moscow, 1965, p. 188. See also V. Cherniavskii, "Optimalnyi otraslevoi plan" [The Optimum Sector Plan], *Ekonomicheskaia gazeta* [Economic Gazette], August 8, 1964, p. 19.

ing was done for the 1963 annual plan and for the two-year plan for 1964-65.[2]

A different procedure was used in preparing an input-output table (124 by 124) for the last year of the 1966-70 five-year plan. The intersectoral balance was calculated before the five-year plan itself was drafted. The effect on the final version of the plan is not known either.[3] Other less aggregative balances were also drawn up for 1970, one in physical terms by the Chief Computing Center of Gosplan. According to the head of the Center, N. I. Kovalev, the number of products included was 730, but according to I. Evenko it was around 600.[4]

For various reasons, these input-output tables, calculated and drawn up in advance, are inadequate to control the coherence of the plan. The figures are of necessity aggregates and are based on the assumption that aggregated products are homogeneous, which is hardly the case.[5] Technical coefficients are not well known, even for the retrospective calculations. They are essentially based on the so-called "funded" and centrally distributed products. As the number of sectors in an input-output table increases, the difficulties in gathering data grow more than in simple proportion. They also grow when one moves from a retrospective to a prospective table. Coefficients are taken as constant and independent of the level of production, and little is

2. Kovalev, *Ekonomisty i matematiki*, p. 188.

3. The number of sectors in the balance for 1970 is 124 according to some authors (of which 112 are industrial) and 129 according to others in the same source (A. N. Efimov and L. Ia. Berri, eds., *Metody planirovaniia mezhotraslevykh proportsii* [Methods of Planning the Proportions Between Sectors], Moscow, 1965, pp. 91 and 117). It seems that several alternative balances were prepared.

4. Kovalev, *Ekonomisty i matematiki*, p. 189; and I. Evenko, "Problemy vnedreniia ekonomicheskoi kibernetiki v upravlenie promyshlennostiu SSSR" [Problems in Introducing Cybernetics in the Administration of Soviet Industry], *Voprosy ekonomiki* [Problems of Economics], No. 8, 1965, p. 127. We should note that Kovalev's information dates from March, 1964, and Evenko's from July-August, 1965. On this subject, see also Marie-Louise Lavigne, "La diffusion des méthodes mathématiques appliquées à la planification en U.R.S.S.," *Le Courrier des Pays de l'Est*, November 12, 1965, pp. 19-34.

5. The complexity of Soviet industrial production today is discussed later (see pp. 53-54).

known about the possibilities of substitution of the material inputs.[6] Besides, the technical coefficients transmitted to central authorities are by no means necessarily accurate since enterprises have a direct interest in maintaining a safety margin. Finally, a source of error lies in the very process of iteration, in which more remote relations are neglected, and also in the fact that the nomenclature of 50 to 60 per cent of the products has been revised in a few years.[7]

THE IMPRECISE NATURE OF THE OPTIMUM

Any authoritarian regime claims that the economic plan it carries out is the best possible one, *i.e.*, the optimum plan. That was the case of the Soviet regime under Stalin. Indeed, Stalin did not particularly care to define with any precision the criterion of that optimum—at one time it could be the progress of collectivization, at another the increase in production of certain key commodities like steel or electric power, at still other times the increase in aggregate gross production in constant (1926/27) prices.

In recent years, economists from the Eastern Bloc have started questioning what the criterion for the optimum should be. The following criteria have been suggested by various authors: growth in national income (L. A. Vaag, K. Plotnikov, Oskar Lange);[8] growth in national income while maintaining a specified

6. See John Michael Montias, "Central Planning in Soviet-Type Economies, An Introduction to Basic Problems," in *The Soviet Economy in Theory and Practice* (Columbia, Mo.: School of Business and Public Administration, University of Missouri, 1964), pp. 9-17.

7. V. Pugachev, "Voprosy optimalnogo planirovaniia narodnogo khoziaistva s pomoshchiu edinoi gosudarstvennoi seti vychislitelnykh tsentrov" [Problems of Optimal National Economic Planning Using a Single National Network of Computing Centers], *Voprosy ekonomiki*, No. 7, 1964, p. 93.

8. L. A. Vaag, *Sovershenstvovat ekonomicheskie metody upravleniia khoziaistvom* [Improve the Economic Methods of Managing the National Economy], Moscow, 1964, p. 76; K. Plotnikov, "Zadacha Nr. 1" [Problem Number One], *Ekonomicheskaia gazeta*, January 13, 1965, p. 3; Oskar Lange, *Problèmes d'économie socialiste et de planification* (Rome, 1963), pp. 14 and 16. The criterion of national income is accepted by many other authors in the Soviet Union and in countries of the Eastern Bloc.

structure (V. Cherniavskii);[9] growth in gross national product;[10] multiple criteria, the optimum being measured by the weighted deviation of these criteria from the actual indexes (Smekhov);[11] maximum growth of consumption funds relative to expenditures on labor and capital (Bronislav Mints).[12]

Thus far, no agreement on a national criterion has been reached.[13] In any case, such an agreement can only be of theoretical importance as long as the Soviet price system is maintained. But to make price reform a prerequisite would be an even greater difficulty, since for the time being in the Soviet Union there is no solution in sight for bringing prices closer to costs; the efforts of such economists as Kantorovich and Novozhilov face formidable obstacles.[14]

Even if these problems of criteria and prices were solved, one wonders whether a real optimum plan could be adopted under

9. "One should accept as a criterion of the optimum for a national plan the maximization of national income with a set proportion between the part spent and the part accumulated." See V. Cherniavskii, "Kriterii optimalnosti" [Criteria of the Optimum], *Ekonomicheskaia gazeta*, March 17, 1965, p. 9.

10. Mentioned by Vaag, *Sovershenstvovat ekonomicheskie metody*, pp. 72-77, among the criteria proposed in the Soviet Union.

11. B. Smekhov, "O kriterii optimalnosti narodno-khoziaistvennogo plana" [On the Criteria of the Optimum for National Economic Plans], *Voprosy ekonomiki*, No. 1, 1965, p. 126.

12. B. Mints also mentions several restricting conditions, such as the ability of the consumption funds to satisfy public needs, the duration of maximization, the need for accumulation, the average length of the working day, and full employment. See B. Mints, "Kriterien der Optimalisation auf verschiedenen Stufen der sozialistischen Volkswirtschaft" (unpublished lecture, presented at the Gösing Colloquium on September 28, 1965, at the Österreichisches Ost- und Südosteuropa Institut). See also B. Mints and V. Psheliakovskii, "Uravneniia sotsialisticheskogo nakopleniia (dinamika nakopleniia i maksimizatsiia potrebleniia)" [Equations of Socialist Accumulation (the Dynamics of Accumulation and Maximization of Consumption)] in V. S. Nemchinov (ed.), *Primenenie matematiki v ekonomicheskikh issledovaniiakh* [Application of Mathematics in Economic Research], Moscow, 1965, III, pp. 303-11.

13. This point is brought up by Academician Trapeznikov in his article in *Pravda*, August 17, 1964, in which he emphasizes that the absence of such a criterion precludes the general use of electronic computers in the preparation of the plan.

14. This problem is beyond the scope of this book. For further detail on it, see Henri Denis and Marie Lavigne, *Le problème des prix en Union Soviétique* (Paris, 1965).

the administrative system of planning, for choice of an optimum plan assumes that alternative variants of the plan have been prepared and openly discussed. It is not clear who, in a country under a single party system like the Soviet Union, could present an alternative plan since that would be tantamount to questioning Party policy. The "optimum" for an administrative plan can never be more than a choice of means for carrying out a governmental policy already determined, and the number of "constraints" is so large as to make the concept of optimum entirely relative.[15]

CONTROVERSY ABOUT THE MERITS OF ADMINISTRATIVE PLANNING

The defects of the administrative planning system have long been known in the Soviet Union, but there has been no agreement on who is to blame and to what degree. Some Soviet authors blame the defects on Stalin's errors:

"Stalin's interference in planning work, his purely arbitrary goals, and his adjustments of the plans without regard for material possibilities often deprived whole sections of the plan of all economic meaning and lowered the standards of economic science. As a result, the national economy could not develop in accord with plans, and the results of efforts by the people were reduced. Various persistent and prolonged economic difficulties that became apparent could not be explained away as due to problems of economic growth, which Stalin invoked so many times to hide his errors."[16] This explanation, which was offered mainly after the Twentieth and the Twenty-second Party Congresses, seems to have since lost a great deal of its weight. Stalin has been gone for fourteen years, but the defects in the administrative planning system remain. Hence other explanations are gaining wider general acceptance.

15. The word "optimum" is somewhat abused these days in Soviet economic writing. It is often applied to various government measures on the structure of production, introduction of technical innovations, etc., without any evidence that these measures are indeed "optimal."

16. See S. Starostin and E. Frolov, "Ekonomicheskoe razvitie i sovershenstvovanie planirovaniia" [Economic Development and Improvement in Planning], *Kommunist*, No. 17, 1962, p. 17.

The most frequent explanation is the assumed link between the planning system and the level of maturity of the Soviet economy. Oskar Lange, for example, argued that the need to concentrate resources on promoting growth of heavy industry, combined with poor industrial management, makes introduction of a war economy automatically necessary at a given stage of growth. He added, however, that with the building up of a modern industrial economy, such a system tends to become obsolete since a more complex economy requires a more sophisticated planning system.[17] This view is shared by several Soviet economists, who draw from it the conclusion that today administrative directives must be replaced by economic instruments to control implementation of the plan and who therefore demand fundamental changes in the system. We shall say more later about propositions and partial reforms in this direction.

It must not be forgotten, however, that the need for radical reform and for a flexible economic planning system is advocated by only some Soviet economists. Their ideas come to the fore only at the moments when official Party policy emphasizes the need for certain reforms. But official policy shows few signs of being influenced by their ideas, and one even encounters warnings against excessive hopes in that direction. Such a warning was addressed to the "reformers" in an editorial in *Ekonomicheskaia gazeta* that was designed to prepare public opinion for the reforms that Kosygin was to announce in his speech of September 27, 1965.[18]

The editorial in *Ekonomicheskaia gazeta* challenges the very need to abandon administrative for economic methods in running the national economy. It rejects the views of the authors who claim that administrative methods suit certain historical conditions while economic methods suit others; these views, it says, could only lead to confusion. According to that editorial, socialist production cannot do without administrative directors, just as an orchestra cannot do without a conductor. The orders given by

17. Cited by Alec Nove, *The Soviet Economy* (London, 1961), p. 146.

18. "Ekonomicheskie zakony i rukovodstvo khoziaistvom" [Economic Laws and Management of the National Economy], editorial in *Ekonomicheskaia gazeta*, September 15, 1965, p. 2.

administrative agencies ensure a unity of will and make it possible to unify all the workers into a monolithic group. The whole must form an economic mechanism working with the precision of a fine instrument. In order to obtain that precision, it is necessary to see to it that the administrative directives have a scientific basis, that they express correctly the needs of production, and that they obey economic laws.

One wonders to what extent that position reflects a durable policy on reform. Rather it seems to be a tidal phenomenon: the failure of administrative reform brings forth an upsurge of discussions on the need for reforming the planning system; and the hesitations and difficulties encountered in that field bring back the problem of administrative reform. It seems, therefore, necessary to examine first the administrative reforms and then the proposed fundamental reforms of the whole planning system, in order to study later the scope of the changes that have really taken place.

CHAPTER 2. Recent Administrative Reforms

It is generally assumed that in every system of centralized planning there must exist a central agency which prepares plans and coordinates those drafted by lower economic units. Two systems of planning are generally distinguished: (1) the authoritarian or administrative planning system, in which orders are transmitted and resources are allocated by the central authorities, and (2) the flexible or indicative planning system, which uses prices, money, credit, and fiscal policy as essential instruments for intervention in the economy.

The existence of a central planning agency, which has and uses the necessary power to prepare plans for the whole economy and a complete program for future activity, is an indispensable prerequisite of a centrally planned system. Centralization without an over-all plan is a poor substitute for planning. If a government does not know what it is to do, it can claim for itself the right to do anything at any moment.[1]

Another situation may equally well occur, and it is quite common: the central planning agency, while preparing plans and putting them into operation, may not dispose of adequate political and economic power. In that case, the central planning agency risks being subjected to various pressures which, by reducing its power of decision, may force it to draft poorly coordinated plans and thus compromise the chances of their fulfillment. It is, therefore, of interest to see whether there really exists in the Soviet Union a central planning agency with such powers and whether Gosplan could actually be considered such an agency.

It seems to the point to examine the real powers wielded by Gosplan, the changes resulting from recent reforms, and the planning powers held by other agencies of the economic administration.

1. Czeslaw Bobrowski, *Formation du Système Soviétique de Planification* (Paris and The Hague, 1965), p. 28. Bobrowski was in charge of Poland's Central Planning Office from 1945 to 1949.

GOSPLAN'S PLACE IN THE HIERARCHY OF CENTRAL POLITICAL AND ECONOMIC AGENCIES

The first limitation of Gosplan's power comes from the Party. Party leaders consistently try to restrict Gosplan's range of activity to technical expertise while keeping the right to make decisions in their own hands. This idea was repeated recently by Khrushchev when he claimed that "Gosplan must become the economic barometer of the Party and react quickly to every new and progressive element in our economy."[2]

Although Party control over economic activities is officially exerted through the Politburo (formerly Presidium) and the Party Secretariat, in reality a parallel administrative structure is superimposed by the Party upon the economic agencies. As of June, 1965, the following sections, whose activities were concerned exclusively with economic matters, were assigned directly to the Politburo and the Secretariat of the Central Committee:[3] agriculture in the republics (F. D. Kulakov); chemical industry; construction (A. E. Biriukov); defense industries (I. D. Serbin); economic relations with the countries of the Socialist Bloc (P. I. Miroshnichenko); heavy industry (A. P. Rudakov); light industry, food industry, and trade (P. I. Maximov); machine-building (V. S. Frolov); transportation and communications (K. S. Simonov); finance, trade, and planning agencies. In addition, there was an office for the Russian Republic with its own economic sections. Offices for Transcaucasia and Central Asia, created under the Central Committee in November, 1962, have since been abolished, as have the offices for industry and construction (A. P. Rudakov), for chemical and light industries (P. N. Demichev), and for agriculture (V. I. Poliakov).[4]

Certain sections of the Politburo and Secretariat, although basically political and administrative bodies, have power in economic matters as well. This is the case, for instance, for the

2. Speech at the Plenary Session of the Party Central Committee of February 14, 1964. See N. Khrushchev, *Izvestia*, February 15, 1964, p. 5.

3. The names of chairmen are given in parentheses. Cited from "Post Khrushchev Changes in USSR Council of Ministers and CPSU Apparatus (Pre-September 1965 Plenum)," *The ASTE Bulletin*, Summer, 1965, p. 19.

4. *Ibid.*

section for army and navy general administration (A. A. Epishev), the section for relations with the Communist parties of the Socialist Bloc countries (Iu. V. Andropov), and the committee for science and education (N. F. Krasnov).[5] Until December, 1965, the Party and State Control Committee (A. N. Shelepin) also had these multiple powers. But the transformation of that committee into the National Control Committee (*Komitet narodnogo kontrola SSSR*) and the replacement of Shelepin by P. V. Kovanov on December 9, 1965, make it impossible for the time being to evaluate the position of this new agency.[6]

In November, 1962, Khrushchev tried to strengthen further the Party's control over the economy by dividing up Party agencies at the republic and province level between the offices of industry and construction, on the one hand, and of agriculture, on the other. This measure seems to have failed; and after Khrushchev's downfall in November, 1964, it was rescinded by the Party Central Committee, also purportedly to strengthen the role of the Party.

The power wielded by the Party in economic matters would be sufficient in itself to prevent Gosplan from being a central planning agency. Equally important is the fact that, within the hierarchy of economic agencies, the position of Gosplan is much weaker than it should be for an agency responsible for central planning of the economy.

Both in December, 1963, under Khrushchev (Chart 1) and in August, 1966, under Kosygin (Chart 2), the chairman of Gosplan had the rank of a vice chairman in the Council of Ministers; and in that capacity he had to share power with several colleagues. Indeed, there were eight vice chairmen in March, 1963, and nine in June, 1965, December, 1965, and August, 1966, as can be seen in the following tabulation:[7]

5. *Ibid.*

6. *Pravda,* December 10, 1965, p. 2.

7. Based on Michel Lesage, "La structure du gouvernement soviétique," *Le Courrier des Pays de l'Est,* April 23, 1964, p. 39; Michel Lesage, Georges Sokoloff, and Jean-Pierre Saltiel, "La réforme de la gestion de l'économie soviétique–l'administration économique et le statut de l'enterprise," *ibid.,* November 4, 1965, p. 17; *The ASTE Bulletin,* Summer, 1965, p. 18; *Pravda,* December 10, 1965, p. 2, and August 4, 1966, pp. 1-2.

Area	March, 1963	June, 1965	December, 1965, and August, 1966
Agriculture	D. S. Polianskii	D. S. Polianskii	[8]
Party and State Control	A. N. Shelepin	A. N. Shelepin	[8]
Relations with the Council to Help Countries of the Eastern Bloc	M. A. Lesechko	M. A. Lesechko	M. A. Lesechko
U.S.S.R. Gosplan	P. F. Lomako	P. F. Lomako	N. K. Baibakov
U.S.S.R. Sovnarkhoz	V. E. Dymshits	V. E. Dymshits	
Supplying Materials and Equipment	[9]	[9]	V. E. Dymshits
U.S.S.R. Gosstroi	I. T. Novikov	I. T. Novikov	I. T. Novikov
Coordination of Scientific Research	K. N. Rudnev	K. N. Rudnev	V. A. Kirillin
Armaments	L. V. Smirnov	L. V. Smirnov	L. V. Smirnov
Other functions		V. N. Novikov[10]	V. N. Novikov[10]
Other functions			N. A. Tikhonov[11]
Other functions			M. T. Efremov[11]

8. D. S. Polianskii became First Vice Chairman of the Council of Ministers at the end of September, 1965; A. N. Shelepin was released from his duties as Chairman of the Party and State Control Committee in December, 1965, to devote full time to work on the Party Secretariat. The Party and State Control Committee was then renamed the National Control Committee, but its chairman, P. V. Kovanov, was not made a vice chairman of the Council of Ministers.

9. Before the reforms of October 2, 1965, the functions of the State Committee on Supplying Materials and Equipment were actually performed by U.S.S.R. Sovnarkhoz.

10. V. N. Novikov was appointed Chairman of the Supreme Council of the National Economy in March, 1965, replacing D. F. Ustinov, who was appointed to the Party Secretariat. However, Novikov did not get his predecessor's rank of First Vice Chairman on the Council of Ministers and had to be content with that of an ordinary Vice Chairman. After elimination of the Supreme Council of the National Economy, V. N. Novikov preserved his vice chairmanship, but his new duties are still unclear (*Izvestia*, October 3, 1965, p. 2).

11. The duties of N. A. Tikhonov and M. T. Efremov have still not been clarified. In June, 1965, Efremov was First Secretary of the Stavropol Party Committee, a Candidate to the Politburo, and a member of the Party Bureau for the Russian Republic (*The ASTE Bulletin*, Summer, 1965, p. 19).

It is obvious that the chairman of Gosplan cannot have the final voice even in the Restricted Committee composed exclusively of vice chairmen of the Council of Ministers. His peers are just as interested in economic matters as he is, and there is no reason for his views to prevail over theirs. Arbitration is probably carried out at a higher level—that of the Council's chairman and first vice chairmen.

Until Khrushchev's downfall in October, 1964, there were three first vice chairmen of the Council: Mikoyan, Kosygin, and Ustinov.[12] New positions were then given to Mikoyan and Kosygin, and only Ustinov remained a first vice chairman. He was replaced by Mazurov in March, 1965, when he was promoted to the Party Secretariat. On October 2, 1965, Polianskii was named as a second first vice chairman. Today the central governmental direction of the Soviet economy is therefore in the hands of three men: Chairman Kosygin and First Vice Chairmen Polianskii and Mazurov. Gosplan has the role of an advisor, not a central planning agency.

The Council of Ministers is an agency which, at least officially, must make the major decisions. It is normal that every one of its members should take an important part in decision-making in his particular field. As can be seen from Charts 1 and 2, practically all economic interests are directly represented on the Council and can thus defend their special interests on an equal footing, again officially, when Gosplan coordinates plans. In case of a conflict of interests, Gosplan acts as an expert rather than an arbiter; final decisions are left to the first vice chairmen of the Council or to an even higher level.

The position of Gosplan within the Council could have been strengthened in March, 1963, when most sector state committees were subordinated to that agency (Chart 3). But that measure was offset by subordination of Gosplan itself to the newly created Supreme Council of the National Economy (V.S.N.Kh.),[13] as well as by the fact that chairmen of the state committees were *ex*

12. Lesage, *Le Courrier des Pays de l'Est*, April 23, 1964, p. 39.

13. On the powers of the Supreme Council of the National Economy, see p. 37.

Chart 1. Composition of U.S.S.R. Council of Ministers as of December 19, 1963[a]

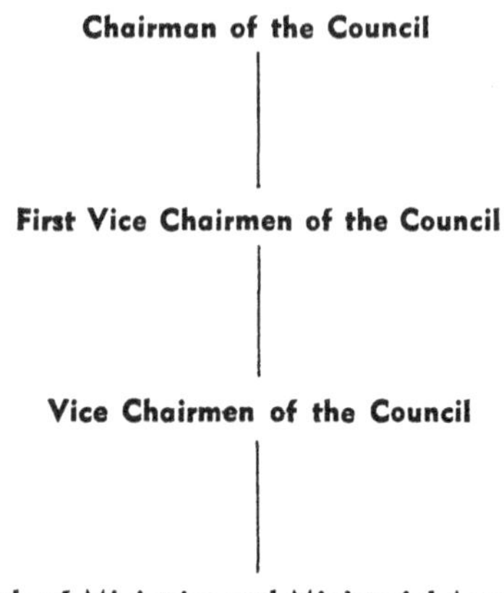

Heads of Ministries and Ministerial Agencies

All-Union Ministries
- Foreign Trade
- Maritime Fleet
- Means of Communication

Union-Republic Ministries
- Secondary and Higher Education
- Public Health
- Foreign Affairs
- Culture
- Defense
- Telephone and Telegraph
- Agriculture
- Finance
- Ministerial Agencies
- State Bank
- Central Statistical Administration

Chairmen of Republic Councils of Ministers
- Russian Republic
- Ukraine
- Belorussia
- Kazakhstan
- Georgia
- Uzbekistan
- Azerbaidzhan
- Lithuania
- Moldavia
- Latvia
- Kirghizia
- Tadzhikistan
- Armenia
- Turkmenia
- Estonia

Chairmen of Autonomous State Committees[b]

Supreme Council of the National Economy (V.S.N.Kh.)[c]
Council of the U.S.S.R. National Economy (U.S.S.R. Sovnarkhoz)[d]
State Committee on Construction (Gosstroi)[d]
Committee on the State Plan (Gosplan)[d]

Chart 1 (concluded)

State Committee for the Coordination of Scientific Research[d]
Party and State Central Committee
Committee on Labor and Wage Problems
Committee on Radio and Television
Committee on Motion Pictures
Committee on Publications
Committee on Trade[e]
Committee on Procurements[e]
Committee on Foreign Economic Relations
Committee on Foreign Cultural Relations
Committee on State Security

Individuals with the Rank of U.S.S.R. Minister[f]

2 Vice Chairmen of the V.S.N.Kh.
6 Chairmen of State Committees attached to V.S.N.Kh.
1 First Vice Chairman of U.S.S.R. Sovnarkhoz
2 Vice Chairmen of U.S.S.R. Sovnarkhoz
1 Chairman of the State Committee attached to U.S.S.R. Sovnarkhoz
9 Chairmen of State Committees attached to Gosstroi
2 Vice Chairmen of Gosplan
12 Chairmen of State Committees attached to Gosplan
1 Chairman of the State Committee on Irrigation and Hydraulic Agriculture

Agencies Directly Under the Council Whose Chairmen Were Not Automatically Ministers

Central Office of Civil Aviation[g]
State Committee on Irrigation and Hydraulic Agriculture[h]

---

[a] See *Pravda*, December 20, 1963, p. 2. Composition confirmed at a meeting of the Supreme Soviet on December 16-19, 1963.

[b] According to Article 70 of the Soviet Constitution (see *Pravda*, December 20, 1963, p. 2), chairmen of these state committees belong to the Council of Ministers, since they are created and abolished by the Presidium of the U.S.S.R. Supreme Soviet. Other state committees were created by the Council of Ministers and placed under the jurisdiction of V.S.N.Kh., U.S.S.R. Sovnarkhoz, Gosplan, and Gosstroi. See note f.

[c] The chairman (D. F. Ustinov) was *ex officio* a first vice chairman of the Council of Ministers.

[d] Chairmen were *ex officio* vice chairmen of V.S.N.Kh. (See *Ekonomicheskaia gazeta*, January 4, 1964, p. 34, and *Pravda*, March 14, 1966.)

[e] Chairmen had the rank of U.S.S.R. minister.

[f] The decree of January 11, 1963 (see footnote 49) awarded the rank of U.S.S.R. minister to chairmen of state committees (probably state commit-

Notes to Chart 1 (concluded)

tees for economic sectors). Nominations were made on an individual basis, but the Secretary of the Presidium of the Supreme Soviet, M. P. Georgadze, specified the functions of most of the people nominated. See *Pravda*, December 20, 1963, pp. 2-3.

The structure of central agencies of economic administration and the list of chairmen of state committees with their ranks were given in *Ekonomicheskaia gazeta*, January 4, 1964, p. 34. It can be seen from that list that not all chairmen had the rank of U.S.S.R. minister. After publication of the list in *Ekonomicheskaia gazeta*, the State Committee for the Chemical and Petroleum Industry was broken up into three state committees by sectors that were under the jurisdiction of Gosplan. See note f to Chart 3.

[g] The chairman, E. F. Loginov, did not have the rank of U.S.S.R. minister, personally or *ex officio*.

[h] The chairman had the personal rank of minister. This committee had two other state committees under its jurisdiction: one on cotton growing in Central Asia and the other on irrigation and the building of state farms in Central Asia. See *Pravda*, December 20, 1963, p. 3, and *Ekonomicheskaia gazeta*, January 4, 1964, p. 34.

Chart 2. Composition of U.S.S.R. Council of Ministers After Restoration of Industrial Ministries on August 3, 1966[a]

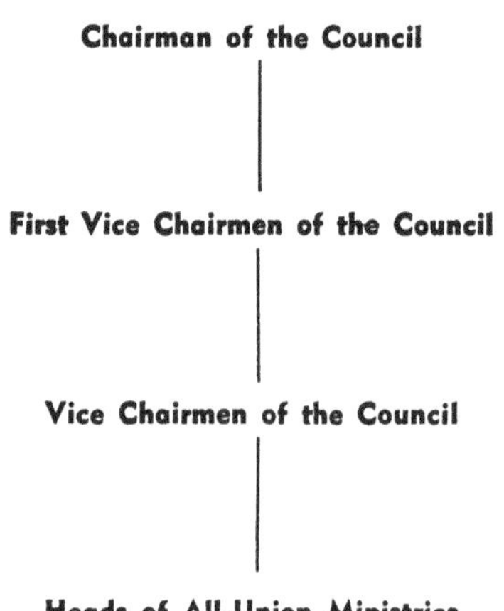

Aeronautics Industry
Automobile Industry
Foreign Trade
Gas Industry
Civil Aviation

Medium Machine-Building
Machine Tool and Tooling Industry
Machine-Building for Construction, Road Construction, and Communal Economy

Chart 2 (continued)

Machine-Building for Light Industry, Food Industry, and Current Consumer Goods Industry
Maritime Fleet
Defense Industry
General Machine-Building
Construction of Instruments, Means of Automation, and Management Apparatus
Means of Communication
Radio Industry
Shipbuilding
Construction of Tractors and Agricultural Machinery
Construction of Means of Transportation
Heavy Machine-Building, Construction of Machines for Power and Transport
Machine-Building for Chemical and Petroleum Industries
Electronic Industry
Electrotechnical Industry

Heads of Union-Republic Ministries

Higher and Specialized Secondary Education
Geology
Public Health
Foreign Affairs
Culture
Light Industry
Wood, Cellulose, Paper and Woodworking Industry
Irrigation and Hydraulic Agriculture
Assembly Work and Special Construction
Meat and Dairy Industry
Petroleum Extraction
Petroleum Refining and Petroleum Chemical Industry
Defense
Food Industry
Building Materials
Fishing Industry
Telephone and Telegraph
Agriculture
Trade
Coal Industry
Finance
Chemical Industry
Nonferrous Metal Industry
Ferrous Metal Industry
Power and Electrification

Chairmen of Republic Councils of Ministers

Russian Republic
Ukraine
Belorussia
Kazakhstan
Uzbekistan
Georgia
Azerbaidzhan
Lithuania
Moldavia
Latvia
Kirghizia
Tadzhikistan
Armenia
Turkmenia
Estonia

Chart 2 (concluded)

Chairmen of Autonomous State Committees[b]

Committee on the State Plan (Gosplan)
State Committee on Supplying Materials and Equipment (Gossnab)
State Committee on Construction (Gosstroi)
State Committee on Science and Technology
State Committee on Labor and Wage Problems
State Committee on Professional and Technical Training
State Committee on Procurements of Agricultural Products
State Committee on Foreign Economic Relations
State Committee on Forestry (lesnoe khoziaistvo)

Chairmen of Other State Committees and Agencies Directly Under the Council

State Bank
Central Statistical Administration
Union for Sale of Agricultural Produce (Soiuzselkhoztekhnika)
Committee on National Control
Committee on State Security

---

[a] See *Izvestia*, October 3, 1965, p. 1; *Pravda*, December 10, 1965, p. 2; *Ekonomicheskaia gazeta*, No. 49, 1965, pp. 24-25; *Pravda*, August 4, 1966, pp. 1-2.

When industrial ministries were restored, most individual nominations for the rank of minister lost their usefulness. A decree of the Presidium of the Supreme Soviet of October 9, 1965, therefore removed the rank of minister from those who were not actually in charge of ministries. See *Pravda*, December 10, 1965, p. 2.

Certain state committees of the Council of Ministers (radio and television, motion pictures, publications, foreign cultural relations) were demoted at that time to ordinary committees under the Council, and their chairmen were removed from Council membership. In addition, the chairmen of two agencies (U.S.S.R. Bank for Financing Investments and the Central Office of the Hydro-Meteorological Service) and of the following committees were no longer on the Council as of August 3, 1966: prices (now under Gosplan); inventions and discoveries; standardization, weights, and measures; use of atomic energy; and geological deposits.

On the other hand, a new state committee of the Council—on forestry—was added.

To understand the changes clearly, compare *Ekonomicheskaia gazeta*, No. 49, 1965, pp. 24-25, and *Pravda*, August 4, 1966, pp. 1-2.

[b] See note b to Chart 1. When the Supreme Council of the National Economy (V.S.N.Kh.) and U.S.S.R. Sovnarkhoz were abolished, several state committees formerly under their jurisdiction either obtained the rank of ministries or were put under the direct jurisdiction of the Council of Ministers.

officio members of the Council (Chart 1). It is true that the chairman of Gosplan was himself a vice chairman of the Council; but, as has already been pointed out, he shared that rank with several others whereas Ustinov, then Chairman of V.S.N.Kh., was one of three first vice chairmen.

The re-establishment of industrial ministries in place of the sector state committees and the abolition of V.S.N.Kh. and the U.S.S.R. Council of the National Economy (U.S.S.R. Sovnarkhoz), which took place on October 2, 1965, do not seem to have had much effect on Gosplan's position within the Council of Ministers. Gosplan's chairman remains one of many Council vice chairmen, and the raising of sector state committees to the rank of ministries was done mainly at the expense of U.S.S.R. Sovnarkhoz. Thus Gosplan remains torn between the directives of the Party Politburo and the government, on the one hand, and the pressures from ministries and republics (which it cannot resist), on the other.

FLUCTUATIONS IN GOSPLAN'S POWER

The difficulty in fixing the power of a planning commission is inherent in the very nature of planning. A clear distinction between formulation and implementation of a plan exists only in principle. In practice, a plan must be continually adjusted while being carried out. But adjustments are made primarily at the demand of those carrying out the plan, and they thereby acquire the initiative in reformulating the plan as required by every adjustment of sufficient importance.

Another problem is posed by the nature of the various planning functions. Four basic functions may be distinguished: (1) long-range planning; (2) annual or quarterly current planning; (3) planning of supplies; (4) statistical control of fulfillment of the plan.

At the end of the war, these four essential planning functions belonged to Gosplan (see Chart 4), but soon the last two were removed from its jurisdiction. Supplying of materials and equipment is the area in which planning and management are most closely interlinked. While the plan for supplying materials and

Chart 3. Planning and Management Agencies Under the Jurisdiction of the Supreme Council of the National Economy (V.S.N.Kh.), as of April, 1964

V.S.N.Kh.

State Committees for Production[a]
Gas Industry
Medium Machine-Building
Power and Electrification

State Committees
Coordination of Scientific and Research Work[b]
Aviation Technology
Defense Technology
Radio Electronics
Shipbuilding
Utilization of Atomic Energy
Inventions and Discoveries
Standardization, Weights and Measures, Measuring Instruments
Geology

Central Office for Agricultural Technology

Bank for Financing Investments (U.S.S.R. Stroibank)

State Committee for Mining Resources

U.S.S.R. SOVNARKHOZ[b]

State Committee of the Fishing Industry

Republic Sovnarkhozes[c]
R.S.F.S.R.
Ukraine
Belorussia
Georgia
Azerbaidzhan
Lithuania
Moldavia
Latvia
Armenia
Estonia

Sovnarkhozes of 47 Economic Regions[c] (as of January 11, 1964)[d]

Note: The organizations in the first panel were under the direct jurisdiction of the V.S.N.Kh.; those in the next three panels, under its indirect jurisdiction through the intermediary of the designated agencies.

Source: *Ekonomicheskaia gazeta*, January 4, 1964, p. 34, and April 11, 1964, p. 38.

[a] Various construction enterprises or agencies were directly subordinated to state committees for production.

[b] Chairmen were *ex officio* vice chairmen of V.S.N.Kh. See note d in Chart 1.

[c] The Sovnarkhozes of the Russian Republic and the Ukraine controlled those of their economic regions (twenty-four for the Russian Republic and seven for the Ukraine). The other republic Sovnarkhozes were mingled with those of their economic regions. Note that for the four republics of Central Asia (Uzbekistan, Kirghizia, Tadzhikistan, and Turkmenia) there was only one Sovnarkhoz.

[d] There were originally (after the November, 1962, reforms) 41 Sovnar-

Chart 3 (concluded)

U.S.S.R. GOSPLAN[b]

State Committee for Professional and Technical Training

State Committees by Sectors[e]

Heavy Machine-Building, Construction of Machines for Power and Transport
Machine-Building for Chemical and Petroleum Industries
Construction of Automobiles, Tractors, and Agricultural Machinery
Machine Tool Industry
Production of Instruments, Means of Automation, and Management Apparatus
Electrotechnical Industry
Ferrous and Nonferrous Metal Industry
Fuel Industry
Chemical Industry[f]
Petroleum Extraction[f]
Wood, Paper, Cellulose Industry, and Logging
Light Industry
Food Industry
Petroleum Refining and Petroleum Chemical Industry[f]

Councils of Coordination and Planning of Large Economic Regions[g]

Baltic region
Transcaucasia

Republic Gosplans[h]

U.S.S.R. GOSSTROI[b]

State Committees for Production

Construction of Means of Transportation
Assembly Work and Special Building
Construction for the Economic Region of Central Asia

Central Office for Construction on the National Level

(Soiuzglavstroikomplekt)

State Committees

Building Materials
Civilian Construction and Architecture
Machine-Building for Construction, Road Construction, and Communal Economy

Republic Gosstrois[i]

khozes, which replaced the 101 former Sovnarkhozes. Later the Sovnarkhoz of the Kazakh Republic was broken up into seven separate Sovnarkhozes (see *Ekonomicheskaia gazeta*, January 11, 1964, p. 34).

[e] The sector state committees were responsible for economic policy of the whole sector and directly controlled the Offices of Studies and Projects.

Notes to Chart 3 (concluded)

Their powers were considerably increased after the reforms of November, 1962, and March, 1963.

[f] The State Committee for the Chemical and Petroleum Industry was broken up in January, 1964, into three state committees under the jurisdiction of U.S.S.R. Gosplan: one for the chemical industry, the second for petroleum extraction, and the third for petroleum refining and the petroleum chemical industry. See *Pravda*, January 26, 1964, p. 4.

[g] These councils were created in 1961 after division of the country into seventeen large economic regions. (There are at present eighteen large economic regions plus the Moldavian Republic, which does not belong to any other region. See G. A. Ivanov in *Planovoe khoziaistvo*, No. 11, 1963, pp. 89-90.) After creation of the new enlarged Sovnarkhozes in November, 1962, the Councils of Coordination of the ten regions in the Russian Republic and of the three regions in the Ukraine were eliminated. In Kazakhstan the functions of the Council of Coordination were taken over by the Council of Ministers of this republic (see Jan Pawlik in *Gospodarka Planowa*, No. 10, 1963, p. 55). The Councils now in existence—for the Baltic countries and Transcaucasia—are under the jurisdiction of U.S.S.R. Gosplan. In fact, according to M. V. Breev (ed.), *Planirovanie narodnogo khoziaistva SSSR* [Planning of the U.S.S.R. National Economy], Moscow, 1963, p. 119, the Councils of Coordination for the large regions are under the jurisdiction of U.S.S.R. Gosplan or republic Gosplans.

[h] Since Gosplan is a union-republic agency, there is a double subordination for the republic Gosplans—to U.S.S.R. Gosplan and to the relevant republic Council of Ministers. At the lower republic level there are Gosplans of the autonomous republics, and Planning Commissions of province (*oblast*) or territory (*krai*) and of district (*raion*) or city. See Breev (ed.), *Planirovanie narodnogo khoziaistva*, p. 116.

[i] Since March, 1963, U.S.S.R. Gosstroi (State Building Agency) has been a union-republic agency; that is, it controls, along with the republic Councils, the republic Gosstrois.

equipment is an essential part of the general plan under a system of centralized planning by government authorities, it is impossible to make decisions about supplies for the whole year. Often these decisions are made on a daily basis, and thus the work of the corresponding planning agencies bears a close resemblance to that of management.

Independence of statistical services from the planning and managerial agencies seems to be important to the central authorities. In the Soviet Union statistics are above all a means of control, and it would be risky to leave to planners and managers the power of controlling their own work.

The fusion of long-range and current planning in one single

Chart 4. Organization and Powers of Central Agencies for Planning and Managing the Soviet Economy, 1945-1966

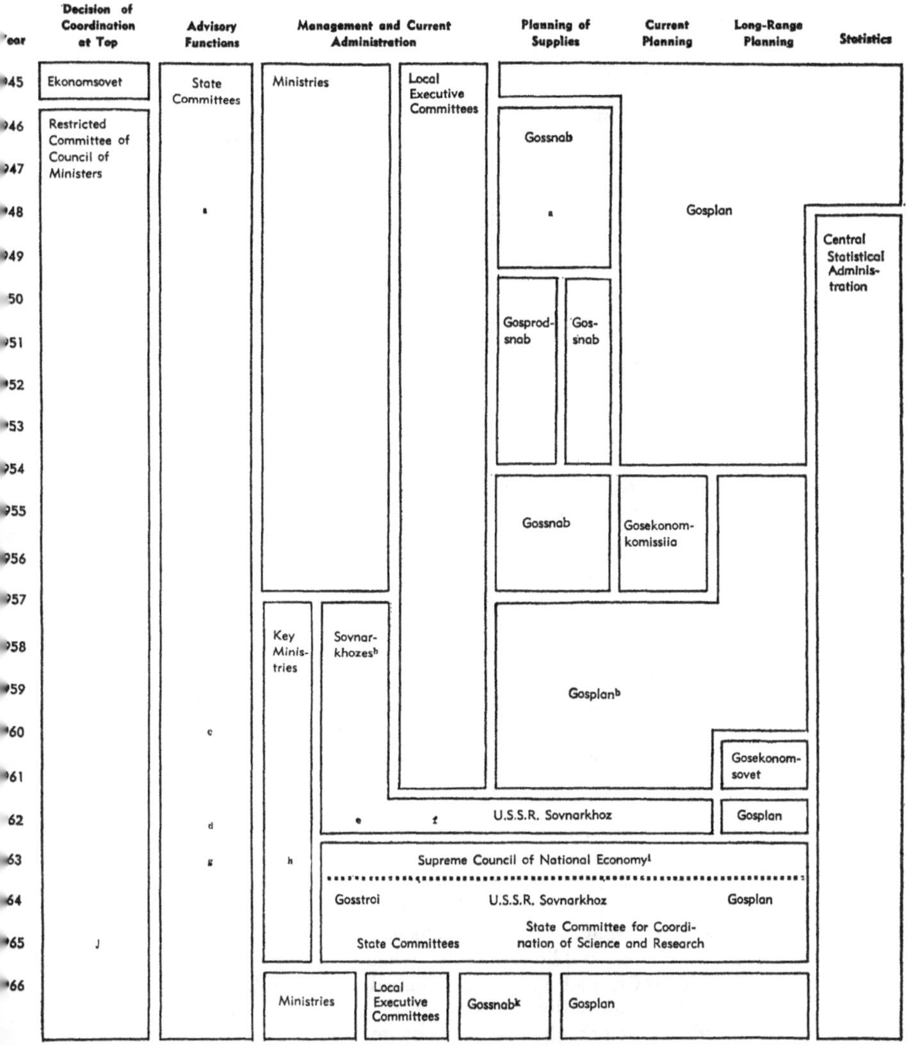
Decision of Coordination at Top
Advisory Functions
Management and Current Administration
Planning of Supplies
Current Planning
Long-Range Planning
Statistics
Ekonomsovet
Restricted Committee of Council of Ministers
State Committees
Ministries
Local Executive Committees
Gossnab
Gosplan
Central Statistical Adminis-tration
Gosprod-snab
Gos-snab
Gossnab
Gosekonom-komissiia
Key Minis-tries
Sovnar-khozes
Gosplan
Gosekonom-sovet
U.S.S.R. Sovnarkhoz
Gosplan
Supreme Council of National Economy
Gosstroi
U.S.S.R. Sovnarkhoz
Gosplan
State Committees
State Committee for Coordi-nation of Science and Research
Ministries
Local Executive Committees
Gossnab
Gosplan

[a] The State Committee for New Technology (Gostekhnika) was created in 1948. Its functions had previously been handled by Gossnab (State Committee for Supplying Materials and Equipment).

Notes to Chart 4 (continued)

[b] The powers of Gosplan were considerably increased during 1958-62, to a large extent at the expense of the Sovnarkhozes, so that Gosplan acquired some functions in the realm of plan fulfillment or current management. The central sales services of former ministries were made part of Gosplan and were entrusted with drawing up delivery plans among republics and with setting prices for goods and services.

[c] The number of state committees increased considerably, particularly in 1962. The functions remained essentially advisory, but the need was felt to coordinate management of the different branches of industry. By November, 1962, state committees existed for all branches of industry.

[d] The reform of November 24, 1962, gave to state committees several planning functions and also certain management functions for their sectors.

[e] After its creation, U.S.S.R. Sovnarkhoz controlled the Sovnarkhozes of the economic regions (whose number was reduced from 101 to 41 in November, 1962) and most of local industry through the regional Sovnarkhozes. The main construction functions were transferred to U.S.S.R. Gosstroi. The division of power between U.S.S.R. Sovnarkhoz and Gosplan in the November, 1962, reforms is not clear. It seems that U.S.S.R. Sovnarkhoz was to control at the source the essential functions of current planning.

[f] After the November, 1962, reforms, the Sovnarkhozes controlled local industry except for artisans, who remained under the jurisdiction of local executive committees. No precise division of power between the Sovnarkhozes and the local executive committees could be found in the sources that were consulted.

[g] The March, 1963, reforms did not change the functions of the state committees, but the legal status of several committees was changed so that they came under the Supreme Council of the National Economy, U.S.S.R. Sovnarkhoz, U.S.S.R. Gosstroi, and Gosplan. Some state committees continued to report directly to the Council of Ministers (see Charts 1 and 2).

[h] Several ministries with military interests (medium machine-building, transport equipment, and geology) were transformed into state committees and subordinated to the Supreme Council of the National Economy or U.S.S.R. Gosstroi.

[i] On the hierarchical structure of the agencies under the Supreme Council of the National Economy, see Chart 3.

[j] See *Izvestia*, October 3 and 10, 1965.

[k] The planning of supplies became the responsibility of Gosplan apparently for the roughly 14,000 products distributed by agencies for general direction of interrepublic deliveries, which between November, 1962, and September, 1965, had been subordinated to U.S.S.R. Sovnarkhoz. These agencies have, since the abolition of the U.S.S.R. Sovnarkhoz, been subordinated to Gossnab. The former chairman of U.S.S.R. Sovnarkhoz, V. E. Dymshits, became chairman of Gossnab. The latter's job in principle is solely to carry out plans for supplying materials and equipment drawn up by Gosplan and to distribute production not distributed by Gosplan. But it is evident that, in supplying materials and equipment on the basis of the

Notes to Chart 4 (concluded)

priorities of the moment, both Gossnab and its management affect plans. The law of October 2, 1965, making decisions of Gossnab obligatory for ministries (which control funds), is quite clear on this point. On the supplying of materials and equipment, see fourth section of Chapter 5 and footnote 70 in Chapter 4.

agency also presents many inconveniences. Current annual planning and the numerous adjustments of plans, always very urgent, absorb practically all the efforts of Gosplan, leaving no time for careful study of long-range prospects as they relate to the changing state of affairs—the moving conjuncture—in the national economy. There has been, therefore, a tendency not to adjust long-term plans in force and to pay little attention to them in drawing up annual plans. The authorities' efforts to remedy such defects by continuous planning will be described in the next chapter.

Despite these inconveniences, Soviet authorities tried on two occasions to unite the three essential functions of planning in a single agency: in 1953, following Stalin's death, when the fusion of the ministries took place; and again in 1957, when economic management was reorganized on a regional basis and the Sovnarkhozes (Councils of the National Economy) were established. A third attempt was made in October, 1965, after the abolition of the U.S.S.R. Sovnarkhoz. Sharing of power among several agencies also has drawbacks: lack of coordination between annual goals and available resources as well as between annual and long-range plans. To cope with this situation, Soviet authorities often created new posts of responsibility with broad powers and entrusted them to persons believed to be more dynamic.

With reorganization of the economy on a regional basis, concentration of power within Gosplan had still another justification. Because of elimination of economic ministers, various coordinating tasks were transferred to sectoral departments of Gosplan (Chart 5).[14] These departments acquired considerable importance, and their heads became members of the Council of

14. Some managerial powers of Gosplan were in fact inherited from the late Gosekonomsovet, which, under M. G. Pervukhin, used to exercise control over technical ministries. See Basile Kerblay, "Les propositions de Liberman pour un projet de réforme de l'entreprise en U.R.S.S.," *Cahiers du Monde Russe et Soviétique*, No. 3, 1963, p. 302.

Ministers. Gosplan became the principal agency controlling and coordinating the work of the new Sovnarkhozes, acting through the Councils of Ministers and Gosplans of the republics.[15]

Weakness of the regional economic system resulted in further strengthening of Gosplan over the years 1958-62. The Sovnarkhozes were accused of defending their local interests, of compromising interrepublic delivery plans, and of diverting investment funds and resources from the national interest. Sales services of former ministries (Glavsbyt) were subordinated to Gosplan, and a Central Directorate of Interrepublic Deliveries was created under it. After January 22, 1959, Sovnarkhozes were deprived of the right to appropriate material resources and investment funds, that right being given to the Gosplans and Councils of Ministers of the republics. However, with the creation in June-July, 1960, of Sovnarkhozes for the large republics—the Russian Republic, the Ukraine, and Kazakhstan—the right to allocate material resources was given to these bodies and taken away from the Gosplans of the corresponding republics.

The power of Gosplan, which had also been entrusted with price control and the right to determine customers and suppliers of enterprises, became so great that it practically controlled management of Sovnarkhozes. After long-range planning was entrusted in 1960 to a newly created agency, the Gosekonomsovet (the State Economic Committee), Gosplan became in effect a sort of a super-Sovnarkhoz for the entire Soviet Union. However, officially it had no right to control the over-all activities of Sovnarkhozes, which still came under the republic Councils of Ministers (sometimes through the intermediary of an all-republic Sovnarkhoz).

Seen from this viewpoint, the reforms of November, 1962, essentially confirmed an existing situation. The decision reached at the Plenary Session of Party Central Committee stipulates:

15. Jan Pawlik, "Reorganizacja systemu kierowania i zarzadzania gospodarka narodowa w ZSSR" [Reorganization of the Direction and Administration of the U.S.S.R. National Economy], *Gospodarka Planowa*, No. 8-9, 1963, pp. 58 and 61. "Nowe zasady kierowania i zarzadzania gospodarka narodowa ZSRR" [New Principles of Managing the U.S.S.R. National Economy], *ibid.*, No. 2, 1966, pp. 37-42.

"To improve long-range planning of the national economy and to guarantee direction of the fulfillment of annual plans, it is indispensable to assure the best possible delimitation of functions of the central planning agencies.

"To this end, the functions of U.S.S.R. Gosplan, until now responsible for the year-to-year fulfillment of long-range plans, must be transferred to a new agency, U.S.S.R. Sovnarkhoz, empowered with such administrative functions as are indispensable; and the State Economic Committee must be transformed into U.S.S.R. Gosplan, whose duty will be long-range planning."[16]

The point was emphasized by Khrushchev in his speech of November 19, 1962:

"In order to define with greater precision the functions of these agencies [Gosplan and Gosekonomsovet], they must be fitted into the present structure of planning and management of the national economy. It is desirable that Gosplan should take over long-range planning, which is now the function of Gosekonomsovet; while fulfillment of annual plans, which today is the responsibility of Gosplan, should be turned over to U.S.S.R. Sovnarkhoz."[17]

The statements were not too clear, however, on the drawing up of annual plans. Since the intention was to introduce continuous planning with five-year plans divided into annual slices to be corrected every year (see below), the idea may have been that annual plans were to be replaced by ever-improved versions of the long-range plans. That is to say, the former annual planning would be replaced by current planning, which would consist essentially in executing plans and adjusting them in the course of the year.

It is not certain, however, whether this interpretation is correct. In any case, the decree of January 11, 1963, issued by the Party Central Committee and the Council of Ministers entrusted Gosplan with the functions of both long-range planning and pre-

16. *Izvestia,* November 24, 1962, p. 2.

17. N. S. Khrushchev, *Stroitelstvo kommunizma v SSSR i razvitie selskogo khoziaistva* [Building of Communism in the U.S.S.R. and the Development of Agriculture], Moscow, 1963, VII, p. 373.

paring annual plans.[18] This definition of powers for Gosplan was confirmed at the meeting of the Party Central Committee in March, 1963.[19]

The new powers of Gosplan consisted in preparing current (annual or two-year) plans, setting wholesale prices for industrial and agricultural products, setting rate schedules and retail prices, and determining consumption norms for fuel and raw materials and norms for use of equipment. Gosplan was also to coordinate plans for the Soviet Union with those for other countries in the "socialist camp" and to supervise execution of the plan—particularly regarding putting new production facilities into operation, introducing new techniques, etc.[20]

A clearer distinction was made between Gosplan's work in drawing up studies and in preparing compulsory plans. The first stage was to be preparing forecasts of developmental trends and studying the coherence of directives. The second stage was to be preparing the plan itself, in cooperation with all interested agencies, for a limited number of compulsory indexes that would have to be submitted for government approval.[21]

The reforms of October 2, 1965, were described by Kosygin as intended to give more importance to Gosplan. The creation of ministries was to increase Gosplan's role in coordinating the projects of various sectors. In reality, though, there is no evidence of the strengthening of Gosplan, except for its emancipation from supervision by the now-abolished Supreme Council of the Na-

18. "O dalneishem uluchshenii organizatsii planirovaniia razvitiia narodnogo khoziaistva SSSR" [On Further Improvement in the Organization of Planning of the U.S.S.R. National Economy], *Sobranie postanovlenii pravitelstva SSSR* [Collection of Decisions of the U.S.S.R. Government], No. 1, Art. 4, 1963, cited by A. A. Pushkin and I. Krasko "Rukovodstvo deiatelnostiu sovnarkhozov i organizatsiia planovoi raboty v promyshlennosti v novykh usloviiakh" [Management of the Work of the Sovnarkhozes and Organization of Planning Work in Industry in the New Conditions], *Sovetskoe gosudarstvo i pravo* [Soviet State and Law], No. 7, 1963, p. 101.

19. *Pravda*, March 14, 1963.

20. "Razvitie leninskikh printsipov organizatsii narodnokhoziaistvennogo planirovaniia" [Development of Leninist Principles of Organizing National Economic Planning], *Planovoe khoziaistvo*, No. 4, 1963, pp. 3-5.

21. Pushkin and Krasko, *Sovetskoe gosudarstvo i pravo*, No. 7, 1963, p. 102; and *Planovoe khoziaistvo*, No. 4, 1963, p. 4.

tional Economy (V.S.N.Kh.), a supervision that was actually more theoretical than real. Its jurisdiction over planning supplies of material and equipment remains partial,[22] and its new State Committee on Prices seems to have a more autonomous status than its former Office of Prices.[23]

Kosygin stressed the importance of the republic Gosplans. Until November, 1962, these Gosplans concerned themselves exclusively with plans for enterprises directly under the jurisdiction of their particular republic and local authorities. After that date, they were to supervise the execution of all plans for the republic's economy.[24] The law of October 2, 1965, specifies that the republic Gosplans should prepare plans for the economic program of their particular republics and republic ministries, while limiting themselves to suggestions for the preparation of plans by the U.S.S.R. ministries. The defense industry is, moreover, explicitly removed from the jurisdiction of republic Gosplans.

Before the reforms of October 2, 1965, the jurisdiction of republic Gosplans was rather vaguely defined, and it remains uncertain whether they actually prepared plans or only made suggestions for industries under direct jurisdiction of the central government (*i.e.*, under the Supreme Council of the National Economy—see Chart 3). It is more likely that their function was limited to mere suggestions and also that even then the defense industry had been completely removed from their influence. But even if the Gosplans' authority remains formally unchanged, it has changed in fact; some industries that were until October 2, 1965, under the Sovnarkhozes are now under the jurisdiction of ministries (especially machine-building industries—see Charts 1, 2, and 3). Therefore, the republic Gosplans are limited to making suggestions in matters where they had formerly had a direct responsibility for preparations of plans.

22. See note k of Chart 4.

23. The representative of the State Committee on Prices—along with the representatives of Gosplan, the Ministry of Finance, and other agencies—was a member of the commission that was to determine which enterprises were to transfer to the new system of management in 1966. See V. F. Garbuzov in *Pravda*, December 8, 1965, p. 4.

24. M. V. Breev (ed.), *Planirovanie narodnogo khoziaistva SSSR* [Planning of the U.S.S.R. National Economy], Moscow, 1963, p. 120.

Chart 5. Internal Organization of Gosplan Before the Reforms of November, 1962

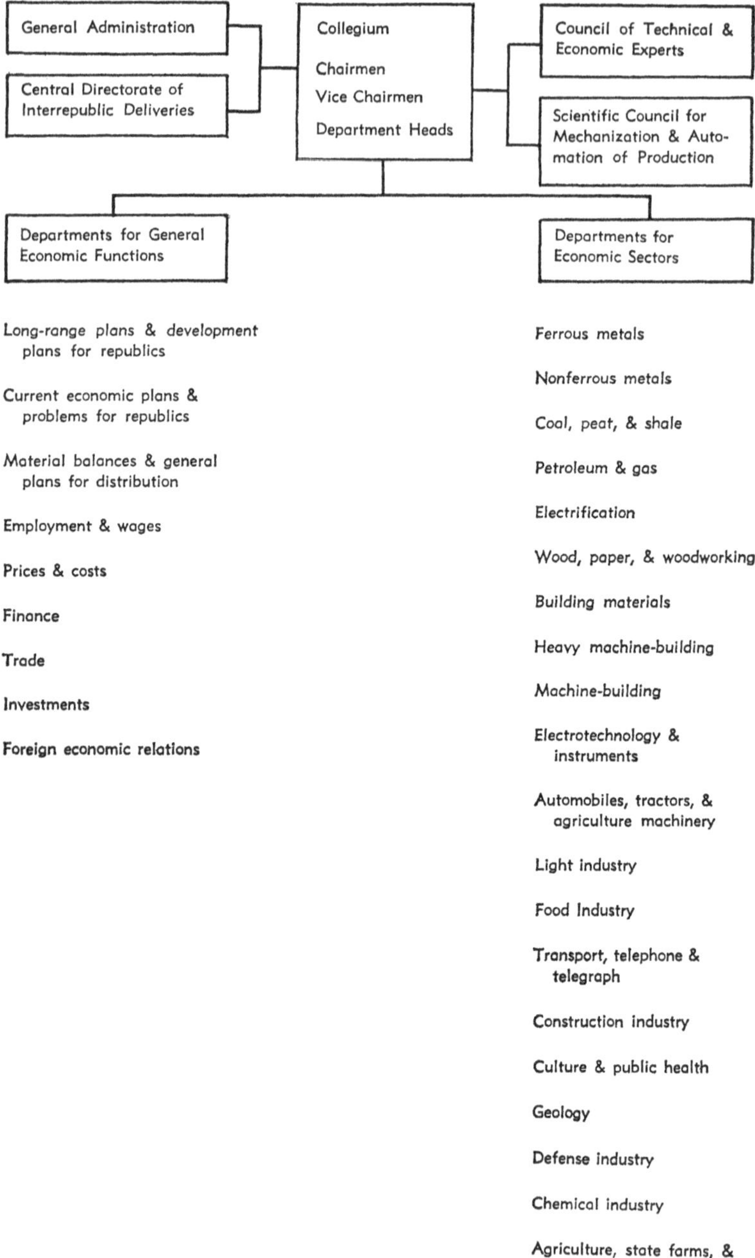

Source: A. N. Efimov, *Perestroika upravleniia promyshlennostiu i stroitelstvom v SSSR* [Reorganization of the Administration of Industry and

Source to Chart 5 (continued)

Construction in the U.S.S.R.], Moscow, 1957, p. 85. I. A. Evenko, *Voprosy planirovaniia v SSSR na sovremennom etape* [Problems of Planning in the U.S.S.R. at the Present Stage], Moscow, 1959.

The question of the responsibilities of republic Gosplans is part of a larger one: relations between Gosplan and ministries or, in other words, relations between current planning and management. The reforms of October 2, 1965, do not seem to provide an answer.

GOSPLAN'S INTERNAL ORGANIZATION AND DECISION-MAKING AUTHORITY

Preparation of a central plan requires a certain amount of arbitration by the planning office when plans for basic economic units, various sectors, etc., are coordinated. Until November, 1962, the body charged with that arbitration (see Chart 5) was the Gosplan Collegium, which consisted of thirty to thirty-five members with the simulated rank of U.S.S.R. minister.[25] This body thus consisted of quite a large number of important officials and was likely to produce rather impersonal decisions.

Since the Collegium had to resolve a large number of problems requiring special knowledge, it had to have the respect not only of Gosplan's technical personnel but also of various research institutes and bureaus of studies that cooperated with it. Around 1958, there were 323 scientific bodies subordinated to Gosplan, the republic Gosplans, and the Sovnarkhozes. These scientific bodies had 19,000 scientific workers, 16,000 of whom came directly under the jurisdiction of the Gosplans.[26] It is quite obvious, therefore, that their work could not be closely con-

25. See I. A. Evenko, *Voprosy planirovaniia v SSSR na sovremennom etape* [Problems of Planning in the U.S.S.R. at the Present Stage], Moscow, 1959, p. 35.

26. *Ibid.*, p. 32. In May, 1962, the Moscow section of U.S.S.R. Gosplan alone had a staff of twenty-seven hundred persons, ninety of whom were assigned to the Office of Prices, according to a report from the Soviet Union by the French mission under Louis Dufau-Perès, *Cahiers de l'I.S.E.A.*, Series G, August 18, 1963, p. 11.

trolled and that the coordination of plans had to consist as much in bargaining as in studying various dossiers.

The internal reorganization of Gosplan that took place after the reforms of November, 1962-March, 1963, reflected shifts in the responsibilities of that agency rather than changes in its working methods. It lost control of the Central Directorate of Interrepublic Deliveries, which was placed under the jurisdiction of U.S.S.R. Sovnarkhoz (created in November, 1962). Its sectoral departments lost much of their importance in coordinating plans after creation of sectoral state committees (see Chart 6); the heads of the former departments lost their rank as U.S.S.R. ministers and the chairmen of the new committees acquired it. It is also probable that many of the research institutes formerly under Gosplan were attached to state committees.

The decline in importance of Gosplan's departments was accompanied by a reduction in their number (see Charts 5 and 6). In principle there was merely a transfer of jurisdiction within the framework of Gosplan since most sectoral state committees were placed under its control (see Charts 3 and 4). In fact, however, the subordination of the state committees was purely formal since their chairmen sat on the Council of Ministers. The chairman of Gosplan was only first among equals, and one wonders whether he had sufficient power to impose his views.

After March, 1963, it became obvious that the situation was rather abnormal and that the sectoral state committees would have to be either combined with corresponding sectoral departments of Gosplan (if the system of regional management were strengthened) or made into ministries (if the system of sectoral management prevailed). Since the latter system came into effect when industrial ministries were re-established by the law of October 2, 1965, an internal reorganization of the Gosplan seems inevitable in view of the complete rearrangement of the economic administration. No information on such a reform was available as late as December, 1965. The sectoral state committees, which have become ministries, are no longer under Gosplan. The Office of Prices has become the State Committee on Prices attached to Gosplan, so that it now has greater autonomy.[27] One wonders whether the Council of Coordination and Planning of Large Economic Regions will survive the abolition of Sovnarkhozes, and whether the new ministers will replace former chairmen of state committees on Gosplan (see Chart 6). At any rate, a "scientific" balancing of planning powers on the central level may still concern the Soviet leaders for a while.

PLANNING AUTHORITY OUTSIDE GOSPLAN

Since the Soviet plan concerns the entire economy, it is natural that all political and economic organizations should cooperate in preparing it. In a broader sense, all agencies and even all Soviet citizens cooperate in planning. Obviously, it would be impossible to mention all these activities.

Party and Parliament. The role of the Communist party of the Soviet Union in economic management, mentioned earlier, could be traced out only through a special study. In principle, the Party has unlimited rights of all sorts, rights it can exercise only in part precisely because of their unlimited nature. The result is continual interference and intervention by the Party which limit considerably the powers delegated to Gosplan.

Another "sovereign" power in planning is wielded by both the Supreme Soviet and the republic Soviets. The plan is considered a legislative act, and since 1957 it has been submitted to the Soviets for parliamentary ratification. In reality, though, the rights exercised by the Soviets in planning have been very modest. The plan has been rapidly examined by the budgetary commissions of both the Soviet of the Union and the Soviet of Nationalities, and by the economic committee of the latter. These committees, although permanent in principle, were overburdened with work, and creation of a number of subcommittees (ten to twelve in the Supreme Soviet) did not remedy this defect. Parliamentary approval of the plan has taken place after a few days of cursory discussion, and the approved text has then undergone

27. See footnote 23 above.

important revisions in the course of the year through simple decrees of the Council of Ministers. The Supreme Soviet, the republic Soviets, and their Presidiums have not been consulted on these revisions or notified of them.

This practice has stirred up protests in the Soviet press recently; voices have been raised in favor of increasing the control over planning by the Soviets (parliament) as representatives of the public. It has been proposed that more detailed texts of the plan be submitted for parliamentary examination and that consultation with the Presidiums be obligatory when important adjustments are made in the approved plan.[28]

As a result of these criticisms, raised most frequently inside the Party, Brezhnev—speaking as Secretary General of the Party—suggested in his address of March 29, 1966, to the Twenty-third Party Congress that new, permanent committees be created in the Supreme Soviet. These committees came into existence on August 2 and 3, following a report by N. V. Podgorny to the First Session of the Seventh Supreme Soviet.[29] Out of a total of ten permanent budgetary committees created in each of the two chambers of the Supreme Soviet (the Soviet of the Union and the Soviet of Nationalities), the following seven were to be particularly concerned with economic questions: plan and budget; transportation and telecommunications; production of construction materials; agriculture; health and social security; education, science, and culture; and trade and services. The three other committees were those on law, foreign affairs, and mandates. We may note that the former Economic Committee of the Soviet of Nationalities was discontinued.

Membership in the committees has been increased. For each chamber, there are fifty-one members in the committee on the plan and budget, forty-one members in the committees on agri-

28. S. Dosymbekov, "Voprosy kompetentsii Verkhovnykh Sovetov Soiuznykh Respublik v oblasti planirovaniia (na materialakh Kazakhskoi SSR)" [Questions of the Jurisdiction of the Supreme Soviets of the Federal Republics in Matters of Planning (Based on Materials of the Kazakh Republic)], *Sovetskoe gosudarstvo i pravo*, No. 10, 1963, p. 43.

29. See N. V. Podgornyi, *Pravda*, August 3, 1966, p. 3, and August 5, 1966, pp. 3-4.

culture and on transportation and telecommunication, and thirty-one members in each of the others. The objective is to achieve a more careful examination of the plan and budget, a stricter control over the activities of ministries and administrative agencies, and a broader policy of hearings on ministerial reports and recommendations.[30]

The creation of these new permanent committees certainly strengthens parliamentary powers in the formulation of plans. But it also adds one more turn in the already tortuous path of plan making, and it is difficult to see how the government could take account of parliamentary objections requiring important revisions of the plan. In the case of the five-year plan for 1966-70, for example, examination by the Supreme Soviet is not to take place until December, 1966. If important revisions were then called for, the plan would be delayed six months to a year and would then apply only to the three years 1968-70. Even greater difficulties would be encountered in getting annual plans under way. One may reasonably wonder how much difference parliamentary arbitration will make in the planning powers.

Supreme Council of the National Economy. Between March, 1963, and October, 1965, Gosplan's decisions were submitted to the further arbitration of V.S.N.Kh. (see Chart 3). It would be quite difficult to ascertain the nature of this arbitration. V.S.N.Kh. had direct control over certain state committees and acted only as a coordinating agency for the activities of Gosplan, U.S.S.R. Sovnarkhoz, and Gosstroi. According to Mazurov's recent explanation, V.S.N.Kh. was concerned exclusively with industrial and construction problems, whereas Gosplan was concerned with the planning of the national economy as a whole.[31]

When the chairman of V.S.N.Kh. was made a first vice chairman of the Council of Ministers, he seemed to acquire great authority over economic activities of the country. It therefore came as a surprise when Ustinov, an expert on armaments, was

30. *Ibid.*, August 3, 1966, p. 3.
31. *Izvestia*, October 2, 1965, p. 2.

Chart 6. Internal Organization of Gosplan After the Reforms of November, 1962, and March, 1963 (approximate data)

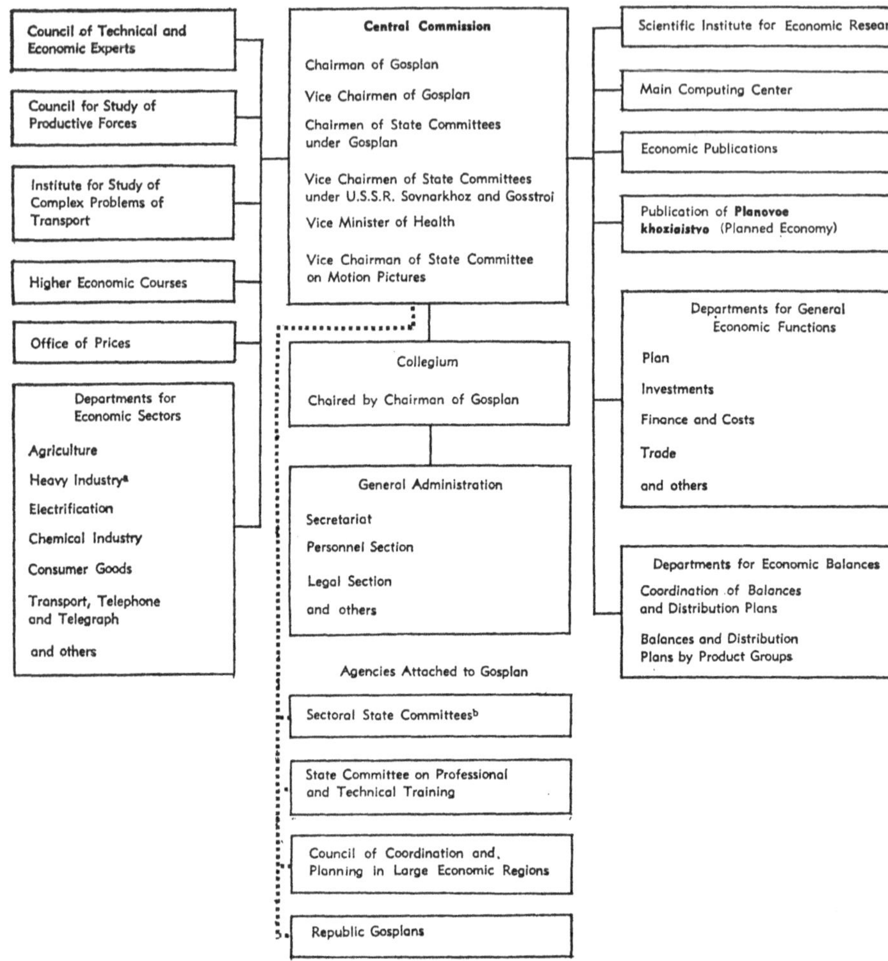

Note: ——— = agencies under the direct jurisdiction of Gosplan
- - - - = agencies under the indirect jurisdiction of Gosplan

Source: *Planovoe khoziaistvo*, No. 4, 1963, p. 9; Breev (ed.), *Planirovanie narodnogo khoziaistva*, p. 118; *Ekonomicheskaia gazeta*, January 11, 1964, pp. 16 and 43; V. V. Laptev (ed.), *Pravovye voprosy planirovaniia promyshlennosti v SSSR* [Legal Problems in Planning U.S.S.R. Industry], Moscow, 1964, pp. 81-95.

Notes to Chart 6

[a] This section drafts plans for the following industries: coal, petroleum, ferrous metals, nonferrous metals, geological prospecting, lumber, and building materials (see *Planovoe khoziaistvo*, No. 4, 1963, p. 9).

[b] The list of these state committees is given in Chart 3.

appointed to that position, since he was not even a member of the Politburo. As a rule, such a high position in the government is accompanied by a correspondingly high one in the Party hierarchy.

During the December, 1963, session of the Supreme Soviet, it also came as a surprise that the main speech presenting the plan was delivered by Gosplan Chairman P. F. Lomako, whereas the chairman of V.S.N.Kh.—theoretically the senior economic agency—played only a secondary role.[32] The trend toward re-establishing industrial ministries weakened V.S.N.Kh. even further. On March 2, 1965, eight of the committees under it were released from its control and turned into ministries, and on March 26, Ustinov resigned from his post upon being chosen Secretary of the Party Central Committee. Considering the criticism of that body by Kosygin and Mazurov when it was abolished, one may conclude that its coordinating functions had been rather ill-defined and that it had not been exercising its power for some time before being abolished.

U.S.S.R. Sovnarkhoz. The responsibilities for planning were better defined in the case of U.S.S.R. Sovnarkhoz, created in November, 1962. In addition to having direct control over the forty-seven regional Sovnarkhozes (see Chart 3) that supervised preparation and execution of plans at the enterprise level, it had some functions, taken over from the former Gosplan, that were essential to planning, such as supplying materials and equipment, determining suppliers and customers, and controlling all inter-republic deliveries.[33] It also had authority to revise plans of

32. The other important speech at that session of the Supreme Soviet was the presentation of the budget by V. F. Garbuzov, the Minister of Finance (see *Pravda*, December 17 and 20, 1963).

33. Breev (ed.), *Planirovanie narodnogo khoziaistva*, p. 119; also *Planovoe khoziaistvo*, No. 4, 1963, p. 5.

republics and of various sectors, to make changes in the allocation of funds for investment, and to discontinue production for which there was not sufficient demand.[34] Despite the fact that the fixing of norms was within Gosplan's jurisdiction, the Research Institute on Organization of Management and Fixing of Norms came under U.S.S.R. Sovnarkhoz, so that the latter could exert a strong influence on Gosplan.

Reduction in the number of compulsory indexes in the national plan considerably increased the planning powers of U.S.S.R. Sovnarkhoz. Acting on proposals of the republics and other economic agencies, U.S.S.R. Sovnarkhoz confirmed plans for production and distribution of commodities that were not listed in the national plan.[35] In other words, a part of the plan did not go beyond U.S.S.R. Sovnarkhoz.

While being essentially a managerial agency, U.S.S.R. Sovnarkhoz also played an important role in preparation of the plan. The plans drafted by Gosplan concerning development of the national economy and foreign trade were submitted to U.S.S.R. Sovnarkhoz for preliminary study before being submitted to the Council of Ministers for final approval.[36]

While the division of power between U.S.S.R. Sovnarkhoz and Gosplan did not seem to present any major difficulties at the national level, it did at the republic and province levels.[37] From November, 1962, on, republic Gosplans prepared plans for the entire economy of the republic and not, as before, just for those enterprises and organizations that were administratively depen-

34. Pawlik, *Gospodarka Planowa*, No. 8-9, 1963, p. 62.

35. *Planovoe khoziaistvo*, No. 4, 1963, p. 5.

36. *Ibid.*, p. 6; and Breev (ed.), *Planirovanie narodnogo khoziaistvo*, p. 119.

37. Abram Bergson, *The Economics of Soviet Planning* (New Haven and London, 1964), p. 146, mentions the imprecise distinction between responsibilities of the Gosplans and Sovnarkhozes in the republics. Interventions of U.S.S.R. Gosplan were just as frequent on the republic level, since it was concerned with allocation of resources not only among but also within republics, even down to individual enterprises. This task was supposed to be carried out "in cooperation with republic agencies" by the Glavsbyt (sales services) of former ministries attached to Gosplan after their abolition in 1957-58. Bergson's remarks apply to the period from 1958 to November, 1962.

dent on the republic and local agencies.[38] They also coordinated the work of state agencies, for which they determined planned goals. In these regards, they had to resolve concrete problems that arose in the course of fulfillment of plans, to direct work of the services of supplies and sales, and to control implementation of the national plan.[39] This state of affairs created confusion about the responsibilities of Sovnarkhoz and Gosplan on the republic or province level and led to *de facto* subordination of republic Gosplans to U.S.S.R. Sovnarkhoz, as opposed to their *de jure* subordination to U.S.S.R. Gosplan and the republic Councils of Ministers. This is a typical example of how difficult it is to distinguish functions of annual and current planning, on the one hand, and management, on the other.[40]

When Kosygin announced on September 27, 1965, that the Sovnarkhoz system was to be abolished, the conflict between responsibilities of planning and management was not resolved. A large share of U.S.S.R. Sovnarkhoz's power in the central allocation of resources was turned over to the State Committee for Supply of Materials and Equipment under the Council of Ministers. V. E. Dymshits, former chairman of U.S.S.R. Sovnarkhoz, was named chairman of that committee. An effort was made to maintain the principle of regional management by creating Directorates for Supply of Materials and Equipment in the republics, those directorates to be subordinated both to the state committee headed by Dymshits and to republic Councils of Ministers.[41] The other responsibilities of U.S.S.R. Sovnarkhoz

38. Breev (ed.), *Planirovanie narodnogo khoziaistva*, p. 120.

39. Pushkin and Krasko, *Sovetskoe gosudarstvo i pravo*, No. 7, 1963, p. 103.

40. Certain authors like Pushkin and Krasko, *ibid.*, advocated limiting the role of republic Gosplans to the preparation of long-range and annual plans. But since the plan cannot be fulfilled without being subjected to continuous changes, it is difficult to see how this suggestion could be accepted without making Gosplan an unrealistic institution. The October 2, 1965, decree on administrative reorganization ignored the suggestion. The republic Gosplans must, in effect, examine the problems arising in the course of fulfillment of the plan and involving several different branches of industry so that they will often be forced to interfere in cases concerning management.

41. Iu. Koldomasov, "Razvitie priamykh khoziaistvennykh sviaziakh i

were transferred to the newly created ministries. Hence two regional planning systems (republic Gosplans and Directorates for Supply) existed, along with the ministerial agencies for each sector on the republic and local level. Definition of powers required special dispositions that were taken after final disappearance of the Sovnarkhozes in 1966.[42]

Gosstroi. The U.S.S.R. State Building Committee (Gosstroi) is another central agency with which Gosplan must share its power in planning (see Chart 3).

After the 1957 reforms, Sovnarkhozes were supposed to manage industry and construction. Actually, construction was largely subordinated to the republic Ministries of Construction. Of the 8,000 building enterprises under the republic Councils of Ministers, only 3,500 were placed under the jurisdiction of Sovnarkhozes, 3,400 under republic Ministries of Construction, and more than 1,000 under local Soviets.[43]

The reforms of November, 1962, extended to both the plan-

sovershenstvovanie raspredeleniia sredstv proizvodstva" [Development of Direct Economic Ties and Improvement of the Distribution of Means of Production], *Voprosy ekonomiki*, No. 11, 1965, p. 14.

42. The 1966 plan was drawn up on the basis of the old economic administrative system with subdivisions by Sovnarkhoz. Regional Sovnarkhozes could therefore not be abolished before this plan was put into operation. According to Henryk Chadzynski, "ZSSR—Rachunek, bodźce, gospodarność" [The U.S.S.R.—Calculations, Incentives, Savings], *Zycie Gospodarcze*, November 7, 1965, p. 1, industrial ministries were to take over management of Sovnarkhozes at the beginning of December, 1965, and to write a report accompanied by a work schedule on December 15, 1965 (as told to Chadzynski by the Chairman of the Russian Republic Gosplan, Ia. Chadaev).

43. M. I. Baryshev, "Noiabrskii (1962 g.) plenum TsK KPSS i dalneishee sovershenstvovanie organizatsionno-pravovykh form upravleniia stroitelstvom" [The November, 1962, Plenary Session of the Party Central Committee and Further Improvement of the Organizational and Legal Forms of Managing Construction Work], *Sovetskoe gosudarstvo i pravo*, No. 8, 1963, p. 81. In the three big republics—RSFSR, Ukraine, and Kazakhstan—the Sovnarkhozes could run general construction enterprises, while special construction and assembly enterprises were placed under the republic ministries of construction. However, in various other republics—Belorussia, Latvia, Lithuania, Kirghizia, Tadzhikistan, Turkmenia, Uzbekistan—all construction enterprises were placed under the republic ministries of construction. See Pawlik, *Gospodarka Planowa*, No. 8-9, 1963, p. 56.

ning and management of construction. All building enterprises that were not managed directly by state committees for production were placed under the republic Ministries of Construction.[44] At the same time, an important role in planning was given to a newly created agency called U.S.S.R. Gosstroi, which was to be "responsible for fulfillment of investment plans throughout the country, while coordination of the technical policy for construction remained under the jurisdiction of state committees and republic construction agencies."[45]

In practice, Gosstroi has, in investment planning, a role comparable to that of U.S.S.R. Sovnarkhoz in industrial planning. In collaboration with the republics, it prepares plans for subcontracting agencies specialized in construction and plans for model projects.[46] In cooperation with Gosplan, Gosstroi examines estimates of construction made with imported equipment and norms for expenditure and inventories of construction materials. It presents to Gosplan requests for high-priority construction to be entered in the drafts of the national plan. It also cooperated with U.S.S.R. Sovnarkhoz in drawing up plans for production and distribution of building materials. It helps the State Committee on the Coordination of Science and Research to prepare plans for research in its field.[47] It also has the right to revise allocation of investment funds, materials, and equipment among republics and branches of industry.[48]

The essential functions of Gosstroi were apparently not changed by the reforms of October 2, 1965. It has, however, lost control over several state committees that were promoted to ministries: construction of means of transportation; assembly work and special construction; building materials; and machine-building for construction, road construction, and communal economy.

44. *Ibid.*, pp. 58 and 62.

45. Decree of the Party Central Committee and the Council of Ministers on "Improvement in the Management of Capital Construction," *Sobranie postanovlenii*, No. 1, Art. 5, 1963 (cited by Baryshev, *Sovetskoe gosudarstvo i pravo*, No. 8, 1963, p. 86).

46. Breev (ed.), *Planirovanie narodnogo khoziaistva*, p. 119.

47. *Planovoe khoziaistvo*, No. 4, 1963, p. 7.

48. Pawlik, *Gospodarka Planowa*, No. 8-9, 1963, p. 62.

State Committees. The reforms of November, 1962, considerably increased the responsibilities of state committees, which until then had acted essentially in an advisory capacity. Their position in the hierarchy of economic agencies also improved because their chairmen obtained ministerial status and became members of the Gosplan Collegium (in the case of committees affiliated with Gosplan). One vice chairman from each committee participated in the management of U.S.S.R. Sovnarkhoz, supervising fulfillment of plans for introduction of new productive capacities, etc.[49] In other words, state committees took over several functions of the former ministries, and they were often chaired by former ministers for the same sectors.[50]

The planning function of the state committees was to prepare plans for the entire country. This work was based on regional projects presented by republic Councils of Ministers. The state committees determined the volume and nomenclature of production, productivity indexes, and costs. They also helped prepare plans for scientific work in their sectors and examined proposals of plans for introducing new technology as presented by the republic Councils of Ministers. In the latter field, their responsibilities went beyond planning since they had the power to distribute material and technical means for investments.[51]

Several responsibilities of the state committees were on the border line between planning and management. They took part in determining and approving norms for the use of raw materials and fuel, in planning the training of qualified personnel (engineers and technicians), and in checking on adherence to planned technological processes by enterprises. In some cases, state committees managed directly the work of enterprises or agencies subordinated to them, particularly in the case of state committees for production.[52] The sectoral state committees had direct con-

49. "On the Increased Role of the State Committees and on Their Responsibility for Developing Industries," *Sobranie postanovlenii*, No. 1, Art. 3, 1963, decree of January 11, 1963 (cited by Pushkin and Krasko, *Sovetskoe gosudarstvo i pravo*, No. 7, 1963, p. 105).

50. N. Khrushchev, *Izvestia*, April 26, 1963.

51. *Planovoe khoziaistvo*, No. 4, 1963, p. 8.

52. See Chart 3, note a.

trol over scientific institutes placed under them in November, 1962, and over some industries considered particularly important. They could also, jointly with the Sovnarkhozes, manage pilot enterprises.[53]

Ministries. After the reforms of October 2, 1965, almost all former state committees for production became ministries. According to Kosygin, the old state committees' powers were inadequate. Plans for new technology were studied and passed upon by some agencies (state committees), plans for production and investment by others (Gosplan and Gosstroi), and plans for supplying materials and equipment by still another (U.S.S.R. Sovnarkhoz). The re-establishment of industrial ministries was designed to remedy this dispersion of power: the ministries were to supervise fulfillment of plans, direct production, and resolve problems of technological policy, supply of materials and equipment, finance, employment, and wages.[54]

Industrial ministries became managers of funds allotted for supply of materials and equipment. They were also given direct control of the scientific research institutes in their respective sectors. Obviously, industrial ministries have inherited virtually all the powers of former state committees for production, as well as many powers of the former U.S.S.R. Sovnarkhoz. They have therefore considerable power in planning.

Republic Councils of Ministers. When the regional system of economic management was introduced in 1957, the role of republic Councils of Ministers in the administration and management of the economy increased considerably. However, their power was more limited in the preparation of plans because Gosplan was not legally obliged to take their suggestions into account.[55] The reforms of November, 1962, strengthened the role of republic Councils in planning, the decree of January 11, 1963, stipulating that Gosplan must take into account proposals for

53. Pawlik, *Gospodarka Planowa*, No. 8-9, 1963, pp. 60-61.

54. A. Kosygin, *Pravda*, September 28, 1965.

55. Pushkin and Krasko, *Sovetskoe gosudarstvo i pravo*, No. 7, 1963, p. 101.

plans presented by republic Councils and incorporate them into a coherent regional and sectoral framework.[56]

The republic Councils of Ministers were an important link in the Soviet planning system because the republic Gosplans and Sovnarkhozes were directly subordinated to them. Each Council of Ministers approved the plans prepared by the Sovnarkhozes for gross and marketed production and for the output of principal commodities in physical terms. In addition, approved plans for specialization and cooperation of enterprises, transportation of goods, costs, and allocation of raw materials and equipment. Finally, it made general appraisals of the work of the republic Sovnarkhozes.[57]

In the speech of September 27, 1965, announcing reforms in economic administration, Kosygin declared that the Party Central Committee and the Council of Ministers had adopted a resolution entrusting the republics with new responsibilities in planning, investment, finance, employment, and wage policies. One may, therefore, assume that some of the responsibilities of Sovnarkhozes have been transferred to the republic Councils of Ministers. However, certain other responsibilities of Sovnarkhozes in industry have been transferred to all-union ministers and probably also to union-republic ministries. In order to draw more specific conclusions, one must wait for the reforms of October 2, 1965, to be put into operation.

The list of planning powers exerted by agencies other than Gosplan is not complete. One could mention the important control power wielded by the National (formerly Party and State) Control Committee, the financial control exercised by the Ministry of Finance and the banks, and the statistical control exercised by the U.S.S.R. Central Statistical Administration. However, this brief survey of the responsibilities of the various agencies of the Soviet state is sufficient to see the limits to the

56. Decree "On the Further Improvement of the Organization of Planning of the U.S.S.R. National Economy," cited by Pushkin and Krasko, *ibid.*

57. *Ibid.*

power of the central planning agency, which, in theory, should be Gosplan.[58]

58. Limitation of the powers of Gosplan has also resulted from failure to codify the legal texts regulating the planning process. Those texts are "numerous, poorly coordinated, and often even contradictory." See P. Fedoseev, *Pravda*, December 9, 1962, cited by Pushkin and Krasko, *Sovetskoe gosudarstvo i pravo*, No. 7, 1963, p. 102.

CHAPTER 3. Continuous Planning

The idea of "continuous planning" (*nepererivnoe planirovanie*) was introduced to the public by Khrushchev in his speech before the Supreme Soviet on May 7, 1957:

> In reviewing the work of our planning agencies, it must be pointed out that one of the serious flaws of our planning system is that from one year to the next, from one five-year plan to the next, each time, we begin planning almost from scratch. The year draws to a close and some of our enterprises and construction sites do not have plans for the coming year until the last moment or even until the very end of the current year. Life is a continuous activity, whereas plans are cut off at certain fixed calendar dates. Planning must be organized in such a way that the essential features of the plan for the following year should be known in the course of the current year and that the principal features of the forthcoming five-year plan, or at least the essential data for its first years, should be known while the current five-year plan is still in force.
>
> Most enterprises are built over the course of several years. For that reason, when planning, we must not only consider what we shall need during the present five-year period, but also look into the future and try to see and study the prospects for the forthcoming five years.[1]

These ideas were taken up officially, and a government decree of December, 1960, as well as a planning conference in March, 1961, tried to put "continuous planning" into practice. Finally, the decree of January 11, 1963, stipulated:

> The plans for development of the national economy are drawn up for five-year periods and are subdivided by year, by sector, by republic, and by large economic region.
>
> On the basis of goals of the five-year national economic plan and taking account of the state of its fulfillment, of new needs, of scientific and technological progress, of new resources in primary raw materials and other reserves of

1. *Zasedaniia Verkhovnogo Soveta SSSR Chetvertogo Soiuza* [Sessions of the U.S.S.R. Supreme Soviet of the Fourth Legislature], 7th Session, Stenographic Transcript, Moscow, 1957.

> the national economy—indispensable corrections are introduced (and approved) in the annual plans and their semiannual subdivisions.
>
> In order to ensure continuity of planning in annual plans, the principal targets of economic growth for the year after the five-year plan are established at the same time, so that the prospects of national economic growth are always established for a five-year period.[2]

It is interesting to see to what extent this technique of continuous revision of the targets of the long-range plans is new in the history of Soviet planning and then to examine the reforms actually carried out after 1960.

NEW TECHNIQUES OF LONG-RANGE PLANNING

The need for a continuous formulation of long-term prospects—five, seven, even fifteen or twenty years in advance—apparently does not spring solely, as Khrushchev claimed, from difficulties caused by the transition from one five-year plan to the next. It also stems from the impossibility of accurately foreseeing the evolution of an economy and the effects of decisions that are made. In fact, every adjustment of any importance in a plan requires revision of virtually all indexes, whether in the current annual plan or in the remainder of the current five-year plan. Continuous planning is, therefore, necessary even if the terminal year of the plan is maintained and not pushed ahead.

Soviet planners of the 1920's and 1930's were well aware of these problems. The draft of the First Five-Year Plan, prepared jointly by Gosplan and the Supreme Council of the National Economy in 1925, was revised every year until 1929. Every year it proved necessary to make a draft for the coming five-year period. Thus, the plan for 1925/26-1929/30 was superseded by one for 1926/27-1930/31, later by one for 1927/28-1931/32, and finally by one for 1928/29-1932/33. The improvement in planning techniques and the fact that the text of the First Five-Year Plan did not receive official approval until May, 1929, certainly

2. "On Further Improvement of the Organization of Planning of National Economic Growth," in K. I. Orliankin (ed.), *Sbornik reshenii po selskomu khoziaistvu* [Collection of Decisions on Agriculture], Moscow, 1963, p. 663.

justified continuing preparatory work and drafting new variants. Changes in planned targets resulted mostly from changes in economic outlook, revisions of Party and governmental economic policy, and postponement of the terminal year of the plan in order always to have a five-year period ahead.[3]

After the First Five-Year Plan was adopted by the Fifth Congress of the Soviets on May 29, 1929, it became obvious that quite substantial revisions were needed. The government, having proclaimed that the five-year plan was the law of the land and hence binding on all citizens, was very reluctant to admit that its plan was already obsolete. Nevertheless, the control figures (annual plan) for 1929/30 differed considerably from the targets written into the five-year plan for that year. With Stalin's emphasis on the collectivization of agriculture, on "the forward leap" in heavy industry, and on a national policy of independence from foreign markets, a general revision of the five-year plan became essential; and all governmental agencies got down to work on it in the spring of 1930. Instead of devising new plans for the five years ahead, they revised only the targets for the terminal year—1932/33—of the First Five-Year Plan. The revised parts of the plan became the Three-Year Plan for 1930/31-1932/33 or, after the adoption of the calendar year in the Soviet Union, 1931-33.[4]

During the years 1930 and 1931, the Soviet Union went through a period of feverish activity when the pace of collectivization and the building of new factories could not possibly be planned with any precision. The work of planners lagged behind reality, and only a few isolated three-year plans (1931-33) for certain sectors were drawn up without being properly fitted into an over-all plan of the national economy. To save time, the government started working on a second five-year plan for 1933-37 in 1931. Actually, at the outset this was a six-year plan since the first year, 1932, was considered as a year of "preparation."[5]

3. For details, see E. Zaleski, *Planification de la Croissance et Fluctuations Economiques en U.R.S.S.*, Vol. I, 1918-1932 (Paris, 1962), pp. 48-56.

4. *Ibid.*, pp. 108-11.

5. *Ibid.*, pp. 194-97.

After numerous revisions in this second five-year plan during 1931-34, it was officially adopted and published in November, 1934. In 1935 and 1936 new revisions became necessary, and the annual plans for these years departed considerably from the corresponding versions in the Second Five-Year Plan. Nevertheless, no over-all revision of the Second Five-Year Plan was ever published, and it is doubtful whether one was ever made. In 1936 and 1937 the economic outlook had already changed considerably, and planners were looking forward to preparation of a third five-year plan for 1938-42.

Continuous long-range planning was also practiced during the latter period. A first draft was ready in 1937, and a revised draft was published in the spring of 1939. There was probably a further revision in 1940, but it was never published. In any case, in 1941 the Soviet government was mainly interested in the long-range plan for 1943-57 and in the new five-year plan for 1943-47; it gave no thought to revising targets of the Third Five-Year Plan for 1942.[6]

During the years 1945-52, Soviet long-range planning was not very advanced. It was only after Stalin's death in 1953 that multi-year plans similar to the continuous prewar planning began to be published frequently. Khrushchev's idea of continuous planning involved considerable improvements over previous practices. Adjustments and revisions in plans were no longer to be carried out in an isolated fashion by some central planning or management agencies, but were to be approached in an orderly, coordinated way in order to draft a new coherent variant of the general plan that would each time give the prospects for several years ahead. The new goals were no longer to be derived by extrapolating existing trends in individual sectors, but were instead to permit greater expansion in sectors of rapid growth, such as the chemical industry. The terminal year of the five-year plans was to lose its mystical significance thanks to continuous preparation of long-range plans for five-year periods.

Continuous planning, as defined by Khrushchev, remained

6. E. Zaleski, *Planification de la Croissance et Fluctuations Economiques en U.R.S.S.*, Vol. II, 1933-1952 (in preparation).

nothing more than a blueprint. In 1961 the Council of Ministers charged the republic Councils, the ministries, and other interested agencies with preparation of the basic indexes of national economic growth for 1966 and their submission to the State Economic Committee (Gosekonomsovet) by November 15, 1961, at the latest. To make that possible, Gosekonomsovet had to supply republic Councils of Ministers with necessary forms and schedules as well as control figures for 1966. Though the forms were sent in 1961, it was necessary to wait until the end of January, 1962, for the control figures. The 1962 annual plans for individual republics therefore had to be drafted without taking into account goals for the Soviet Union as a whole as envisaged by the control figures for 1966. The republics went on preparing the 1966 plan, but, in the output of certain commodities and in the installment of new facilities, their drafts turned out considerably different from the corrected versions of the Seven-Year Plan, which at that very time were being adjusted in republic Gosplans and in Gosekonomsovet. Consequently, it proved necessary to suspend work on the long-range plan for 1966, and the republics proceeded with preparation of their annual plans for 1963 without benefit of a five-year perspective for the year 1967.[7]

The Soviet government has given up, at least for the time being, preparing long-range plans every year for the next five years. The March 13, 1963, decree ordered preparation of a new five-year plan for 1966-70 and of a plan for the "preliminary" years 1964-65.[8] Controversies about the role of heavy industry, changes in leadership after Khrushchev's downfall, poor harvests, and the international situation were no doubt responsible for the slow preparation of the 1966-70 plan. Many variants of this plan were probably considered, and the one published in part in February, 1966, and discussed during the Twenty-third Party Congress does not seem to be final.[9] On June 8, 1966, Kosygin

7. F. Khiliuk, "O nekotorykh voprosakh uporiadochneniia organizatsii planirovaniia" [Some Problems Connected with Bringing Order into Planning], *Planovoe khoziaistvo*, No. 7, 1962, p. 46.

8. *Pravda*, March 14, 1963.

9. "Postanovlenie Plenuma TsK KPSS priniatoe 19 fevralia 1966 g. Proekt Direktiv XXIII sezda KPSS po piatiletnemu planu razvitiia narodnogo

announced that it would be discussed further at the session of the Supreme Soviet on August 2 and 3, but this discussion did not take place.[10] The new committees of the Supreme Soviet established in August will not be able to deliberate on the five-year plan until December, 1966, and by that time the annual plan for 1967 will already be prepared. Hence, they will in effect consider only the plan for the three years 1968-70.

As far as continuous planning is concerned, the situation appears to be very much the same as it was toward the end of 1931, when the early drafts of the Second Five-Year Plan made it possible, to some extent, to lose sight of the initial goals of the First Five-Year Plan. In any case, as now practiced in the Soviet Union, continuous planning resembles prewar planning much more than Khrushchev's ideal concepts.

What, then, are the chances for introducing real continuous planning in the Soviet economy?

The first obstacle is the increasing complexity of the modern industrial system, which imposes long delays in transmission of information through various administration and planning levels and which, for all practical purposes, makes impossible the drafting of any adequately detailed centralized plans. According to Academician A. Dorodnitsyn,[11] the problems of Soviet industrial planning are today 1600 times more complicated than they were in 1928, whereas the planning methods have remained very much the same. Dorodnitsyn claims that the number of relations between indexes in the plan increases in proportion to the square of the number of these indexes. When preparing the plan for the machine-tool industry, which turns out 125,000 types of

khoziaistva SSSR na 1966-1970 gody" [Decision of the Plenary Session of the U.S.S.R. Party Central Committee of February 19, 1966; Draft of the Directives of the 23rd Party Congress on the Five-Year Plan for the Development of the U.S.S.R. National Economy in 1966-1970], *ibid.*, February 20, 1966, pp. 1-6. See also the speeches of Brezhnev and Kosygin at the 23rd Congress in *ibid.*, March 30, 1966, pp. 2-9, and April 6, 1966, pp. 2-7.

10. *Pravda*, June 9, 1966, and August 3 and 5, 1966.

11. *Izvestia*, May 15, 1963, as cited by Leon Smolinski and Peter Wiles in "The Soviet Planning Pendulum," *Problems of Communism*, November-December, 1963, pp. 21-24.

products, planners must take into account 15 billion possible relations (125,000 × 125,000). It is possible to get an idea of the difficulties facing Soviet planners by remembering that the standard classification of all industrial products made today in the Soviet Union includes as many as 20 million items.[12]

The complexities of planning also increase with the growing number of industrial enterprises. Today industrial statistics list two hundred thousand enterprises; the total number of enterprises and organizations with accounting autonomy (*khozraschet*) is almost two million.[13] The increase in the number of industrial enterprises stems directly from technological progress encouraging specialization and outside contracts and brings about disintegration of the old "universal" factories. Automation too has caused the national economy to become more sensitive to disturbances in the supply of raw materials and spare parts while amplifying planning errors. The old practice of feverish last-moment assaults to fulfill or over-fulfill plans (*sturmovshchina*) cannot work in an automated factory.

This evolution has resulted in a disquieting expansion in planning personnel. According to the estimates of N. P. Fedorenko, director of the Central Institute of Mathematical Economics, the actual number of persons engaged in the "sphere of administration" is about twelve million. According to Kovalev, the number of persons engaged in planning and control has risen by about 50 per cent in the course of the past seven years.[14] Ac-

12. *Ekonomicheskaia gazeta*, May 18, 1963, p. 17, as cited by Smolinski and Wiles in *Problems of Communism*, November-December, 1963, p. 24. The number of centrally planned products often varies and data on that subject are rather meager. One must distinguish here products that are centrally *planned* and products that are centrally *allocated* in the supplying of materials and equipment.

13. A. M. Birman, "Za glubokuiu razrabotku problem upravleniia" [For a Detailed Elaboration of Problems of Management], *Planovoe khoziaistvo*, No. 3, 1963, p. 13; and Smolinski and Wiles, *Problems of Communism*, November-December, 1963, pp. 23-24. There are also 400,000 construction sites in the Soviet Union, of which 100,000 are financed by Gosplan. See O. Nekrasov, "Otraslevoi printsyp upravleniia promyshlennostiu i tekhnicheskii progres" [Basic Principle of Industrial Management and Technological Progress], *Voprosy ekonomiki*, No. 11, 1965, p. 8.

14. N. Kovalev, "Nauchnoe planirovanie i ratsionalnaia sistema ekonomi-

cording to V. M. Glushkov, planning work multiplies by the square of production and one would have to multiply by thirty-six the number of economists engaged in planning to attain a sixfold multiple in production in 1980 if planning methods are not changed.[15] Some Soviet authors go even further and claim that, according to certain calculations, if present planning methods were preserved, by 1980 the entire adult population of the Soviet Union would be employed in planning and administration.[16]

Soviet administrators seem to count heavily on mathematical methods and electronic computers as means of coping with the overflow of work resulting from modernization of the national economy. Early in 1964, a decision of the Party Central Committee and the Council of Ministers provided for establishment of a Unified Automatic System of Management.[17] Realization of this project would enable automatic collection and use of economic data, both retrospective and planned. A network of relay posts and computing centers, interconnected and communicating with enterprises, would process the collected data itself.

cheskoi informatsii" [Scientific Planning and a Rational System of Economic Information], *ibid.*, No. 12, 1962, p. 102: "If the present methods of data processing are maintained, in twenty years the planning and control apparatus will grow more than four times while the national economy will receive only a 'starvation diet' of economic data."

15. Speech of K. N. Plotnikov during discussion of a report by L. F. Ilichev, *Vestnik akademii nauk SSSR*, No. 12, 1962, p. 42.

16. "Stroitelstvo kommunizma i planirovanie" [The Building of Communism and Planning], *Planovoe khoziaistvo*, No. 10, 1962, p. 5.

17. M. Polonskii and M. Ippa, "Na putiakh k edinoi sisteme" [On the Road to a Single System], *Ekonomicheskaia gazeta*, February 8, 1964, p. 42; M. Fedorovich, *ibid.*, March 21, 1964, p. 13; V. S. Nemchinov, "Sotsialisticheskoe khoziaistvovanie i planirovanie proizvodstva" [Socialist Management and Planning of Production], *Kommunist*, No. 5, 1964, p. 84.

It is, however, difficult to imagine an input-output table with 18,000 entries, which would in any case risk being inaccurate and becoming obsolete very rapidly. "It is naive to think that it is possible to coordinate perfectly within central agencies the production and material supply plans for hundreds of thousands of enterprises whose links are continuously and inevitably being extended in the course of the production process." N. Razumov, "O polozhenii i pravakh promyshlennogo predpriiatiia" [On the Situation and Rights of the Industrial Enterprise], *Voprosy ekonomiki*, No. 7, 1963, p. 130.

The hope is to form an automatic flow of information from base to center, thereby ensuring immediate control over execution of the plan and, in case of need, preparation of required corrections and adjustments in essential elements of the plan. It is estimated that the Unified Automatic System of Management will be in operation in fifteen to twenty years and that numerous production complexes could then be run with minimal requirements of personnel. Planning work would be liberated from the "manual" methods in use today.

The computing centers are first being installed in Belorussia, Lithuania, the Tartar Autonomous Republic, and the Kiev economic region. In 1962, the Belorussian Computing Center, assisted by the laboratory of the U.S.S.R. Academy of Sciences, worked out matrixes for five hundred industrial enterprises, permitting calculation of a planned balance of production and distribution in Belorussia. It also undertook preparation of a Belorussian input-output table for the year 1970, to complement work being done by central agencies for the country as a whole.

It has been suggested that data processing as such should be dissociated from the network of planning, operational management, and relay posts. Data processing would be based on the present system of the Central Statistical Administration, whose calculating centers would be transformed into electronic computing centers.

It has also been suggested that management systems be distinguished for different levels of economic administration. "Large systems" would apply to sectors, regions, and republics; "medium systems," to enterprises; and "small systems," to certain technological processes of production. Most progress is currently being made in establishing "small and medium automatic systems of management."

In the beginning of 1966, the Unified Automatic System of Management was still in the planning stage. V. N. Starovskii, head of the Central Statistical Administration, stressed the fact that this work should come under the jurisdiction of his agency, but he admitted that it might be possible to create separate networks for sectors and agencies if the various networks were linked together. At the same time he warned against attempting to create an automatic system of computing centers that would issue detailed operational orders to every enterprise, for he considered such ideas against the spirit of the October, 1965, reforms.[18]

According to Starovskii, computing sections and centers (*mashinoschetnye stantsii ili vychislitelnye tsentry*) have been created in all the federal republics and major regions and in more than 650 administrative regions and cities. But he stressed that the handling of basic accounting material is still very complicated and that the problem of mechanization remains to be solved. More than two million persons are engaged at present in this work, not counting engineers, technicians, and other specialists.

One of the most difficult problems remaining is how to coordinate the work of different agencies. Starovskii insists that priority be accorded to his agency in the processing of statistical data. In the decree recently issued by the Soviet government on the distribution of tasks,[19] the Central Statistical Administration is to establish and install a national system of computing centers; Gosplan is to design the system; and an Agency for Constructing and Assembling Computing Centers, established as an autonomous accounting unit (*khozraschet*), is to construct them. The State Committee on Science and Technology, the Academy of Sciences, and the Committee on Standardization, Weights, and Measures also had their functions defined. The creation of scientific bases and the long-range development, design, and installation of the computing centers seem to be too complicated for a precise administrative distribution of functions among the various state agencies. We can therefore expect new assignments to be made and specialized agencies to be

18. See "Gosudarstvennaia set vychislitelnykh tsentrov" [National Network of Computing Centers], *Ekonomicheskaia gazeta*, No. 3, 1966, p. 25.

19. "Ob uluchshenii organizatsii raboty po sozdaniiu i vnedreniia v narodnoe khoziaistvo sredstv vychislitelnoi tekhniki i avtomatizirovannykh sistem upravleniia [On Improving the Organization of the Work to Establish and to Introduce into the National Economy Computational Techniques and Automatic Systems of Management], cited in *ibid.*

created, while organizational and social obstacles to establishment of such a statistical system become more serious than the technical obstacles.

One wonders, however, whether continuous revision of long-range plans would be politically expedient for the Soviet government, even if it were technically feasible. Continuous planning, if efficiently organized, would imply rapid revision of the entire general plan in the case of a moderate disturbance. Government would be obliged to allow all repercussions from every decision to work themselves out. Whereas certain measures (such as the space program, for instance) appear attractive in and of themselves, their repercussions on investments and consumption are not necessarily so popular. It would often be necessary to admit, a bit too soon, that certain parts of the plan, considered as intangible, would have to be abandoned for ideological reasons or for the sake of prestige.

In any case, such an attitude would involve a complete change in the traditional behavior of the Soviet government in the face of economic difficulties. The traditional response has been to sustain outmoded goals, with obstinacy and for as long as possible, by increasing pressure on the public and appealing to "socialist discipline" and patriotic duty. Such behavior reflects a certain philosophy about human motives: while paying lip service to the feelings of civic responsibility in citizens and bureaucrats, one does not place much faith in their strength. To obtain what is desired, government must ask for the most possible. Premature relaxation of goals might cause the zeal of those carrying out the plan to flag—and, besides, they might wonder whether they should continue taking seriously orders that will anyhow be changed tomorrow.

It is much more convenient for the government to pretend to believe in old goals until the very day when it publishes new ones for some remote date. Since the beliefs of government cannot be officially challenged by anyone, even obsolete targets can be useful in a political sense. Those who are really running the economy—the top Party leaders—are probably not aware of the cost of this practice. Continuous long-range planning will be introduced only when the Party feels that the economic advantages to be derived from it outweigh the political advantages derived from the present system.

PROBLEM OF ADJUSTING THE ANNUAL PLAN

The need to adjust annual plans, generally recognized by Soviet authors,[20] arises because it is impossible to have an accurate vision of the real situation, whether present or future. Soviet authorities would like, however, to limit adjustments to those which are really "justified."[21] In continuous planning, some adjustments might be eliminated: those caused by delays in transmitting planned targets to enterprises, by absence of forecasts for the coming year, by absence of long-range plans for enterprises, and by absence of long-term contracts between individual enterprises.

As a general rule, the right to change a plan belongs to the authority that hands it down. According to the decree of May 4, 1958, the plan for gross production was to be "handed down" to the republics by higher authorities. The republic Councils of Ministers then divided up this plan among Sovnarkhozes, ministries, organizations, and lower administrative bodies. These agencies all transmitted the plan to lower units, particularly to individual enterprises, and at the same time issued additional specifications on gross production, construction, and assembly work.[22] According to Article 49 of the September 27, 1957, regulation on Sovnarkhozes, the latter authorities could change production and delivery figures in the annual plan provided that they obtained the consent of the client, made necessary corrections in other indexes of the plan, and did not reduce the

20. F. Khiliuk, *Planovoe khoziaistvo*, No. 7, 1962, p. 47.

21. "Of course, during execution, plans must be adjusted and corrected, but they will no longer be radically revised in the upper echelons of planning agencies," S. Starostin and E. Frolov, "Ekonomicheskoe razvitie i sovershenstvovanie planirovaniia," *Kommunist*, No. 17, 1962, p. 18.

22. "O merakh po uluchsheniiu planirovaniia narodnogo khoziaistva" [On Measures to Improve National Economic Planning], in *Zakonodatelnye akty po voprosam narodnogo khoziaistva SSSR* [Legislative Acts on Problems of the U.S.S.R. National Economy], Moscow, 1961, I., pp. 330-33.

profits paid into the budget.[23] Adjustments could be made in quarterly plans[24] forty-five days before the end of the quarter and in monthly plans twenty days before the end of the month.[25]

It is very difficult to obtain detailed information on the nature and number of adjustments made in plans in the course of a year. Judging from reactions of the Soviet press, their number seems to have increased during recent years, and today they appear to be a major problem. The 1961 annual plan for the Tartar Autonomous Republic is said to have been adjusted "almost 500 times";[26] the annual plan of the Yaroslavl Sovnarkhoz was adjusted 789 times, of which 307 were at the orders of superior authorities. The eleven-month plan for 1961 for the Vladimir Sovnarkhoz was revised 20 times by the superior authorities for production goals, and these revisions made necessary 78 more adjustments in other production goals.[27]

Among adjustments made, one must single out those made at the orders of superior agencies. Changes in government policy, the system of priorities, and all that Khrushchev referred to as "the direction of industry and agriculture by means of campaigns" (*kampaneiskoe rukovodstvo*)[28] are generally responsible for the inconsistent character of the over-all plan and the changing directives:

> The practice of making constant changes and corrections in plans shows that some plans had no proper foundation and were not carefully thought out. The responsibility lies entirely with the planning agencies. This practice reduces the importance of the plan as law for

23. See the decree of the U.S.S.R. Council of Ministers in *ibid.*, p. 172.

24. Until 1963 and since 1965, annual plans have also had quarterly subdivisions, although quarterly and monthly targets are set by separate plans in the course of the year.

25. "O merakh po uluchsheniiu planirovaniia narodnogo khoziaistva," *Zakonodatelnye akty*, p. 332.

26. *Ekonomicheskaia gazeta*, November 17, 1962, p. 2.

27. I. Maevskii and A. Fomin, "Nekotorye voprosy sovershenstvovaniia planirovaniia narodnogo khoziaistva" [Some Questions on Improving National Economic Planning], *Voprosy ekonomiki*, No. 12, 1962, pp. 38-45.

28. N. S. Khrushchev, *Stroitelstvo kommunizma SSSR i razvitie selskogo khoziaistva* [Building of Communism in the U.S.S.R. and the Development of Agriculture], Moscow, 1963, VII, p. 320.

> the enterprise and engenders a scornful attitude toward technological and economic calculations as well as toward the bases of the plan; it also weakens state discipline.
>
> Production and investment plans are often poorly coordinated with plans for supplying materials and equipment. In many cases, in order to make both ends meet, the input norms of raw materials and materials are artificially reduced or equipment and materials that are supposed to be put to use by enterprises only in the third and fourth quarters are included in the resources of, say, the first quarter. The current practice of basing plans on statistical averages makes it impossible to take into account the real capabilities of a particular enterprise.[29]

Even if Gosplan accepts or orders a reduction in goals in physical terms, it is often reluctant to reduce goals in value terms at the same time. Republics and Sovnarkhozes have occasionally succeeded in obtaining such reductions, but in most cases they have been forced to increase the targets in value terms set for the last quarter and to authorize production of goods for which there is no demand.[30] This very common practice, called *vozdushnyi val* or *beztovarnyi val* by the parties to it, represents the price paid by the economy for purely statistical performances.[31]

Plan adjustments were made by the Sovnarkhozes for two major reasons: the need to revise a plan that possibly could not be fulfilled, and the desire to obtain a better performance in the eyes of the authorities. It is obvious that only the first of these reasons was ever given officially.

A plan may be impossible to fulfill for many reasons. The most important are: failure to fulfill the plan for putting new facilities into operation, lack of raw materials or intermediate products, and changes in the demand for certain products. A letter or a telegram from higher authorities in charge of supply-

29. *Ibid.*, pp. 366-67.

30. Khiliuk, *Planovoe khoziaistvo*, No. 7, 1962, p. 48.

31. Starostin and Frolov, *Kommunist*, No. 17, 1962, p. 17. The term *vozdushnyi val* can be translated literally as a wall, rampart, or wave of air, and the term *beztovarnyi val* as an unmarketable wall, rampart, or wave. There is a pun here: the word *val* is an abbreviation for *valovaia produktsiia* (gross production). A proper translation would be "gross production of air" or "unsalable gross production."

ing materials and equipment is sometimes sufficient to justify such changes in the plan.[32]

The desire to make their performance look better often incited Sovnarkhozes to make adjustments in the plan. In planning the production of their enterprises, they often set uneven goals—some obviously too high, others too low. They could then easily argue that, since certain goals are too high, the whole plan for gross industrial output of the Sovnarkhoz in question should be reduced. This practice, as a general rule, enabled them to overfulfill their plan as a whole because the easy targets that were still included could readily be surpassed.[33]

To make their work look bettter, Sovnarkhozes often changed the plans of their enterprises. The plans of the better enterprises were increased in the course of the year, while those of the worse ones were reduced, so that the plan could be more evenly fulfilled. On such occasions, the better enterprises lost their profits and the workers in them their bonuses, because adjustments were not made in labor and wage plans as necessitated by changes in the production plan. In general, the Sovnarkhozes, their subsections, and the trusts tended to change plans so as to make fulfillment of them easier. However, by the end of the year so many changes had been made in the annual plan that none of the planning agencies was capable of registering them. Hence the planning agencies no longer had any knowledge of the adjusted annual plan, which appeared in the form of a document only at the Central Statistical Administration, as the aggregate of all the adjusted plans of enterprises.[34]

PROSPECTS FOR CONTINUOUS PLANNING

To what extent will the reforms under way in Soviet planning—in particular continuous planning—improve current planning and eliminate "unjustified" adjustments? The administrative reforms already indicated and strengthening of planning by sectors could improve internal cohesion of the plan and make some adjust-

32. Khiliuk, *Planovoe khoziaistvo*, No. 7, 1962, p. 49.
33. Starostin and Frolov, *Kommunist*, No. 17, 1962, p. 21.
34. Khiliuk, *Planovoe khoziaistvo*, No. 7, 1962, pp. 49-50.

ments unnecessary. However, organization of the central authority in economic matters remains very complicated. In contrast with the stable political authority represented by the Party Secretariat and Politburo, the economic authorities in general and those concerned with planning in particular are weak, divided among several agencies, and unstable. These agencies—whose average lifespan is two, three, or at most four years—hardly have the time and independence needed to put together coherent plans.

Annual formulation of long-range plans for the coming five years and of shorter-range plans for two years or fifteen months could facilitate transmission of goals to lower agencies and enable them to organize their work for a slightly longer period. Such continuous long-range planning has apparently not yet been put into operation, although the official documents concerning it remain in force. The authorities anticipate that it will be sufficient to correct and adjust the annual sections of the new five-year plan for 1966-70, without preparing new plans for each of these years.[35] For the two years in between (1964-65), a two-year plan and a two-year budget were drafted and presented to the December 16, 1964, session of the Supreme Soviet by P. F. Lomako, Chairman of Gosplan, and V. F. Garbuzov, Minister of Finance.[36]

Lomako emphasized the fact that he had followed the "directives of the Central Committee intended to ensure continuity in planning," although he did not confirm that two-year plans would be prepared every year. Such, nevertheless, seems to have been the opinion of V. Lagutkin, the Vice Chairman of the Russian Republic Sovnarkhoz.[37] The idea of two-year plans,

35. F. Kotov, "Aktualnye problemy razrabotki novogo piatiletnego plana" [Present Problems of Drawing Up a New Five-Year Plan], *ibid.*, No. 5, 1964, pp. 9-10.

36. *Pravda*, December 17, 1963. The drafting of a two-year plan for 1964-65 and of a five-year plan for 1966-70 was ordered by the Party Central Committee directives of March 13, 1963 (see *ibid.*, March 14, 1963).

37. Nemchinov, *Kommunist*, No. 5, 1964, p. 88.

which is not at all new in the Soviet Union, was not pursued by Khrushchev's successors.[38]

Another new aspect in current planning is subdivision of the 1964-65 plan into semiannual periods rather than into quarters, as had been the practice until 1963.[39] This change could bring greater stability to productive linkages, but it is doubtful that it could eliminate the lack of coordination in the plan.

In 1963 the government placed considerable faith in the formulation of two-year plans directly in enterprises, construction sites, laboratories, or study offices. This practice could be connected with the reduction in the number of centrally planned indexes announced on the occasion of the reforms. In fact, this is a step toward decentralization of the planning process, though a relatively small one. In the Russian Republic alone, about three hundred high officials from the Russian Republic Gosplan and Sovnarkhoz and from other republic agencies were sent out "into the field" along with about one hundred officials from U.S.S.R. Gosplan and state committees to help local units prepare and formulate the plan.[40] These representatives of central agencies may have given some critical advice on matters previously within the jurisdiction of enterprises, but it is unlikely that they could have verified actual productive capacities and thereby improved coherence of the plan.

One wonders whether real progress will result from con-

38. In 1957 Gosplan prepared, concurrently with the annual plan for 1958, approximate projections for 1959 that were to be transmitted to the republic Gosplans to help them prepare the annual plan for 1959 and the seven-year plan for 1959-65. See I. I. Kuzmin, *Zasedaniia Verkhovnogo Soveta SSSR* [Sessions of the U.S.S.R. Supreme Soviet], Fourth Legislature, Stenographic Transcript, Moscow, 1958, p. 19.

This practice was not mentioned in the reports on annual plans for later years. In the history of Soviet planning, the idea of two-year plans has been raised from time to time but never carried through with any obvious success. On this subject, see Zaleski, *Planification de la Croissance*, I, pp. 38-39 and 67.

39. "Novym khoziaistvennym planam—vsestoronnee obosnovanie" [A More Solid Foundation for the New Economic Plans], *Planovoe khoziaistvo,* No. 5, 1963, p. 2.

40. Ia. Chadaev, "Sovershenstvovat planovoe rukovodstvo narodnym khoziaistvom" [Improve the Planned Management of the National Economy], *ibid.*, No. 11, 1963, pp. 2-3.

tinuous planning as it is conceived today, *i.e.*, as simultaneous formulation of three plans every year—the annual plan, the plan for the coming year, and the plan for the terminal year of a moving five-year period. Some Soviet authors believe that such a practice is not justified and that it would be very time consuming. They propose replacing that method by correcting each year the annual goals of the five-year plan and letting these corrected goals serve as the annual plan, a practice that would require an accumulation of material reserves and new methods of drafting long-range plans. It would, indeed, necessitate taking into account the fact that the indexes in the long-range plans are not the same as those in the annual plans.[41]

Actually, the Soviet government has been hesitating for a long time between two possible solutions to the problem of how to adjust plans. The first solution, usually adopted, consists in strengthening the control of central authorities, a process that manifests itself in an increase in centrally planned indexes and in products allocated by central authorities. This solution is impractical since representatives of central authorities at the command post cannot take the place of specialists in the field, whose number increases daily as the industrial economy grows more complex. Adjusting the plan often becomes the only way to avoid errors which become more and more grave the longer they are not corrected. The adjustment process becomes an element of flexibility in a system suffering from bureaucratic rigidity. Before complaining about "unjustified" adjustments, one should weigh them against those that enterprise managers might make and against the losses that result from postponing or refusing to make necessary adjustments.

The other solution would be to replace this *de facto* flexibility inherent in plan adjustment by a system that would really be more flexible. Various suggestions have been made along these lines in the Soviet Union, and we shall trace what has happened to them in the next chapter in order to get some idea of the evolutionary prospects of the Soviet planning system.

41. V. Loginov, "Problemy sovershenstvovaniia planirovaniia" [Problems of Improving Planning], *Voprosy ekonomiki*, No. 5, 1963, p. 128.

CHAPTER 4. Proposals for Basic Reforms

The reorganization of managerial and planning agencies and the proposal to introduce continuous planning have in no way challenged the principle of authoritarian, centralized planning; nor have they brought about significant changes in methods of planning at the enterprise level.

The partial nature of these reforms could not have escaped notice by the Soviet economists who wanted more substantial reforms at the time of the discussion of prices, success criteria, and criteria for investment decisions. However, a general debate oriented toward fundamental reforms in the system was still awaited.

RESURGENCE OF DISCUSSION ON REFORMS

Such a debate did not "explode" until the fall of 1962 during discussion of the theses of Professor E. G. Liberman on planning at the enterprise level. It might seem inappropriate to use the word "explode" for a debate carefully initiated by the Party and fully supported by the official press and Party apparatus. But an explosion did seem to take place, and the authorities had to devote some time to the task of defining the permissible limits of debate.

Although ushered in by the Party, discussion of the Liberman theses revealed a general undercurrent in favor of reforms. In the middle of 1962, fulfillment of the Seven-Year Plan was encountering various difficulties and causing lively dispute during preparation of the annual plan for 1963. By the financial law of 1961, the government had reduced the authority of enterprise managers to make investments "outside the plan." This restraint was resented as a step backward and the source of all the trouble.[1] Moreover, all sources for financing decentralized investments were reduced by half, starting January 1, 1962.[2]

1. Basile Kerblay, "Les propositions de Liberman pour un projet de réforme de l'entreprise en U.R.S.S.," *Cahiers du Monde Russe et Soviétique*, No. 3, 1963, p. 305.

2. Henri Wronski, "La localisation des forces productives en URSS," *Revue d'Economie Politique*, No. 1, 1964, p. 401.

Resurgence of discussion on reforms resulted directly from deterioration of material incentives within enterprises. In the case of staff, engineers, and technicians with fixed salaries, the material incentives had come primarily from bonuses received when the plan for marketed production was fulfilled or overfulfilled.[3] After 1959 bonuses were paid only for fulfillment or overfulfillment of the plan for costs; and they were also made contingent on fulfillment of plans for gross output, assortment, and all the other principal productive indexes. By comparison with the situation before 1959, bonuses were substantially reduced, the additional prerequisites having made them much harder to obtain.[4] It is not surprising that the share of bonus payments in the basic salaries of engineers and technicians fell from 26.4 per cent in 1959 to 19 per cent in 1960, 13.2 per cent in 1961, and 11.6 per cent in 1962.[5]

The wage reform introduced during the years 1957-60 contained similar provisions for workers. Bonuses for exceeding norms had given flexibility to the system by enabling enterprises themselves to raise the wages of piece workers. The reforms of 1957-60, taking account of the incidence of technical progress, substantially reduced the number of piece workers. Their fraction of all workers fell from 73 to 61 per cent for industry as a whole; in certain sectors, such as the petroleum and chemical industries, the drop was much greater.[6] As a result, a very large number of workers could no longer expect higher earnings unless there were a general revision of the basic schedule of wage rates, which rarely occurred.

Reform of the bonus system was therefore in order, and bonus

3. Provided other goals, such as gross production, cost reduction, etc., were fulfilled. See V. F. Maier, *Zarabotnaia plata v period perekhoda k kommunizmu* [Wages During the Transition Period to Communism], Moscow, 1963, p. 228.

4. *Ibid.*, p. 229.

5. L. Zotova and V. Bazanova, "Materialnoe stimulirovanie i vysokie planovye zadaniia" [Material Incentives and High Planned Goals], *Planovoe khoziaistvo*, No. 10, 1963, p. 2.

6. In petroleum refining, the proportion of workers paid by piecework dropped from 63 to 12 per cent after the reforms; in petroleum extracting, from 51 to 21 per cent; and in the chemical industry, from 59 to 36 per cent (Maier, *Zarabotnaia plata*, p. 161).

reform had to be considered within the general framework of the problem of material incentives for workers. But it was impossible to discuss material incentives without bringing up the subject of reforms in enterprise planning. Hence, discussion focused on that problem in the fall of 1962, with the encouragement of government and Party. Since a Soviet enterprise is merely a basic cell in a system operated from above, it soon became evident that essential reforms in the management of enterprises entailed fundamental reforms in the whole system, reforms which had political, economic, and social implications that were not at all approved by the Party.

CRITICISM OF PLANNING AT THE ENTERPRISE LEVEL

The discussion of planning at the enterprise level could not fail to raise the question of the enterprise's freedom of action. The quality of the plan imposed upon the enterprise from above and used as the basic criterion of its efficiency, therefore, had to be examined initially.[7]

The first objection to the present system was its inability to generate an objective method for calculating a *composite index* that would accurately reflect the work of the enterprise. Much of the blame must be borne by the higher agencies' practice of sending down the ensemble of calculations made in formulating the plan as obligatory indexes.[8] As a corrective, the compulsory indexes (gross value of output, output in physical terms, labor productivity, costs, profits) were supplemented by accounting indexes,[9] such as production per ruble of fixed capital or output

7. In Soviet parlance, one must distinguish the "plan of the enterprise" and the goals assigned to the enterprise. The latter are referred to as "planned assignments" (*planovye zadaniia*) and are part of orders given to lower agencies. The expression "planning for enterprises" is also often used. These expressions are used, for instance, by A. G. Zverev, "Protiv skhematizma v reshenii slozhnykh voprosov" [Against Sketchiness in Deciding Complex Questions], *Voprosy ekonomiki*, No. 11, 1962, pp. 94-97; and V. Laptev, "Planirovanie i prava predpriiatii" [Planning and Rights of the Enterprise], *ibid.*, No. 6, 1963, p. 27. There are many more such examples.

8. V. Nemchinov, "Zainteresovat predpriiatie v bolee napriazhennom plane" [Interesting the Enterprise in a Tauter Plan], *ibid.*, No. 11, 1962, p. 100; Laptev, *ibid.*, No. 6, 1963, pp. 27-28.

9. The accounting indexes are, in principle, mere calculations made for

per unit of capacity. Taken by themselves, these indexes hardly yield a better answer to the crucial question of enterprise efficiency.[10] The multitude of planned indexes handed down from above and their often contradictory nature bring about continuous intervention in management of the enterprise, stifle its initiative, and prevent optimal utilization of its resources.[11]

In addition to being too detailed, the plan imposed on an enterprise is often arbitrary, making no allowance for special conditions in each productive unit.[12] Moreover, the plan is an unfair criterion of efficiency because it takes as a starting point the results of the preceding year, thereby penalizing the enterprise that did good work last year.[13]

To all these defects must be added the lack of coordination and internal consistency in the plans. The norms on which balances are based are not very satisfactory;[14] balances are not

---

internal use and have no binding force. Since, however, higher agencies are interested in some of these indexes, they use them in fact in evaluating the results of work in the enterprise. Hence the accounting indexes become "unofficial" criteria of efficiency that, without being formal orders, limit the enterprise's freedom of action.

10. L. Vaag and S. Zakharov, "Platnost proizvodstvennykh fondov i pribyl predpriiatiia" [Payments for Use of Productive Capital and Profits of the Enterprise], *ibid.*, No. 4, 1963, p. 89.

11. Nemchinov, *ibid.*, No. 11, 1962, p. 100.

12. "The principal defect of planning is, above all, the well-known leveling of a stereotyped nature, planning according to general indexes that are not differentiated, without taking into account the specific nature of the various sectors and individual enterprises. Such plans, lacking precision and based on ready-made formulas, become a serious impediment to our economic growth." (A. Vorobeva, "Iskhodnoi bazoi stimulirovaniia mozhet byt tolko plan" [Only the Plan Can Be the Basis for Incentives], *ibid.*, No. 11, 1962, p. 102.)

13. See *ibid.*, p. 102; B. Sukharevskii, "O sovershenstvovanii form i metodov materialnogo stimulirovaniia" [On Improving the Forms and Methods of Material Incentives], *ibid.*, p. 14; and Vaag and Zakharov, *ibid.*, No. 4, 1963, p. 89.

14. "The critical drawback in planning lies in the outdated character of norms. The setting of norms was already unsatisfactory before and has deteriorated even further in the past few years. Therefrom stem the inadequacy of the technological and economic foundations of plans for individual enterprises, the failure to coordinate plans for production and supplies, and the frequent changes in plans—all of which generate lack of confidence in plans on the part of the collective body of the enterprise and explain why it cannot regard the plan as a law or as a directive that must be

based on planned cost reductions;[15] and the tautness of plans, which has increased during the last few years,[16] creates bottlenecks. The poor quality of plans imposed upon enterprises causes frequent adjustment and general instability of the plans.[17] These adjustments, often partial, only add to the inconsistency of plans and often penalize workers who are not responsible.[18] To these essential defects must be added such "minor" ones as the lack of longer-range plans for enterprises[19] and of adequate control over execution of the plan.[20]

Adoption of the plan as a criterion of performance implies that it plays a decisive role in the awarding of bonuses to the personnel. The defects of plans are communicated to the bonus system and are amplified even further by various conditions restricting payment: the preconditions for establishment of an enterprise's incentive fund and for payment of bonuses; the

---

unconditionally executed." G. Kosiachenko, "Vazhnoe uslovie uluchsheniia planirovaniia" [An Important Condition for Improving Planning], *ibid.*, No. 11, 1962, p. 109.

15. M. Bor, "O povyshenii nauchnogo urovnia planirovaniia narodnogo khoziaistva" [On Raising the Scientific Level of National Economic Planning], *ibid.*, No. 3, 1963, p. 5.

16. Zotova and Bazanova, *Planovoe khoziaistvo*, No. 10, 1963, p. 2.

17. K. Plotnikov, "B chem prav i neprav E. G. Liberman" [In What Respects Liberman Is Right and Wrong], *Voprosy ekonomiki*, No. 11, 1962, p. 114; L. Alter, "Sviazat stimulirovanie s perspektivnym planirovaniem predpriiatiia" [Link Up Incentives with Long-Range Planning of Enterprises], *ibid.*, p. 117; N. Razumov, "O polozhenii i pravakh promyshlennogo predpriiatiia" [On the Situation and Rights of the Industrial Enterprise], *ibid.*, No. 7, 1963, p. 131. A. M. Birman, *Nekotorye problemy nauki o sotsialisticheskom khoziaistvovaniiu* [Some Problems in Managing a Socialist Economy], Moscow, 1963, pp. 47-48.

18. Changes in plans for production and for costs are often not accompanied by corresponding changes in financial indexes, so that enterprises are kept from fulfilling plans for profits and budgetary payments, and deprived of resources for their incentive fund. See L. L. Rotshtein, "Uluchshit finansovoe planirovanie v sovnarkhozakh" [Improve Financial Planning in the Sovnarkhozes], *Voprosy ekonomiki*, No. 11, 1962, p. 119.

19. Alter, *ibid.*, p. 117. On this point, see also Razumov, *ibid.*, No. 7, 1963, p. 130: "We know that at the present time there are no approved long-range plans for either the Sovnarkhozes or the enterprises; there are only rough drafts of plans as adopted by superior agencies. Thus one is practically forced each time to formulate the annual plan from scratch."

20. Bor, *ibid.*, No. 3, 1963, p. 11.

measures of performance used as a basis for calculating the bonuses, on the one hand, and the indexes whose fulfillment determine whether they will be paid, on the other; the limitation of aggregate bonus payments imposed by the plan for the wage fund; and so on.[21]

Defective plans imposed from above are not, however, the only cause of inefficient work by the enterprises. Lack of autonomy and above all indeterminacy of rights expose the enterprise to constant interference by superior agencies in affairs theoretically reserved to it, often depriving the enterprise of the results of its work. Not unusual are the practices of redistributing assignments or resources among enterprises of the same sector or of the same region in the course of the year, or simply of preempting financial resources from the accounts of an enterprise.[22]

Deprived of its essential rights and subjected to many different pressures, the Soviet enterprise is on the bottom rung of the bureaucratic ladder; enterprises are separated from the decision-making agencies by the many stages through which they must solicit appropriation of funds.[23] Buyer and seller are separated by a long line of offices and organizations that receive, check, and accept requests; that distribute funds among republics

21. "Voprosy uluchsheniia sistemy materialnogo stimulirovaniia predpriiatii" [Questions of Improving the System of Material Incentives in Enterprises], *ibid.*, No. 10, 1962, p. 147; D. Onika, "Plan i materialnoe stimulirovanie" [The Plan and Material Incentives], *ibid.*, No. 11, 1962, p. 30. The present defects in the bonus system are described particularly in the articles advocating its reform.

22. Birman, *Nekotorye problemy*, pp. 29 and 35. Many authors emphasize this point. According to E. Liberman, "Planirovanie proizvodstva i normativy dlitelnogo deistviia" [Planning of Production and the Standards of Long-Range Action], *Voprosy ekonomiki*, No. 8, 1962, p. 105, "the decisions of superior agencies are often not coordinated among themselves, so that costly work is required to re-examine the plan and correct it." According to B. Sukharevskii, "Sotsialisticheskoe predpriiatie i narodnoe khoziaistvo" [The Socialist Enterprise and the National Economy], *ibid.*, No. 5, 1963, p. 38, "one must condemn the practice, backed by decisions of republic Councils of Ministers or Sovnarkhozes, of using an enterprise's funds to make up for insufficiency of working capital in lagging enterprises and to finance work that has no connection with the activity of the enterprise in question."

23. Liberman, *ibid.*, No. 8, 1962, p. 105.

and individual enterprises; and that issue notifications, delivery certificates, etc. For example, documents for the distribution of tires must be processed through thirty-two stages; those for ball-bearings, through twenty; those for instruments, through twenty-five; and those for cardboard, through fifteen. Whenever a change is made in the plan, that long procedure must be re-enacted. The granting of delivery certificates takes as a rule three to four months, and it is only then that seller and buyer may officially contact each other to discuss specific conditions of the order, technical and other.[24]

Many authors emphasize that this situation creates a clash of interests between the individual enterprise and the economy as a whole.[25] Enterprises have no special interest in making the most economical use of resources. They are not interested in the price at which they buy, as long as that price is legally sanctioned, since all expenses enter into planned costs, the plan "covering everything."[26]

The introduction of new techniques is delayed because it entails specialization and cooperation with other larger and more diversified enterprises; this specialization in turn makes the enterprise plan more dependent on supplies of materials and equipment. Since 30 per cent of the work stoppages in enterprises result from deficiencies of supply, it is easy to see why an enterprise hesitates to embark on such a course.[27]

This state of affairs obviously does not create a climate favorable to growth in efficiency. The divergent interests of the individual enterprise and the economy engender distrust in the higher agencies, causing them to bombard the enterprise with new directives and instructions; and this only sharpens further the clash of interests inherent in the system.[28] The very definition

24. Razumov, *ibid.*, No. 7, 1963, p. 129.

25. Sukharevskii, *ibid.*, No. 11, 1962, p. 25; E. Manevich, "Premirovat za fakticheskoe snizhenie sebestoimosti produktsii" [Bonuses for Actual Reduction in Production Cost], *ibid.*, p. 93; Nemchinov, *ibid.*, p. 100; Liberman, *ibid.*, No. 8, 1962, pp. 104-5; and Birman, *Nekotorye problemy*, pp. 43-45.

26. Liberman, *Voprosy ekonomiki*, No. 8, 1962, p. 110.

27. E. Rusanov, "O glavnom pokazatele raboty predpriiatiia" [On the Main Index of the Enterprise's Work], *ibid.*, No. 11, 1962, p. 130.

28. Liberman, *ibid.*, No. 8, 1962, p. 112; and Birman, *Nekotorye problemy*, p. 58.

of efficient work becomes vague. Why work hard when it is much simpler to work out an "easy" plan? Some directors do not believe in economic efficiency of an enterprise as something objective, but rather as what they themselves create. If they lower the plan, an enterprise will operate efficiently with old equipment and obsolete methods; if they raise the plan of even the best-equipped enterprise, it may become rated as inefficient.[29]

THE PRINCIPAL SCHOOLS OF THOUGHT ON REFORM

Although all the Soviet economists agree on the defects in the present system, they differ sharply on the reforms that should be introduced to change it.

Advocates of Greater Centralization. The use of electronic computers should, according to some Soviet economists, make it possible to calculate in physical terms the total needs of an individual enterprise. The over-all national plan would be a gigantic survey of the requirements in physical or "natural" terms of all enterprises. Such a calculation in natural terms would distinguish a planned economy from a capitalist economy, which is forced to use indexes in value terms.[30]

According to Fedorovich, a professor at the Sergei Ordzhonikidze Institute of Economic Engineering, the failure to process the huge bulk of available information is due only to the inadequate methods used today by planning agencies. Rather than decentralizing, he proposes giving up computation on paper and putting centralized economic planning on "electronic rails." The computers themselves, using programs formulated for them in advance, would draw up the optimum variant of the national plan for regions and enterprises and later would analyze and evaluate its execution.[31]

Fedorovich believes that, as of today, all prerequisites exist

29. Liberman, *Voprosy ekonomiki*, No. 8, 1962, pp. 111-12.
30. Birman, *Nekotorye problemy*, pp. 19-21.
31. M. Fedorovich, *Ekonomicheskaia gazeta*, November 3, 1962, p. 39, and November 10, 1962, p. 6. Leon Smolinski and Peter Wiles, "The Soviet Planning Pendulum," *Problems of Communism*, November-December, 1963, pp. 26-27.

for installation of a nationwide cybernetic system. In any system of centralized administration, the basic unit would be the industrial enterprise, which would serve higher agencies as the primary source of information and as the direct recipient of orders. Enterprises and workshops could be completely automated in the next twenty years. That would require "not only the use of superior computational techniques but also more complex administrative techniques, on which the cybernetic system of management must rely since it attains its goal directly, without human intervention, with a greater or smaller variety of choices determined by the flow of information fed into the system."[32]

Some mathematical economists like Natan E. Kobrynskii, deputy chief of a Gosplan section, believe that the way to improve planning is "to move to optimal methods of planning" by mechanizing calculations and using electronic computers. On the issue of centralization versus decentralization, Kobrynskii is quite vague; he says that "centralization accompanied by decentralization" is what is needed. While insisting that the optimum must be based on a single criterion, he refuses to identify the criterion, saying that is the task of economic science.[33]

Other mathematical economists, while enthusiastically supporting the introduction of electronic computing methods, clearly criticize the tendency toward centralization. Thus Academician Anatolii Dorodnitsyn, director of the Computing Center of the Academy of Sciences, states that introduction of a unified system of management "should not be confused with absolute centralization." For him, a unified system of management implies existence of a single goal, whereas centralization implies detailed operational management of production from the center as well as formulation of goals and general plans. Such a system, he says, is possible only in the abstract. It is inconceivable in practice no matter what machines are used and no matter how powerful they

32. Report on statement by M. Fedorovich in "Forsirovat primenenie matematiki v ekonomike" [Speed Up the Application of Mathematics to Economics], *Voprosy ekonomiki*, No. 1, 1963, p. 96.

33. *Ekonomisty i matematiki za kruglym stolom* [Economists and Mathematicians at a Round Table Discussion], Moscow, 1965, pp. 122-25.

are. Hence Dorodnitsyn supports a decentralized system in which each element has assigned functions.[34]

For Academician V. M. Glushkov, complete centralization is justified only as an abstract concept. In practice such centralization encounters innumerable limitations upon its efficiency. According to him, preparation and execution of a plan must be distinguished. Execution cannot be divorced from the principle of material interest, needed to stimulate initiative in the lower ranks, or from decentralized choice of managerial methods.[35]

The concept of centralization is also strongly criticized by I. S. Malyshev. It is an illusion, he argues, to imagine that production and distribution can be planned directly in physical terms—that the plan can specify how much of everything is to be produced, what inputs are to be used, and how the products are to be distributed. Such a concept, he feels, is merely a throwback to the customs of the commune (*obshchina*) or the peasant household, wholly inapplicable to an economy with tens of millions of workers. It is true, he says, "that some mathematical economists and statisticians, particularly those unfamiliar with economic theory, believe that mathematics and electronic computers will make it possible to draw up a program and plan the entire economy in an 'optimal' way, using physical quantities. But this is a utopia, and often a most bizarre utopia."[36]

Malyshev then illustrates the defects in such a concept by the way in which an increase of one hundred kilograms in meat production per capita was programmed for achievement in "three or four years." The required total increase in meat was found by multiplying the forecast population by one hundred kilograms. Then coefficients for the yield of meat per head of cattle or hogs were used to derive the required volume of slaughtering. The required livestock herd was next derived from the ratio of slaughtering to herd. From the required herd and various other coefficients came the required fodder and barn space. It then remained only to apportion requirements among administrative

34. *Ibid.*, pp. 118-22.

35. *Ibid.*, pp. 129-33.

36. I. S. Malyshev, *Ekonomicheskie zakony sotsializma i planirovanie* [The Economic Laws of Socialism and Planning], Moscow, 1966, p. 26.

regions in order to set precise goals. Such a system of "direct administrative planning" scarcely amounts to rational planning, Malyshev notes. It ignores such things as realistic prospects for investment in collective farms, for incomes of both collective farm and farmers, and for effective demand on the part of the public for the planned output of meat.[37] Malyshev points out that planning can be economically rational only by making use of "indirect economic procedures," economic laws, and material incentives.[38]

Agreeing with these views, various Soviet economists advocate calculations in value terms. Central planning should be based, according to them, on balances in values, representing major categories, shares, and rates of growth. Electronic computers would be used to find the interrelationships among these magnitudes. However, the initiative of enterprise managers and workers would no longer be stimulated by targets in the national plan but rather by material incentives, by prices based on economic factors, and by the system of finance and credit.[39]

Several proposals for reform have been guided by these basic ideas. It is of interest to discuss three of them; all three attempt to rid the plan of its rigidity and mystique, but each tends to orient the Soviet system toward a different path. These new ideas were voiced by Liberman, Vaag and Zakharov, and Nemchinov.

Liberman's Proposals. The theses formulated in August and September of 1962 by Evsei G. Liberman, professor at the Kharkov Institute of Economic Engineers, are not really new. They had already been published, in part at least, in two articles in *Kommunist* in 1956 and 1959.[40] In any case, the publicity accorded to his article in *Pravda* on September 9, 1962,

37. *Ibid.*, pp. 26-27.

38. *Ibid.*, p. 28.

39. Birman, *Nekotorye problemy*, pp. 19-21.

40. Liberman, "O planirovanii promyshlennogo proizvodstva i o material'nykh stimuliantakh ego razvitiia" [On Planning of Industrial Production and of Material Incentives for Its Growth], *Kommunist*, No. 10, 1956, pp. 75-93; Liberman, "Ob ekonomicheskikh rychagakh vypolneniia plana promyshlennostiu SSSR" [On Economic Levers for Fulfillment of the Plan for U.S.S.R. Industry], *ibid.*, No. 1, 1959, pp. 88-93.

was not at all justified by any changes in his earlier theory.[41] Liberman's system, which is a compromise between the requirements of a central authority and the needs of individual enterprises, rests on three basic ideas: (1) the enterprise should have the greatest degree of autonomy, both in planning and in management, compatible with the system; (2) the operation of an enterprise should be oriented toward greater "profitability"; and (3) an important distinction should be made between planning at the enterprise level and planning within the governmental economic apparatus.

In all his cited articles, Liberman demands greater latitude in planning for the enterprises. Back in 1956, he wrote: "The assignments planned centrally for an enterprise should be limited and not too detailed. . . . Planning should be streamlined and ministries freed from the task of controlling in detail the plans of factories."[42]

In 1956 Liberman also made a distinction between quantitative and qualitative indexes in the planned goals imposed from above. The quantitative indexes—volume and assortment—of production should be communicated to the factory every year, along with a quarterly distribution. However, indispensable details and specifications of deadlines for deliveries should be determined by contracts between suppliers and customers.[43] The qualitative indexes imposed from above should consist of a composite index of "profitability," average wages, norms for labor expenditures, and productivity indexes. The enterprise would thus have a goal set from above that leaves it enough freedom to formulate its own plan aimed at minimum costs.[44]

Liberman's 1959 proposals were made in the same spirit. The indexes for the volume and assortment of production are always to be imposed from above. However, supplying of equipment and materials by plan should be replaced, in the case of impor-

41. Liberman, "Plan, pribyl, premiia" [Plan, Profits, Bonuses], *Pravda*, September 9, 1962, p. 3. See also Liberman, *Voprosy ekonomiki*, No. 8, 1962, pp. 104-12. It was the *Pravda* article that was most publicized.

42. Liberman, *Kommunist*, No. 10, 1956, pp. 77 and 89.

43. *Ibid.*, p. 77.

44. *Ibid.*, p. 83.

tant deliveries, by direct long-term contracts established in conformity with plans and, in the case of minor deliveries, by procurements from bases operated by Sovnarkhozes or similar agencies. As to qualitative indexes, Liberman wanted to preserve, in particular, output per ruble of productive capital, labor productivity, and cost per ruble of marketed production evaluated in comparable wholesale prices.[45]

In his September, 1962, proposals, Liberman advocated centralized determination of not only the volume and assortment of production, but also the quality of products and the deadlines for deliveries, the last to be fixed for enterprises after taking account of "direct contacts between suppliers and customers."[46] This position would seem to be a retreat from his previous views. At the same time, he proposed that the powers of central agencies be enumerated and limited, specifying in particular that all other plan indexes formulated by the central agencies should be transmitted only down to the Sovnarkhozes or similar entities, since it would be useless to distribute them to enterprises. He also specified that the goals for labor productivity, employment, wages, costs, profits, investments, and introduction of new techniques should be determined directly by the individual enterprises themselves.[47]

In the 1956 proposals, the standard of "profitability"—defined as "the ratio of the value of production in wholesale prices to its cost"—was to be determined by the central authorities, but it was to be established in the form of long-term standard ratios for groups of enterprises of the same type. These standard ratios were to remain in force as long as wholesale prices remained unchanged and were not to be altered more than once every five years.[48] Incentive payments to workers would depend on the degree to which the long-range profitability standard was at-

45. Liberman, *ibid.*, No. 1, 1959, pp. 89-91.

46. This phrase is rather vague, and Liberman does not talk of replacing centralized supplying of materials and equipment by trade. Such a proposal was made by Nemchinov, *Pravda*, September 21, 1962. The vagueness of this part of Liberman's proposals was pointed out by Alec Nove, "The Liberman Proposals," *Survey*, April, 1963, pp. 112-18.

47. Liberman, *Pravda*, September 9, 1962, p. 3.

48. Liberman, *Kommunist*, No. 10, 1956, pp. 82-83.

tained, as conditioned by fulfillment of current plans for volume and quality of production and of existing contracts between enterprises.[49] The same principles were formulated by Liberman in an article in 1959. However, the long-range profitability standard was replaced by long-range standards for qualitative indexes (output per ruble of productive capital), labor productivity, and "production profitability" (cost per ruble of marketed production).[50]

The originality of Liberman's proposals of September, 1962, lies, above all, in his method of calculating profitability. It is defined as the ratio of profits to fixed and working capital.[51] Maximization of profits becomes once again the only source of incentive funds and bonuses. The long-range profitability standards, established centrally for as long as wholesale prices remain constant, are, as in preceding versions, the basic criterion of efficiency; they determine payments into incentive funds and hence aggregate bonuses. These payments, just as in the earlier versions, are all conditioned on fulfillment of the targets planned centrally for the enterprise. Liberman, however, is a bit more precise on the subject of payments into incentive funds. The scale given as an illustration and applicable to the machinery industries links the incentive fund to both the profitability percentage and the volume of fixed capital.[52]

Liberman emphasizes the worker and public interest: "What is good for society is good for every enterprise."[53]

In his September 9, 1962, article, Liberman was much more precise about the role of central agencies in the planning process. They would use all the essential tools of planning: prices, finance, budget, accounting, major investments, all indexes in value and units of labor, and the basic indexes in physical terms. They would also determine the fundamental proportions in production, distribution, and consumption. But, except for those specified above, all indexes would be transmitted only to Sovnarkhozes (or

49. *Ibid.*, p. 88.
50. Liberman, *ibid.*, No. 1, 1959, pp. 90-91.
51. Liberman, *Pravda*, September 9, 1962, p. 3.
52. *Ibid.*
53. *Ibid.*

similar agencies), local executive committees, or institutions when control figures were handed down. Sovnarkhozes or their counterparts would no longer be simple transmitting agencies but would become instead centers where all the threads of basic planning crossed. They would also be in a position to check and improve enterprise plans without changing profitability norms. Planning "based on the results of the preceding year" would no longer be possible.[54]

Price reform is considered by Liberman a prerequisite for his proposed reforms. His long-range profitability norms are, however, tied to constancy of wholesale prices. He asks that prices be set for new products so as to make them profitable for producers as well as for consumers.[55]

The Concepts of Vaag and Zakharov. The idea that an enterprise should guide its activities by the profit motive is not new in Soviet literature. It has been advocated for quite some time by such authors as Z. Atlas, I. Malyshev, L. Vaag, V. Sobol, V. Cherniavskii, and S. Zakharov.[56] It has also been advocated by some Polish economists, such as W. Brus, whose ideas on the subject have appeared in Soviet journals.[57] Calculation of profitability as the ratio of profit to fixed and working capital of an enterprise had already been recommended in 1949 by Atlas and in 1951 by Vaag.[58] Some Polish economists such as Henryk Fiszel had suggested interest charges for use of capital as early as

54. *Ibid.*; see also Liberman, *Voprosy ekonomiki*, No. 8, 1962, pp. 104-5.

55. Liberman, *Pravda*, September 9, 1962, p. 3.

56. On this subject, see Marie L. Lavigne, *Le capital dans l'économie soviétique* (Paris, 1961), especially "L'évaluation des facteurs productifs," pp. 57-126.

57. W. Brus, "Iz opyta primeneniia stimulov materialnoi zainteresovannosti v Polskoi Narodnoi Respublike" [From the Experience of Introducing Material Incentives in the Polish People's Republic], *Planovoe khoziaistvo*, No. 12, 1961, pp. 74-83. According to Brus, profits should be the only criterion by which to judge the operations of an enterprise.

58. Z. V. Atlas, *Khozraschet, rentabelnost i kredit* [Accounting Autonomy, Profitability, and Credit], Moscow, 1966, p. 14. Atlas' proposals were made in *Izvestiia otdeleniia ekonomiki i prava Akademii Nauk SSSR* [Reports of the Economics and Law Section of the U.S.S.R. Academy of Sciences], No. 5, 1949, p. 387. Vaag's proposals were made at a 1951 conference on price setting in the Soviet Union whose proceedings have not been published.

1956.[59] The most interesting feature of their ideas is the search for conditions under which the aggregate of decisions made by economic units could theoretically lead to an optimal solution. A summary of these views was presented by Vaag and Zakharov during discussion of the Liberman theses.[60]

Vaag and Zakharov hold that reforms must be based on principles of price formation. They advocate use of a formula of "prices of production" that would cover "total social outlays." "Price of production" is defined as average planned unit cost in a given industry plus unit profit as derived from a rate for the entire economy.[61] That is, $C = (S + r_n K) + E$, where C is the "price of production," S is the usual cost of production not including charges for fixed capital, K is total investment, E is profit, r_n is the single standard coefficient of the efficiency of investment for the entire economy, and $(S + r_n K)$ is "total outlays for production"—all expressed per unit of output.

To price according to these principles, the Soviet government would have to introduce three basic reforms. First, a minimum interest or rental rate for fixed and working capital, the same for the entire economy, would have to be introduced. According to calculations of Gosplan's Institute of Electronic Devices for Management cited by Vaag and Zakharov, the average surplus value per ruble of productive capital is 20 per cent in the Soviet economy.[62] Second, all fixed capital would have to be reevaluated so as to obtain, at the time of movement to the new system of price formation, a 20 per cent return on fixed capital in all enterprises.[63] Third, all prices would have to be translated into "prices of production," including the rental rate of 20 per cent for productive capital. According to further calculations of the Institute, prices of producer goods would have to be increased by 80 per cent if the present level of prices for consumer goods were maintained. Payments under the turnover tax

59. Henryk Fiszel, *Zagadnienie cen i rachunku ekonomicznego* [The Problem of Prices and Economic Calculations], Warsaw, 1956.

60. Vaag and Zakharov, *Voprosy ekonomiki*, No. 4, 1963, pp. 88-100.

61. *Ibid.*, pp. 92-93.

62. *Ibid.*, p. 92.

63. *Ibid.*, p. 97.

would be replaced by rental payments for use of productive capital.[64]

After these reforms, enterprise profits could rise only by virtue of increased production, reduced costs, or improved efficiency in use of productive capital. In all these cases a rise in profits would represent a rise in real national income.[65]

The Vaag-Zakharov system presupposes other conditions that would be necessary in order for the decisions of economic units to lead to optimal solutions. Indeed, under given conditions of supply and demand, only a regime of perfect competition, established spontaneously or imitated ideally, would yield maximum product and minimum factor costs. The same conditions would then be required for the difference between the value and cost of production, which constitutes profit.[66]

The Vaag-Zakharov proposals would affect the price system. Once the principle of profit maximization is accepted, the implications for pricing policy can be strictly established. It has recently been demonstrated that there is only one constellation of factor prices implicit in competitive equilibrium.[67] In any case, it would be necessary to accept a pricing policy based not only on labor value but also on utility. The Soviet mathematical economists have reduced somewhat the customary resistance to calculations based on utility, but lack of necessary data and difficulties in calculation even with electronic computers would make application of their suggestions very difficult.[68] At any rate, such an ideal price system would present an obstacle that a planner would find difficult to overcome. If he conformed to its demands, he would lose control over price formation; if he refused to conform, his decisions would cause deviations from

64. *Ibid.*, p. 96.

65. *Ibid.*

66. Alfred Zauberman, "Liberman's Rules of the Game for Soviet Industry," *Slavic Review*, December, 1963, p. 737. For a theoretical demonstration of this hypothesis, Zauberman refers to Robert Dorfman, Paul Samuelson, and Robert Solow, *Linear Programming and Economic Analysis* (New York and London, 1958), pp. 366 and 404 ff.

67. *Ibid.*, as cited by Zauberman, *Slavic Review*, December, 1963, p. 738.

68. *Ibid.*, pp. 740-41.

optimal solutions and discordant microeconomic and macroeconomic policies.[69]

While the concepts of Vaag and Zakharov rest on a solid theoretical base, the implied reforms in planning methods are not so clear. The one thing that they insist upon is that the incentive fund of an enterprise be based on the amount of profits rather than on the wage fund, as it now is. It would no longer be necessary to impose upon enterprises a plan for costs or to subject them to rationing of equipment and material. Allocation by means of so-called "funded" (*fondiruemye*) products[70] would be replaced by contracts drawn up between enterprises; contracts would include penalty clauses for breach of deadlines and other stipulations.[71] As to the indexes in the plan, Vaag and Zakharov consider that "the work of the enterprise as a whole will no longer be regulated by dozens of indexes because it will suffice for the enterprise to improve a single index, that of profit."

Introduction of the principle of rent on fixed capital should, according to the authors, also have a "beneficial effect on investment planning." The authors have, however, failed to specify how far the autonomy of the enterprise should go in investment planning.[72]

The ideas of Vaag and Zakharov resemble those of Liberman in postulating a real autonomy for the industrial enterprise and advocating adoption of profit as the motivating agent and essential criterion of an enterprise's activity. There are, however,

69. *Ibid.*

70. Before 1958, products were distinguished as "so-called funded products, centrally planned products, and products planned on a decentralized basis. Since April, 1958, the distinction has applied to products supplied centrally and allocated by U.S.S.R. Gosplan, industrial products allocated by the republics, products allocated through a decentralized procedure, and farm produce subjected to a special regime," Philippe Bernard, "Destin de la planification soviétique," *Economie et Humanisme* (Paris, 1963), pp. 102-3.

71. In a pamphlet written a little later, L. A. Vaag, *Sovershenstvovat ekonomicheskie metody upravleniia khoziaistva* [Improve the Economic Methods of Running the National Economy], Moscow, 1964, p. 45, the author advocates the general practice of direct contractual links between enterprises and establishment of their plans on that basis.

72. Vaag and Zakharov, *Voprosy ekonomiki*, No. 4, 1963.

considerable differences between the two sets of ideas. For one thing, the views of Liberman on the questions of capital and pricing policy are much less rigorous than those of Vaag and Zakharov. Liberman actually avoids the problem of price reform by introducing long-range norms of profitability. The price paid for use of capital proposed by Vaag and Zakharov is rather implicitly accepted by Liberman, and subsidies for investments would apparently be preserved in the latter's system. The essential problem of equalizing profit norms has also been avoided by Liberman.[73]

There is still another disagreement between Liberman and Vaag-Zakharov, on the question of how the incentive fund of an enterprise should be constituted. In both cases profitability is calculated as the ratio of profit to the productive capital of the enterprise.[74] But Vaag and Zakharov suggest that payments into the incentive fund should be based on absolute profits, whereas Liberman wants them to be based on both the profitability ratio and aggregate productive capital. Vaag and Zakharov contend that Liberman's solution would cause an artificial inflation of productive capital and would inhibit some investments that had low or limited profitability rates but that, nevertheless, could realize sizable absolute profits.[75]

Generally speaking, the ideas of Vaag and Zakharov, like those of other economists advocating adoption of the profitability criterion together with substantial price reforms, are characterized by a scientific rigor. Liberman's ideas seem to leave more room for considerations of opportunity. However, they all cope inadequately with the problems arising out of the dominant role played by central authorities in formulating and implementing the plan.

73. Zauberman, *Slavic Review*, December, 1963, p. 737.

74. Vaag and Zakharov note that two methods have been advocated in the Soviet Union to calculate "profitability." Their own method consists in subtracting the rent for productive capital from profits before calculating the "profitability" rate. Other Soviet economists propose gross profit as the basis for the same calculation. See Vaag and Zakharov, *Voprosy ekonomiki*, No. 4, 1963, p. 99.

75. *Ibid.*, p. 100.

Nemchinov's Ideas.[76] An effort was made by Academician Vasilii Nemchinov to reconcile reformist views with the necessity of keeping basic decision-making powers in the hands of central planners. According to Nemchinov, social goals should be made to correspond to the interests of the basic units. "What is in the interest of society ought to be in the interest of its members."[77] It is, however, vain to try to obtain this harmony of interest mechanically by means of planned indexes that are the same for all stages of administration and management. To try is to assume implicitly that the national plan is nothing more than the sum of all plans for basic units.

Such a primitive concept of the relation between basic units and the aggregates of which they are parts leads to a petrified mechanical system in which all parameters of management are imposed a priori and the entire system is operated from above at every moment and in every place. Life itself proves these concepts to be false by imposing necessary correctives and by rendering supposedly immutable indexes flexible and pliable.[78]

The success of reforms does not depend on discovery of perfect indexes but on the correct distribution of functions, rights, and obligations among the various links in the chain of planning and implementation. A correct distribution can be achieved only in a system in which complete accounting autonomy (*khozraschet*) is guaranteed to enterprises and in which planned commands are replaced by orders for goods placed with enterprises.

Reforms must be made in all three phases of the planning process: (1) formulation of plans, (2) execution of plans, and (3) management of the economy.

76. See V. Nemchinov, *Ekonomiko-matematicheskie metody i modeli* [Methods and Models of Mathematical Economics], Moscow, 1962, pp. 43 and 51-52; Nemchinov, *Voprosy ekonomiki*, No. 11, 1962, pp. 100-2; V. Nemchinov, *O dalneishem sovershenstvovanii planirovaniia i upravleniia narodnogo khoziaistva* [On Further Improvement in Planning and Managing the National Economy], Moscow, 1963; V. Nemchinov, "A problema est!" [The Problem Is Still With Us], *Literaturnaia gazeta*, March 12, 1964; V. Nemchinov, "Sotsialisticheskoe khoziaistvovanie i planirovanie proizvodstva" [Socialist Management and Planning of Production], *Kommunist*, No. 5, 1964, pp. 74-87.

77. Nemchinov, *O dalneishem sovershenstvovanii*, p. 11.

78. Nemchinov, *Kommunist*, No. 5, 1964, pp. 75-76.

As to formulation of plans, a clear distinction must be made between plans to be drawn up by central authorities and those to be drawn up by individual enterprises. The central authorities should not try to determine all possible indexes and intersectoral relations for every moment, every region, and every productive unit. They should be concerned primarily with planning final production and reducing considerably the number of compulsory indexes contained in control figures. This reduction would be compensated for by an increase in the number of "accounting" indexes calculated for internal use of administrative bodies.

Nor should the central authorities try to set all prices. Only the prices of a limited group of the most important products should be set centrally, either directly or by means of coefficients linking one price to another. These prices should be fixed for a long period of time and sustained by a stabilization fund. A second group of products would have prices controlled by managerial agencies (organizations or institutions) and approved by the Supreme Council of the National Economy or its counterpart. A third group, consisting of goods that are not mass produced, would have prices determined by the producing enterprises themselves.

Indexes calculated by central authorities would not be handed down to enterprises as mandatory targets. The system of administrative orders would be replaced by one of economic regulations. The cardinal problem would then be to reconcile central planning with the "self-administration, self-organization, self-guidance, and self-development of the planning system."[79] Such reconciliation could be obtained by means of orders placed with enterprises by planning agencies. Every enterprise would first report on the conditions under which it was prepared to carry out a given order, specifying the assortment, quality, time limits, and

79. Nemchinov, *Ekonomiko-matematicheskie metody i modeli*, p. 51. In this passage, Nemchinov criticizes the views of the Polish sociologist Ossowski, who maintains that planning must be reconciled with "the fascination of spontaneity." Nemchinov sees no role for spontaneity in the economy and specifies that he is talking of a well-defined reconciliation between central directives and local decisions, a reconciliation that would ensure evolution of the system toward precise goals.

price. These would be real offers made by enterprises. Planning and managerial agencies would respond by placing their orders under conditions most advantageous to them.[80]

As to execution of the plan, planned goals would be incorporated in contracts made with individual enterprises. Incorporation would be neither mechanical nor automatic. It would occur through direct relations among enterprises within the system of state trade, thus replacing the present system of allocating materials and equipment which has been responsible for scarcity.[81] The assemblage of orders, specifying delivery schedules, would replace annual plans now forced on the enterprises. Such a system would avoid the inconvenience involved in making new decisions for every year.

New needs that would be revealed by calculation of annual plans on the national level would be transmitted to the enterprises by means of new orders and through adjustments in orders already placed. When such an adjustment of the orders proved impossible, the plan made by central agencies would have to be changed.

The most important innovation in the new system would be the introduction of mutual obligations on the part of enterprises, on the one hand, and of planning and managerial agencies, on the other. The superior agencies would be responsible for errors and disparities in plans and would be obliged to purchase the entire production that had been ordered at prices specified in the contracts.[82]

Nemchinov realized very well that contracts freely entered into by enterprises could not correspond with centrally planned goals. He foresaw, however, various arrangements that would improve the likelihood of accord. First of all, there would be

80. Nemchinov, *Kommunist*, No. 5, 1964, p. 77.

81. In this respect Nemchinov goes further than Liberman, who proposes that central authorities should determine the suppliers and the customers for basic products.

82. Nemchinov, *ibid.*, No. 5, 1964, p. 78. In his speech of February 28, 1964 (*Pravda*, March 7, 1964, p. 5), Khrushchev too advocated making the superior agencies responsible for errors in plans and in directives issued to collective and state farms (kolkhozes and sovkhozes).

economic legislation that would guide choice on the part of enterprises. It would determine not only total wages and employment conditions or total compulsory payments to collective farmers for their labor days,[83] but also the share of profits to be paid into the budget and the standards of community services to be offered to the public. There would then be social funds, created and used in compliance with economic legislation, that would stimulate certain activities.

The latter funds would actually be only an extension of those already in existence, such as the amortization fund, the enterprise fund, the state reserve fund, and the joint collective farm fund. However, contrary to current practice, these funds would be linked together in a system of mutual interrelations. They would be permanent, not limited (as budgetary allocations are) to the annual period. Long-range norms set by economic legislation would provide for their continuous renewal and for expenditures according to the economic situation.[84]

Nemchinov illustrates the automatic connection between economic activity and the proposed funds through the example of funds designed to stimulate production. Such funds would be fed by payments into the national budget of all profits realized on deficit products whose disposal is easy. On the other hand, enterprises could retain all profits in the case of products for which demand is weak. In agriculture, land would be divided every year into categories, on the basis of which premia would be allocated per quintal of produce delivered to the state or, inversely, payments would be required per hectare for land with good harvests.[85]

As to management, the third phase of planning, each enterprise would establish its plan independently, basing itself on general directives, economic legislation, and contracts made with

83. "Labor day" is the accounting unit used to determine payments to collective farmers. Its size is fixed every year on the basis of the financial results achieved by the individual collective farm. See, on that subject, Henri Wronski, *Remunération et niveau de la vie dans le kolkhoz: Le Troudoden* (Paris, 1957).

84. Nemchinov, *Ekonomiko-matematicheskie metody i modeli*, pp. 5-55.

85. *Ibid.*, p. 55.

suppliers and customers. Nemchinov does not specify what indexes should be imposed upon the enterprise. He merely says that they should be limited in number so as not to stifle the enterprise, with government preferably having to use economic incentives such as prices, credits, and financing.[86] In formulating its plan, the enterprise would take into account the cost of capital on the basis of the interest it would have to pay. It would be guided in its activities by the profit motive, as conditioned by long-range "profitability" norms differentiated by groups of enterprises.[87] In this regard, Nemchinov's ideas are very close to those of Liberman.

The Problem of Autonomy for the Enterprise. The decisions of the Plenary Session of the Party Central Committee of November 23, 1962, advocated greater autonomy for the enterprise and called for the drafting of a statute on the socialist enterprise extending the rights of enterprise managers and assuring workers a more active participation in management.[88] That statute was slow in being promulgated, although the need for it was emphasized on several occasions. It was not until after the Plenary Session of the Party Central Committee of September 27-29, 1965, that the Regulation on Productive Socialist Enterprises was adopted (on October 4, 1965) by the Council of Ministers.[89] The regulation (*polozhenie*) is not a statute (*ustav*), and it is rather

86. In his article in *Kommunist*, No. 5, 1964, Nemchinov does not even mention the indexes that could be imposed on the enterprises. His system, based on replacement of the old annual plan by the assemblage of orders placed with enterprises, hardly seems compatible with one in which planned indexes must reach all the way down to the enterprises.

87. These long-range "profitability" norms do not seem, in Nemchinov's system, to be tied to the price system in effect, as proposed by Liberman. In fact, Nemchinov proposes that they should remain in effect for ten or fifteen years, *Pravda*, September 21, 1962.

88. *Izvestia*, November 24, 1962, p. 2.

89. "Polozhenie o sotsialisticheskom gosudarstvennom proizvodstvennom predpriiatii" [Regulation on Productive State Socialist Enterprises], *Ekonomicheskaia gazeta*, October 20, 1965, pp. 25-29. This decision was announced by Kosygin in his speech of September 27, 1965 (*Pravda*, September 28, 1965). The regulation was translated into French in *Le Courrier des Pays de l'Est*, November 24, 1965, pp. 16-44.

general and ambiguous, making numerous references to "established rules" and "legislation in force."

Before appraising this regulation, we should review the attitudes of proponents of reform on the rights of enterprises. The first point to note is that those proponents want not only fewer mandatory indexes imposed on the enterprise,[90] but also less unpredictable interference by higher agencies in day-to-day activities, the enterprise being left free to decide for itself the best way of using its resources.[91] Although the need for the latter has been accepted generally, the problem of how to protect the enterprise against such interference seems difficult to resolve.

A. M. Birman suggests distinguishing stable indexes that could not be altered over a relatively long period and flexible indexes that could be altered as the need arose.[92] Others suggest that enterprises and the various agencies participating in the formulation of the plan share a mutual responsibility in the conduct of affairs. This view was recently restated by A. N. Kosygin in his speech of September 27, 1965:

"The development of economic methods of industrial management changes the very nature of relations between enterprises and superior agencies. We must give up the habit of thinking that, in the relations between controlling economic agencies and enterprises, the former have nothing but rights and the latter nothing but obligations. The evolution of economic methods of management and the extension of accounting autonomy (*khoz-*

90. The more detailed the planned goals, the more limited the economic and operational autonomy of the enterprise, according to V. Laptev, *Voprosy ekonomiki*, No. 6, 1963, p. 6.

91. Several Soviet economists insist on this point. See Laptev, *ibid.*, pp. 26-31; Liberman, *ibid.*, No. 8, 1962; Razumov, *ibid.*, No. 7, 1963; Birman, *Nekotorye problemy*; see also works by Nemchinov cited in footnote 76 of this chapter.

Recently, in response to an inquiry by the journal *Ekonomicheskaia zhizn*, readers suggested that the enterprise manager be given the right to dispose of various funds as long as he conforms to provisions of the annual technical, industrial, and financial plan (*tekhpromfinplan*). They also suggested that the enterprise be authorized to exclude from its plan products for which there is no effective demand. (*Ekonomicheskaia zhizn*, June 16, 1965, p. 8.)

92. Birman, *Nekotorye problemy*, pp. 47-48.

raschet) in industry make it necessary to introduce mutual rights and obligations in these relations and greater responsibility on the part of both enterprises and agencies directing industry."[93]

Some Soviet commentators believe that an enterprise should have the right to reject production goals from its plan if the needed resources are not assured.[94] Laptev goes even further and suggests introduction of an automatic link between determination of production goals and allotment of necessary resources, and between adjustment of the production plan and modification of all other related goals.[95]

If these principles were adopted by statute, the enterprise would have legal ways of protecting itself against improper goals, *i.e.*, goals not assured by adequate means of implementation. In the first instance, arbitration could be exercised by local executive committees and eventually, no doubt, by other state agencies as well.[96]

The regulation of October 4, 1965, scarcely meets such demands for reform. To prevent any misunderstanding about the status of the enterprise, Article 2 states plainly that it carries out its productive activity "under the direction of the agency above it and in conformity with the national plan."

Practically all important decisions made by an enterprise conform to commands from above; the jurisdiction of the enterprise covers only those areas in which superior agencies do not deem it worthwhile to interfere. Certain provisions of the new regulation make this subordination quite clear. The volume of working capital is set by higher authority and cannot be changed unless the production plan is revised. In the case of that part of the depreciation fund earmarked for capital repairs, the superior agency sets aside up to 10 per cent for use in making repairs in

93. Kosygin, *Pravda*, September 28, 1965, p. 4.

94. Birman, *Nekotorye problemy*, pp. 33-35.

95. Laptev, *Voprosy ekonomiki*, No. 6, 1963, p. 31.

96. Birman, *Nekotorye problemy*, pp. 31-35. In another article, "Mestnye sovety i narodnoe khoziaistvo" [Local Soviets and the National Economy], *Planovoe khoziaistvo*, No. 11, 1964, pp. 75-81, Birman tries to justify intervention by local Soviets on the grounds that they are responsible for proper operation of enterprises situated in their territory. This is a clever position having every chance of being popular.

other, lagging enterprises. Profits of an enterprise are used in accord with detailed instructions of the Council of Ministers, providing for payments into the budget, the enterprise fund, and the consumer goods fund. Investments are made according to plans handed down from above. Materials and raw materials are supplied in conformity with allocation plans and inventory norms determined by superior authority, and contracts between enterprises must conform to that allocation.

The grip of superior agencies is particularly strong in planning. Long-range and annual planned targets are determined by a superior agency in accord with a nomenclature established at the top. The enterprise sets only those prices not set by higher authority. Any operation expected to result in losses requires a special administrative procedure. All decisions concerning bonuses, wage schedules, and norms are strictly regulated. There are very severe provisions for cancellation of bonuses when the planned wage fund is overspent. There is also provision for formation of a group in the enterprise to cooperate with the National Control Committee (Party and State Control Committee until December 9, 1965), as well as for direct inspection by superior agencies and agencies of the National Control Committee.

In the face of all these restrictions, the few concessions made by the regulation of October 4, 1965, seem of little importance. Superior agencies are not permitted to take away working capital allocated to an enterprise in accord with established norms, or to take away more than a limited amount of working capital in excess of norms.[97] They can no longer appropriate sums earmarked for the enterprise fund and distribute them among other enterprises. Housing constructed with the resources of the enterprise fund must be reserved for the personnel of that enterprise. An enterprise may exceed the production goal in its plan only if there is a guarantee that the product can be sold and the required resources are available.

97. Working capital cannot be redistributed except after the annual balance sheet of the enterprise has been drawn up or after an adjustment has been made in the annual plan.

The new regulation also attempts to limit adjustments in the plan, superior agencies being allowed to make them only "exceptionally" and under conditions prescribed by the Council of Ministers. Every adjustment in the plan must be accompanied by an adjustment of indexes based on the plan. The management of the enterprise is authorized henceforward to determine the structure of administrative expenditures and the number of administrative positions without having to record these decisions with financial agencies.[98]

One would search the new regulation in vain for even a trace of the autonomy demanded by some Soviet critics. The enterprise remains as always under the direct control of superior economic agencies; and there is no question of mutual responsibility, of the right to reject plan indexes, or of an automatic link between planned goals and needed resources. Nor is it easy to see, as things now stand, how a Soviet enterprise could turn from one task to another, with the right to make alternative uses of its resources, or how it could protect itself against interference from above.

It is interesting to note that, while the government and higher economic agencies reserve for themselves all essential managerial prerogatives over enterprises, they refuse to accept responsibility for obligations of enterprises (Article 9). Debts of an enterprise that, at the moment of its liquidation, cannot be covered by its assets are simply cancelled (Article 110). In other words, superior agencies reserve the right to force an enterprise to deal with anyone they choose, while disclaiming any responsibility if the customer turns out to be insolvent. Under such circumstances, the financial status of an enterprise can hardly be expected to reflect the efficiency of management. Consequently, multiple success indicators have to be preserved. A true statute of reform for the enterprise is yet to come.

98. Kosygin refers to several of the concessions outlined here in his speech of September 27, 1965 (*Pravda*, September 28, 1965, p. 4).

CHAPTER 5. Obstacles to Basic Reforms

At the center of the debate over reforms lies a controversy about the roles of plan and market in the Soviet economy. In the present centralized system, the plan is an instrument by which the authorities transmit their directives. In economic matters, it imposes the will and preferences of the ruling group, in both a long- and short-run sense, directly on productive units and households. A market exists and even transmits some disturbances, but consumers cannot use it to pass along their demand to productive units.

In the proposed system, the market would be the agent for transmitting all orders. The ruling group would pass along its orders through subsidies, credits, and fiscal exemptions. Consumers would influence production through effective demand generated by their incomes. Government would have strong control over the volume of that demand, but it would have to act in a more flexible way and be bound to a greater extent by its own decisions. All effective demand would have the same weight, and any income payment would have the effect of exerting pressure for production of consumer goods.

Discussion of reforms has somehow bypassed these fundamental issues. As a result of Liberman's compromise proposals, discussion has concentrated instead on the merits of halfway measures that would conserve many essential features of a centralized system. Opponents of reform have consequently adopted the following general line of argument. First, the proposed reforms would be difficult to put into practice and even then would not provide criteria for recognizing efficient enterprises. Second, only the free play of the market could bring about the rational decisions envisaged by proponents of reform, but such a system is incompatible with planned socialism. Third, it is therefore necessary to retain the principle of centralized formulation of all indexes essential for the plan of an enterprise.

The failure of the debate on reforms to come to grips with fundamental issues is merely a reflection of the basic obstacle to reform: an unwillingness to face the political consequences. When the existing political regime may be at stake, there should be little wonder that a cautious approach is taken toward all questions of economic reform.

THE MISPLACED FOCUS ON LIBERMAN'S PROPOSALS

The publicity accorded to Liberman's proposals caused the discussion of issues involved in reforming the planning system to be sidetracked. Attention was concentrated on problems of the enterprise and on ways of making most effective use of workers' efforts, the responsibilities of central political and economic agencies being left in the background.

Discussion has been conducted on the public or quasi-public level, as reported in the daily and weekly press, and the official level within the governmental structure. In the "public" discussion it is of special interest to note the positions taken in *Pravda*, *Izvestia*, and *Ekonomicheskaia gazeta* between the publication of Liberman's proposals on September 9, 1962, and the Plenary Session of the Party Central Committee in November, 1962. The most favorable reactions were by staffs of enterprises, while the reactions by representatives of Sovnarkhozes and officials of higher planning and managerial agencies were much more reserved. Liberman himself was invited to state his views at a discussion organized by the "club" of *Ekonomicheskaia gazeta* and on a radio program.[1]

Another interesting conference was held at the editorial offices of *Ekonomicheskaia gazeta*, attended by such well-known Soviet economists as Nemchinov, Birman, Gatovskii, Zverev, Plotnikov, Cherniavskii, Riumin, and Turetskii.[2] The opinions voiced during that "public" debate are characterized by a certain frankness. However, no agreement or general conclusion was reached.

The important discussion that took place within government

1. *Ekonomicheskaia gazeta*, November 10, 1962, pp. 4-17. B. Kerblay, "Les propositions de Liberman pour un projet de réforme de l'entreprise en U.R.S.S.," *Cahiers du Monde Russe et Soviétique*, No. 3, 1963, p. 308.

2. *Ekonomicheskaia gazeta*, November 3, 1962, pp. 34-43.

agencies was quite a different matter. Only a few details are known about the discussion in the Economic Section of the U.S.S.R. Academy of Sciences, whose results will be examined later. That discussion took place on two different occasions: on September 25-26, 1962, at the Academy's Scientific Council for the Material Stimulation of Production, and on January 7-8, 1963, at a general meeting of the Academy's Division of Economic Science.[3] The September meeting was attended by twenty important economists, but the advocates of fundamental reform were represented only by Academician Nemchinov; Liberman was not invited to take part. The same situation prevailed at the January meeting. In an article published in *Pravda* on November 19, 1962, at the opening of the Party Central Committee's plenary session, L. Gatovskii sums up the conclusions reached and thus confers on them an official status. Another official statement equally critical of Liberman's ideas appeared in *Kommunist*, No. 6, 1962, on the eve of the November plenary session.

The results of the *official* discussion were quite clear. While recognizing that the enterprise should be freed from subjection to superior agencies and that profit should weigh more heavily in the evaluation of an enterprise's work, the specific propositions designed to give the enterprise real autonomy were all rejected *in toto*. Central planning was endorsed for *all* important indexes of the plan: volume of output, assortment and quality of production, designation of suppliers and customers, delivery schedules, employment, wage funds, costs, profits, and investments.

Thus, toward the end of 1962, the reform movement was adjourned *sine die*; only partial reforms—such as the statute on enterprises, material incentives, or criteria for fulfillment of the plan—were discussed in the press.

3. "Voprosy uluchsheniia sistemy materialnogo stimulirovaniia predpriiatii" [Questions of Improving the System of Material Incentives in Enterprises], *Voprosy ekonomiki*, No. 10, 1962, pp. 147-48; "Problemy ekonomicheskogo stimulirovaniia predpriiatii" [Problems of Economic Incentives in Enterprises], *ibid.*, No. 11, 1962, pp. 87-142; "Itogi i perspektivy ekonomicheskikh issledovanii" [Results and Prospects of Economic Research], *ibid.*, No. 3, 1963, pp. 141-42; and L. Alter, P. Krylov, and B. Merochenko, "Nazrevshie voprosy metodologii planirovaniia" [Current Questions of Planning Methodology], *Kommunist*, No. 16, 1962, pp. 64-76.

This eclipse of the advocates of reform was, however, not total. In February, 1964, Khrushchev criticized the practice of simply imposing planned goals on collective and state farms. In March, *Voprosy ekonomiki* (No. 2, 1964, pp. 157-60), the journal of the U.S.S.R. Academy of Sciences, eulogized Academician Nemchinov, one of the principal proponents of reform, on the occasion of his seventieth birthday.

The discussion of reforms was resumed in the press. The signal was given by reports in *Literaturnaia gazeta* beginning in November, 1963, and rejoinders in *Ekonomicheskaia gazeta* (March 7, 1964), that paved the way for Nemchinov's more outspoken article, "The Problem Is Still with Us," published in *Literaturnaia gazeta* in March, 1964. A second article by Nemchinov appeared the same month in the Party's ideological journal *Kommunist.*

Later, in an article in *Pravda* on August 17, 1964, Academician Trapeznikov came out for liberalization of the system and criticized the illusion of mathematicians who would like to save centralization by means of electronic computers. Liberman intervened once again in the debate in *Pravda,* September 20, 1964, insisting that the enterprise be given autonomy and emphasizing that profit cannot be accepted as the criterion of an enterprise's efficiency unless it results from the enterprise's own activity and not from goals imposed from above.

In this renewed discussion, one can clearly distinguish those who favor adoption of profit as the sole criterion of success for an enterprise and those who simply plead for greater autonomy for the enterprise and a reduction in the number of centrally planned indexes. Since condemnation of profit as the sole success criterion in the fall of 1962, direct stands on this subject have become rare. Of the six-hundred-odd letters received in response to Trapeznikov's theses and analyzed in *Pravda* on February 17, 1965 (pp. 2-3), the newspaper mentions only three favoring profit as the sole success criterion, their authors being Nesterenko and Sotchenko of the Ukrainian Republic Academy of Sciences and Remeslennikov from the Kirov region. A similar position was taken by M. Alexeev, manager of the Red October Factory in Odessa, in *Planovoe khoziaistvo*, No. 4, 1965, p. 56.

Most of those favoring profit as the sole success criterion have adopted a more flexible attitude. They have emphasized that profit could be an adequate measure of performance only after a price reform based on "prices of production." The proposals along this line made by Vaag and Zakharov in April, 1963, have already been discussed in the preceding chapter.

Later, Vaag revived the concept, referring to profit as "the economic effect"[4] and arguing that its acceptance as the sole success criterion is dependent not only on price reform but also on abolition of free use of productive capital, on calculation of production actually sold, and on formulation of the enterprise plan on the basis of direct contractual obligations between producers and consumers. In March, 1964, during a conference on the application of mathematics to economics, Malyshev and Belkin asserted that the "profitability" index could be viewed as a synthesizing index, provided that prices correctly reflected outlays of social labor.[5] On that occasion, Kantorovich defended Liberman's theses outright, declaring that adoption of profit as

4. The "economic effect" (E) is defined as the difference between the value of marketed production (C) minus the sum of costs as habitually defined in the Soviet Union (S) and a rental charge for use of productive capital based on the normative coefficient of efficiency (r_nK). Thus, his formula is:

$$E = C - (S + r_nK).$$

See Vaag's "Sovershenstvovat ekonomicheskie metody upravleniia narodnym khoziaistvom" [Improve the Economic Methods of Running the National Economy] in *Obsuzhdaem problemy sovershenstvovaniia planirovaniia* [Let Us Discuss the Problem of Improving Planning], No. 4, Moscow, 1964, pp. 34 and 44-45.

5. "Konferentsiia po primenenii matematiki v ekonomike" [Conference on Applying Mathematics in Economics], *Voprosy ekonomiki*, No. 9, 1964, p. 99.

Many leading Soviet economists, including L. M. Gatovskii, B. M. Kedrov, V. S. Nemchinov, S. L. Sobolev, S. G. Strumilin, T. S. Khachaturov, M. M. Fedorovich, I. S. Malyshev, V. V. Novozhilov, V. M. Glushkov, A. A. Dorodnitsyn, N. I. Kovalev, and A. I. Notkin, took part in that conference.

See also *Ekonomisty i matematiki za kruglym stolom* [Economists and Mathematicians at a Round Table Discussion], Moscow, 1965, 207 pp. (summarized in *Ekonomicheskaia gazeta*, June 20, 1964, pp. 7-9).

the essential criterion of an enterprise's performance would improve the chances of formulating an over-all centralized plan through mathematical optimization.

Pronouncements in favor of greater independence for the enterprise are becoming more and more frequent. They are sometimes expressed in general terms[6] and sometimes in specific ones; the specific pronouncements differ one from another. One favors preservation of centrally planned indexes only for deficit products;[7] a second, only for marketed production, profit, and labor input;[8] a third, only for physical output and profit;[9] a fourth, only for prices, profits, and nomenclature;[10] and so on. Generally speaking, there is a great deal of confusion on this subject.

The general tenor of positions taken on autonomy of enterprises contradicts current practice. The number of indexes in the annual central plan rose from 4,744 in 1940 to 9,490 in 1953, and then fell to 3,390 in 1957 and 1,780 in 1958. This reduction did not enhance the autonomy of enterprises however, since Sovnarkhozes and republic Gosplans added many indexes of their own to those of the central plan.[11] For example, in the Moscow factory for electric bulbs, the number of forms to be filled out rose from fourteen in 1956-57 to forty-two in 1964-65. At the same time, these forms become more and more detailed. One entitled "The Production Plan in Value and Physical Terms" used to have only fifteen lines but now has twenty-four; the form on

6. As examples of articles proposing re-examination of the problem of planned indexes, see "Zalog uspekhov" [Guarantee of Success], an editorial in *ibid.*, February 24, 1965, p. 2; N. Fedorenko, "Vazhnaia ekonomicheskaia zadacha" [An Important Economic Problem], *Pravda*, January 17, 1965, p. 2.

7. S. Iliushin and A. Rutenberg, "Za bolee effektivnye formy khoziaistvovaniia" [For More Efficient Management Methods], *Planovoe khoziaistvo*, No. 1, 1965, pp. 53-54.

8. S. Sergieni, "Ustranit poteri" [Eliminate Waste], *Ekonomicheskaia gazeta*, April 14, 1965, p. 10.

9. B. Smekhov (answering Trapeznikov's proposals), *Pravda*, February 17, 1965, p. 2.

10. Birman and Belkin, *ibid.*, October 14, 1964.

11. Z. V. Atlas, *Khozraschet, rentabelnost i kredit* [Accounting Autonomy, Profitability, and Credit], Moscow, 1966, p. 17.

costs has grown from thirteen lines to twenty-nine.[12] In the Sovnarkhoz of the Central Urals, the plan for production, employment, and costs was set up in 1961 on seventy-three forms with 86,328 indexes. By 1964-65, the number of forms had grown to ninety-eight with 365,230 indexes.[13] In general, a Soviet industrial enterprise has as many as 500 indexes in its annual plan imposed on it from above.[14]

In his speech of September 27, 1965, Kosygin promised to reduce the number of indexes. In order to gauge the chances for success in that endeavor, one must appreciate the obstacles confronting reform and the arguments in defense of the present system.

ARGUMENTS FOR CENTRALIZED PLANNING

The principal argument for maintaining the present system is that it would be impossible to split planning into two parts: one to be carried out administratively and transmitted only down as far as some supervisory level, and the other to be carried out by the enterprise spontaneously, through autonomous decisions on wages, employment, investment, costs, and profits. Such a system, argued advocates of the status quo, would seriously jeopardize national planning as a whole by putting the entire machinery out of gear.[15]

12. Iliushin and Rutenberg, *Planovoe khoziaistvo*, No. 1, 1965, pp. 52-53.

13. "Dva zvena edinoi tsepi" [Two Links in the Same Chain], *Ekonomicheskaia gazeta*, June 16, 1965, p. 15.

14. O. Nekrasov, "Otraslevoi printsip upravleniia promyshlennostiu i tekhnicheskii progress" [The Sector Principle of Managing Industry and Technical Progress], *Voprosy ekonomiki*, No. 11, 1965, p. 3.

15. See, on that subject, several interventions in the course of the discussion organized by the Academy of Sciences, particularly: G. Kosiachenko, "Vazhnoe uslovie uluchsheniia planirovaniia" [An Important Condition for Improving Planning], *ibid.*, No. 11, 1962, p. 111; K. Plotnikov, "V chem prav i neprav E. G. Liberman" [In What Respects Liberman Is Right and Wrong], *ibid.*, p. 113; L. Alter, "Sviazat stimulirovanie s perspektivnym planirovaniem predpriiatiia" [Link Up Incentives with Long-Range Planning of Enterprises], *ibid.*, p. 116; L. Rotshtein, "Uluchshit finansovoe planirovanie v sovnarkhozakh" [Improve Financial Planning in the Sovnarkhozes], *ibid.*, p. 120; and L. Gatovskii, "Sozdat novuiu sistemu stimulirovaniia predpriiatii" [Create a New System of Incentives for Enterprises], *ibid.*, p. 141.

To support their argument, defenders of the present system mentioned certain harmful consequences of the reforms. To start with, the long-range structure of the economy could not be controlled but would be determined by enterprises if the latter were allowed to plan their investments. "How could an enterprise," wonders Sukharevskii, "decide by itself which of its capacities should be developed to satisfy long-range national needs?"[16]

Allegedly, there would also be greater risk of discrepancy between microeconomic and macroeconomic decisions, aggravating existing disproportions:

"If an enterprise whose profits are growing decides upon an investment, it is assumed that it can automatically find the equipment and construction materials it needs. If it increases wages, it is assumed that a corresponding amount of consumer goods has become available. However, such an equilibrium cannot be taken for granted without centralized planning."[17]

According to Zverev, if reforms were introduced, one should expect "more mistakes, less coordination in investment plans, a greater tendency to give precedence to local interests, and therefore greater disparities in industrial development."[18]

The planning of wages by enterprises would make it impossible to maintain throughout the nation a correspondence between the money income of the population and the supply of goods and services available. Whether an increase in the wage fund, and hence in production, takes place in the consumer goods sector or in the producer goods sector is something that cannot be ignored. Thus, it is contended, central planning is indispensable to avoid the danger of inflation, particularly since decentralization of investment would result in an increase in unfinished construction.[19]

16. B. Sukharevskii, "O sovershenstvovanii form i metodov materialnogo stimulirovaniia" [On Improving the Forms and Methods of Material Incentives], *ibid.*, p. 16. See also A. Zverev, "Protiv skhematizma v reshenii slozhnykh voprosov" [Against Sketchiness in Deciding Complex Questions], *ibid.*, p. 95.

17. Sukharevskii, *ibid.*, p. 15.

18. Zverev, *ibid.*, p. 95.

19. See, on this subject, Sukharevskii, *ibid.*, p. 16; I. Kasitskii, "Glavnoe

Other authors believe that reform could lead to a recession. Decentralizing planning and management could slow down growth rates in pilot sectors.[20] Abandoning central planning of manpower could create a problem of employing surplus manpower.[21] There would be a danger of unemployment.

Another troublesome matter would be slackening of discipline. The central plan would lose its psychological impact in rallying the populace and could not serve as the "watchword of battle."[22]

It is interesting to note that the opponents of reform often back their arguments by referring to the experience of foreign countries. According to A. Vorobeva, Czech experiments in decentralizing planning were much more cautious than what Liberman advocates.[23] L. Alter argues that even the French type of indicative planning influences decisions of enterprises by means of centrally directed investments.[24] Some Soviet economists emphasize the fact that capitalist countries use administrative methods indirectly through the governmental apparatus.[25]

—vopros o kriterii pooshchreniia i o planiruemykh predpriiatiiam pokazateliakh" [The Most Important is the Question of the Incentive Criterion and the Indexes Planned by the Enterprises], *ibid.*, pp. 89-90; Kosiachenko, *ibid.*, p. 111; N. Spiridonova, "Istochniki i sistemy premirovaniia" [Sources and Systems of Awarding Bonuses], *ibid.*, p. 125; E. Rusanov, "O glavnom pokazatele raboty predpriiatiia" [On the Main Index of the Enterprise's Work], *ibid.*, p. 130. "At the present time decentralized investments exceed available material resources. If we start, even timidly, allocating material resources to these investments, there would be a considerable expansion of construction and a dispersion of available means. The only possible course would be to limit decentralized investments. But that would be impossible if Liberman's proposals are adopted," Kosiachenko, *ibid.*, p. 111.

According to Plotnikov, unfinished construction accounts for 76 per cent of total investment; and the figure is rising even though there are only 10,000 construction enterprises, half of them at the time under Sovnarkhozes. "What would happen," he asks, "if 200,000 enterprises had the power to decide what to build and how to do it?" (*ibid.*, p. 113).

20. G. Evstafev, "Povysit deistvennost gosudarstvennogo plana" [Increase the Efficiency of the State Plan], *ibid.*, p. 106.

21. Kasitskii, *ibid.*, p. 89.

22. A. Vorobeva, "Iskhodnoi bazoi stimulirovaniia mozhet byt tolko plan" [Only the Plan Can Be the Basis for Incentives], *ibid.*, p. 105; Kosiachenko, *ibid.*, p. 110; Alter, *ibid.*, p. 116.

23. Vorobeva, *ibid.*, pp. 103-4.

24. Alter, *ibid.*, p. 116.

25. Rusanov, *ibid.*, p. 128.

OBJECTIONS TO THE FREE PLAY OF THE MARKET

Defenders of the present system contend that, if government interference were limited to prices, money, and credit, all other variables would evolve spontaneously according to the demand on which the enterprise would base its own plans.[26] The proposed equilibrium would then be one of a logically defined system based on automatic functioning of objective laws and categories.[27] Such a system could only function under conditions of free exchange and prices, *i.e.*, under the unrestricted working of the law of value.[28] But spontaneous functioning of economic laws is inconceivable in a planned economy, and it in no way flows from the objective nature recognized in economic laws.[29] Value should be used as a tool for implementing the plan and not as a point of departure for making decisions. Material interest and profit would guide production imperfectly and could have negative aspects.[30]

It is joint use of administrative and economic methods of transmitting plan directives that has been suggested, although agreement seems purely formal on this score. Many economists certainly do not share Birman's views that certain assignments or norms should be imposed on enterprises and workers only in cases of "dire emergency."[31]

OBJECTIONS TO ABOLITION OF CENTRALIZED ALLOCATION OF RESOURCES

Today, except for enterprises experimenting with "direct links," no enterprise is free to select its suppliers or customers. The con-

26. Alter, *ibid.*, p. 115; and G. Kosiachenko, "Stoimostnye pokazateli plana i povyshenie effektivnosti materialnogo stimulirovaniia" [Cost Indexes of the Plan and Raising the Efficiency of Material Incentives], *ibid.*, No. 5, 1963, p. 92.

27. Rusanov, *ibid.*, No. 11, 1962, p. 127.

28. Vorobeva, *ibid.*, p. 104.

29. Rusanov, *ibid.*, pp. 127-28.

30. *Ibid.*; and Sukharevskii, "Sotsialisticheskoe predpriiatie i narodnoe khoziaistvo" [The Socialist Enterprise and the National Economy], *ibid.*, No. 5, 1963, p. 29.

31. A. M. Birman, *Nekotorye problemy nauki o sotsialisticheskom khoziaistvovaniiu* [Some Problems in Managing a Socialist Economy], Moscow, 1963, p. 23.

tracting parties are designated by the plan or supply offices. The supplying and selling agencies send orders (*nariady*) for delivery of products to suppliers and their customers, the orders being based on the plan for supplies of materials and equipment or for distribution of consumer goods. The *nariad* designates the parties to the contract, obliges them to conclude it, and determines its principal clauses. All decisions are binding, whether issued by the Central Directorate of Interrepublic Deliveries (until October 2, 1965, under U.S.S.R. Sovnarkhoz and thereafter under the State Committee for Supplying Materials and Equipment), by General Directorates of Supplies and Sales within republics, or by local sales agencies.[32]

Allocation of resources is not only authoritarian but also highly centralized, even more so in the last few years. Before the 1957 reforms that introduced the Sovnarkhozes, Gosplan prepared allocational balances for 1,050 so-called "funded" and essential products, whose allocation was controlled by the Council of Ministers. Another 5,000 "centrally planned" products were distributed by the supply agencies attached to the ministries (Glavsbyt). In 1957, these supply agencies were put under the jurisdiction of Gosplan and were named the Central Directorates of Interrepublic Deliveries.[33]

The number of products allocated by Gosplan increased from 12,750 in 1960 to 14,000 in 1961, representing roughly 90 per cent of industrial output.[34]

32. Michel Lesage, "L'évolution du droit des contrats en URSS," *Le Courrier des Pays de l'Est*, May 20, 1965, p. 27. It seems that the General Directorates of Supplies were, after the reforms of October 2, 1965, to be transferred from republic Gosplans to the State Committee on Supplying Materials and Equipment. Sales agencies of Sovnarkhozes were, on the other hand, apparently to be transferred to the appropriate ministries in charge of funds. We cannot be certain about these changes until more information becomes available.

33. See footnote 70, Chapter 4.

34. Henri Wronski, "La localisation des forces productives en URSS," *Revue d'Economie Politique*, No. 1, 1964, p. 401; and G. L. Dubinskii, *Organizatsiia snabzheniia narodnogo khoziaistva v respublike i ekonomicheskom raione* [Organization of the Supplying of the National Economy in Republics and Economic Regions], Moscow, 1964, p. 15.

After U.S.S.R. Sovnarkhoz was created in November, 1962, and the Central Directorates of Interrepublic Deliveries were placed under its jurisdiction, the number of centrally planned and allocated products reached 19,000.[35] This figure is not too reliable, and some authors mention 18,000 centrally planned products[36] or 18,000 centrally allocated products.[37] According to Koldomasov, this figure includes 1,700 of the most important products for which allocation plans are prepared by Gosplan, those of 380 products requiring approval of the Council of Ministers.[38] The discussion of reforms, moreover, has not retarded the continual increase in the number of centrally allocated products, which exceeded 20,000 in July, 1966.[39] But the Deputy Chairman of the State Committee on Supplying Materials and Equipment, V. Lagutkin, announced at that time that 6,000 of these products would henceforth be allocated in a "decentralized" way by regional agencies supplying materials and equipment.[40]

At the enterprise level, the list of centrally planned products is much more detailed because of the specification of nomenclature at lower levels. Thus, while the national plan has only a single entry for cotton fiber, the Central Directorate of Interrepublic Deliveries has fifty-six categories of cotton fiber in its distribution plan. Similarly, for the three entries for wool approved by the Council of Ministers, seventy-eight categories of wool appear in the distribution plan. At intermediary levels of

35. I. Evenko, "Problemy vnedreniia ekonomicheskoi kibernetiki v upravlenie promyshlennostiu SSSR" [Problems of Introducing Economic Cybernetics in the Management of Soviet Industry], *Voprosy ekonomiki*, No. 8, 1965, p. 135.

36. Leon Smolinski and Peter Wiles, "The Soviet Planning Pendulum," *Problems of Communism*, November-December, 1963, p. 17.

37. Iu. Koldomasov, "Razvitie priamykh khoziaistvennykh sviazei i sovershenstvovanie raspredeleniia sredstv proizvodstva" [Development of Direct Economic Links and Improving the Distribution of Producer Goods], *Voprosy ekonomiki*, No. 11, 1965, p. 20.

38. *Ibid.*

39. V. Lagutkin, "Materialno-tekhnicheskoe snabzhenie v novykh usloviiakh" [Supplying Materials and Equipment Under New Conditions], *Ekonomicheskaia gazeta*, No. 26, 1966, p. 4.

40. *Ibid.*

the planning and supplying apparatus, central authorities set plans for 3,240 electrotechnical and optical-mechanical instruments, 24,000 types of heavy machine-building, etc.[41]

The deficiencies of the present system are well known. The unsteady flow of supplies causes work stoppages and jeopardizes fulfillment of the plan; the disruptions spread throughout the economy in a chain reaction.[42] Discrepancies appear between planned production and planned suppliers, and enterprises try to protect themselves against disastrous consequences by stocking additional reserves. The work of agencies in charge of supplying materials and equipment becomes too costly, duplication mounts, and wasteful transportation abounds.

To the advocates of fundamental reforms, it is obvious that the planning system cannot be really improved without doing away with, or at least drastically limiting, centralized allocation of resources. Statements to that effect by Academician Nemchinov and others like Vaag and Zakharov were at first ignored. But reformers returned to the attack in November, 1963, and in the spring of 1964 *Ekonomicheskaia gazeta* conducted an inquiry among high officials of the economic administration.[43] A discussion on this subject was held at the Plekhanov Institute of the National Economy in Moscow in June, 1964, with two prominent advocates of reform—Nemchinov and Birman—attending.[44]

The argument of Nemchinov and Birman is threefold. First,

41. Koldomasov, *Voprosy ekonomiki*, No. 11, 1965, pp. 20-21.

42. E. Lokshin, "Puti sovershenstvovaniia materialno-tekhnicheskogo snabzheniia" [Ways of Improving the Supplying of Materials and Equipment], *ibid.*, No. 2, 1965, p. 39.

43. The reactions of the principal agencies consulted on this subject (the U.S.S.R. and Russian Republic Sovnarkhozes, the U.S.S.R. and Russian Republic Gosplans, and the State Committee on Arbitration) were rather unfavorable. Abolition of centralized supplying of materials and equipment was considered premature in view of the existing shortage of materials, and the consequences of a relaxation in the discipline of the plan were feared (see the article "V povestku dnia: spros, assortiment, kachestvo" [The Order of the Day Is Demand, Assortment, Quality], in *Ekonomicheskaia gazeta*, May 9, 1964, pp. 5-6).

44. "Snabzhat ili torgovat?" [To Supply or to Trade?], *ibid.*, June 27, 1964, pp. 6-11; and "Ne uprazdniat a sovershenstvovat" [Do Not Abolish, But Improve], *ibid.*, September 19, 1964, pp. 7-8.

centralized provision of materials and equipment and authoritarian allocation of resources are theoretically derived from the premise that intermediate products may not be considered as commodities. Stalin used to favor this theory, but it has long been discarded. Trade is in no way incompatible with either socialism or communism, under which the functions of exchange will continue to exist.

Second, from the practical viewpoint, centralized supplying of materials and equipment is a reflection of shortages, but these shortages are themselves the result of faults in the planning system. Enterprises make their requests (*zaiavki*)—*i.e.*, declare their needs—even before they know what their plan will be. This practice tends to produce imbalances. Indeed, preference is given to accounting in physical balances that cannot be equilibrated (*e.g.*, books, textiles), while valuations and the law of value are insufficiently appreciated. In some cases, authoritarian allocation itself creates shortages.

Third, the increase in production and the improvement in calculating balances make it possible to equilibrate needs and resources in plans. There is no reason to believe that the needs of enterprises are more difficult to estimate than those of the population, and the latter are handled by a trade network. The needs of enterprises are, in fact, the more stable of the two and are not subject to fluctuations caused by changing fashion. If centralized supplying of materials and equipment is the result of shortages, the problem should be faced frankly, the allocative expedient viewed as temporary, and progressive movement toward trade in producer goods envisaged. The urgent first step would have to be reform of wholesale prices.[45]

45. Other arguments have also been used in favor of abolishing centralized allocation of materials and equipment. Langshtein (of the Stavropol State Bank) argues that wholesale trade would make formation of fixed capital expensive; Lazarev (from Magadan District), that it would make economic incentives work; Zaostrovtsev (from Leningrad University), that it should be possible to install trade in producer goods for industry when it is accepted for state farms; Kuzmin (from Donetsk), that the time has come to allow free play to the law of value. "We live," Kuzmin writes, "in an age of automation and the law of value must be allowed to play the role of the computer." However, the editors of *Ekonomicheskaia gazeta*

The opponents of reforms reject these arguments.[46] It is true, they respond, that producer goods are commodities and that centralized allocation of materials and equipment is a kind of state trade. However, such trade is different in nature from trade in consumer goods and must therefore be handled differently. State trade in consumer goods closely resembles centralized allocation of resources.[47] Before reaching retail trade, current consumer goods go through various stages of planned distribution. At each stage, the characteristics of centralized allocation of resources are all present (estimation of needs; requests by enterprises; evaluation of resources; determination of delivery orders, funds, time limits; and so on). It is not until the final stage—retail trade—that goods are freely sold to any customer.

The primary argument of defenders of the present system is the need to ensure that claims of high priority—such as those of the defense and chemical industries—are met despite the persistent shortage of producer goods. This argument was advanced by representatives of all the principal agencies consulted in the spring of 1964 by *Ekonomicheskaia gazeta*.[48] The shortage, they contend, is the cause rather than the result of centralized allocation of resources.

One of the strongest defenders of the present system, E. Lokshin, rejects the argument that centralized allocation of resources must be abolished in order to improve the balances. The function of a balance, he argues, is to make clear the resources at the disposal of the state and the needs for them. It cannot be used to

---

protest against these views (see that journal, September 19, 1964, pp. 7-8, and May 9, 1964, pp. 5-6).

46. Among the opponents of reform participating in the discussion organized by the Plekhanov Institute in Moscow, we may mention N. Fasoliak, P. Smirnov, D. Genkin, A. Morozov (head of a Glavk section for allocation of materials and equipment), V. Sadomchev, E. Khrutskii, G. Grigorian, and E. Lokshin. See *ibid.*, June 27, 1964, pp. 9-11.

47. This is Lokshin's view (see *ibid.*, p. 11, and E. Lokshin, "Put sovershenstvovaniia materialno-tekhnicheskogo snabzheniia" [The Way to Improve Supplying of Materials and Equipment], *Voprosy ekonomiki*, No. 2, 1965, pp. 41-42).

48. See footnote 43 above; and *Ekonomicheskaia gazeta*, June 27, 1964, p. 10; *ibid.*, September 19, 1964, p. 7.

show total needs and the production required to satisfy them. Although a bit strange, this argument does have some basis. It is simply an admission by a Soviet specialist that Soviet balances are imperfect and that they have little chance of being substantially improved. Implicitly at least, Lokshin comes to agreement with Nemchinov.

Centralized allocation of resources has also been defended by dictum. Koldomasov, for example, simply asserts that allowing an enterprise to select its suppliers and customers would be a flagrant violation of indispensable conditions, contradicting the very essence of socialist economic planning.[49] Similarly, Khrutskii (of the former U.S.S.R. Sovnarkhoz) asserts that "selling for money is tantamount to producing without a plan"; Professor Grigorian, that "to discontinue centralized allocation of materials and equipment is to break the production process"; and Olshanetskii (chief of the supply service at the Riga Railroad Car Factory), that the proposed reforms would introduce an element of chance into the process of production and distribution.

On the other hand, many Soviet public figures have taken a compromise position. They admit that shortages make direct allocation of resources necessary, but they hold that it is necessary to raise supply to demand by increasing production of deficit goods. The state should reduce the number of products that are centrally distributed, build up stockpiles, and introduce as far as possible a mixture of centralized allocation and trade in producer goods.[50] Professor M. Breev observes that, if Nemchinov's propositions were accepted, centralized allocation would be regulated essentially by prices, the result being an inevitable change in the structure of costs and profits and thereby in the

49. Koldomasov, *Voprosy ekonomiki*, No. 11, 1965, p. 19.

50. See N. Turetskii, A. Filipov, and P. Shein, *Ekonomicheskaia gazeta*, June 27, 1964, pp. 10-11; also Somov and some unidentified responses in *ibid.*, September 19, 1964, p. 7. Some, like M. Alexeev, manager of the Red October Factory, believe that links between suppliers and customers should be extended by gradual stages beginning with enterprises producing consumer goods (see *Planovoe khoziaistvo*, No. 4, 1965, p. 57).

level and structure of prices. Reforms thus involve problems beyond the issue of trade versus centralized allocation.[51]

Although Nemchinov and Birman did not appear to have much support for their arguments during the discussions in June, 1964, this was certainly not the case at a conference jointly organized in July, 1966, by the State Committee on Supplying Materials and Equipment and the editorial staff of *Ekonomicheskaia gazeta.*[52]

Basing their arguments on the September, 1965, resolutions of the Central Committee, the conferees condemned the tendency to reinforce centralized allocation of resources when shortages mount. They claimed that such a rationing system (*kartochnaia sistema*) itself creates shortages by separating planning and distribution processes. Other arguments of Nemchinov and Birman received even stronger support. It was admitted that enterprises submit their requests for equipment and materials (during April through June) before they know their production plans. If they do not later receive the credit needed to finance such expenditures, they simply cancel the requests even though the production plan has been based on them. Such a practice makes it harder and harder to reduce the number of products in short supply.

Henceforward, contracts between enterprises are to link production with consumption and to regulate distribution of products not included in the obligatory list drawn up by superior

51. *Ekonomicheskaia gazeta*, June 27, 1964, p. 9. It should be emphasized that the opponents of fundamental reform usually advocate minor reforms aimed at improving the existing system of supplying materials and equipment. Thus Lokshin, *Voprosy ekonomiki*, No. 2, 1965, pp. 39-49, as well as Smirnov and Shein, advocates creation of a uniform organization for centralized allocation based on the model of state trade. Lokshin, particularly, calls at the same time for decentralizing planning, streamlining bureaucratic procedures for reviewing requests (*zaiavki*) by enterprises, and extending the jurisdiction of Gosplan. He also asks for improved estimation of physical balances, use of mathematical methods and electronic computers, an increase in the number of storehouses, and better supervision of norms for stockpiles. Various small adjustments, such as attachment of suppliers to customers and negotiation of direct contracts within the framework of the allocated funds, are also envisaged by Lokshin (*ibid.*, pp. 39-49).

52. "Ekonomicheskaia reforma i khoziaistvennyi dogovor" [Economic Reform and the Contract], *Ekonomicheskaia gazeta*, No. 30, 1966, pp. 8-20.

agencies. Extended use of contracts is supposed to enable a reduction in the number of centrally planned products.

At the same time, extended use of contracts between enterprises will raise problems that the conferees certainly did not resolve. I. Tanchuk, a member of the State and Law Institute of the Academy of Sciences, suggested distinguishing three categories of contracts: (1) those based on administrative orders (*nariady*); (2) those based on orders from supply agencies; and (3) those made directly between enterprises. Regarding the first and most important category, there is the problem of how to be sure that a contract corresponds to the plan. If the contract is not to be drawn up until an order (*nariad*) is received, there would be no change from present practice. If a preliminary contract is to be drawn up subject to modification after the plan has been adopted, the system may become too cumbersome. Some commentators (*e.g.*, N. Klein) suggest a system whereby a conflicting administrative order (*nariad*)—independently justified—would not automatically nullify a contract, but the conflicts would instead be arbitrated. This solution, which would entail a considerable expansion of arbitrative powers, does not seem to have been adopted. The hope has been expressed, however, that use of administrative orders can gradually be reduced in the spheres of activity in which contracts and orders are in general harmony.

Another element of reform would consist in a change in the characteristic functions performed by regional offices supplying materials and equipment. They would become intermediary supply depots maintaining commercial relations with enterprises and freeing the latter from the necessity of holding excessive inventories. If these depots are to become effective intermediaries, excess inventories in the hands of enterprises will have to be transferred to them. Hence a campaign to reduce excess inventories has been launched, at the displeasure of enterprise managers. The comment of Roshal, head of Glavsnab in the Ministry of Machine-Building for the Chemical and Petroleum Industries, is typical:

"Obviously we must continually develop better methods of supply with the help of supply bases and augment the stocks of regional agencies. But if I were asked my opinion right now on the project of transferring some of our ministry's stocks to Gossnab depots, I would oppose it, although I recognize that it might be useful. Why? Because at present enterprises lack faith in the power of Gossnab."

This attitude led other conferees, like A. Bogomazov, to suggest administrative earmarking of surplus stocks, a proposal in turn criticized on the grounds that such procedures never brought about a reduction in stocks, but on the contrary caused them to increase faster than production.

It is obvious that administrative pressure for reduction of inventories is not consonant with the spirit of the October, 1965, reforms, but how can it be avoided? Is not the enhanced power of enterprises in times of shortages, even though transitory, likely to generate an excessive piling up of inventories?

Whether direct contracts between enterprises become more extensive depends on what is done to reduce the region of activities directed by administrative orders and to strengthen the penalties for failure to meet contractual obligations. The present penalty for missing a scheduled shipment (4.5 per cent of its value) is the same regardless of whether the delay is one day or one month, and it is too small to cover resulting losses. Moreover, inadequate account is taken of delays attributable to railroads, whose fines are far too low relative to losses suffered by enterprises. An offending enterprise manager is also not effectively penalized since he presides over the Committee on Labor Conflicts that assesses penalties in such cases. It has been proposed that the State Arbitration Authority be made responsible for adjudicating conflicts between enterprises and superior agencies, and especially for seeing to it that all plan indexes are carefully coordinated with each other. But these suggestions do not seem to have aroused any definite response.

As a result of official encouragement, it is now widely held in the Soviet Union that materials and equipment should eventually be supplied through the wholesale trade network. The Deputy Chairman of the State Committee on Supplying Materials and Equipment, V. Lagutkin, seems to agree; he says that the problem of circulating commodities can no longer be identified with the problem of allocating existing resources.[53] Hence the ideological barriers to trade in producer goods seem to be lifted, and the practical question of shortages is the only current justification for maintaining rationing through administrative orders.

Under the circumstances, it is hardly surprising that authors like V. Cherniavskii now attack the entire system that supplies materials and equipment, accuse supplying agencies of creating shortages (*tovarnyi golod*), and attribute persisting shortages (as, for example, in the case of ferrous metals) to the unequilibrated nature of plans themselves.[54] Such criticism seems to raise the real problem by indicting the general economic policy of the Soviet government, for the present system of authoritarian allocation of resources is but one means of carrying out that policy.

OBJECTIONS TO EMPHASIS ON PROFIT AND "PROFITABILITY"

The brunt of the attack against the reformers has been aimed at the proposal to use profit as the sole or even the essential and synthetic criterion to assess performance of an enterprise. While agreeing that profit should be given a greater role, the opponents of reform still do not trust indirect planning tools, financial or otherwise. This was the view of the majority at a joint meeting, held in November, 1964, and attended by some 300 Soviet economists, of two science councils of the U.S.S.R. Academy of Sciences: one for Accounting Autonomy and Stimulation of Production and a second for Improvement of Planning Methods and Planned Indicators. The report of this meeting states:

"The majority of participants who spoke supported the view that it is still impossible to express objectively in a single index the numerous economic processes and the particular and special

53. Lagutkin, *ibid.*, No. 26, 1966, p. 4.

54. V. Cherniavskii, "Voprosy sovershenstvovaniia planirovaniia i upravleniia proizvodstvom" [Problems of Improving the Planning and Management of Production], *Voprosy ekonomiki*, No. 6, 1966, p. 26.

aspects of the different sectors of production. The search for a 'universal index' cannot, as experience has shown, lead to desired results. We must have a system of indexes that precisely reflects the essential results of productive efforts by enterprises and that stimulates their work."[55]

Opposition is inspired sometimes by ideological considerations and at other times by practical objections. The most serious ideological objection is that profit is the basic motivational force in the capitalist system and is, therefore, unsuitable for socialism or communism.[56] What counts is production of material goods to satisfy the growing needs of society; fluctuations in value do not necessarily reflect changes in material goods; and people need goods, not exchange value.[57] It should also not be forgotten, other opponents of reform add, that relations between the state and the enterprise in a socialist country cannot be what they are in a capitalist one. The state cannot be viewed as the owner who grants a lease to the enterprise.[58] It has also been said that "profitability" reflects activity in not only production but also distribution,[59] whereas, according to orthodox Marxism, national income should not include services.

55. "Sovershenstvovanie pokazatelei planirovaniia raboty predpriiatii" [Improvement of Planning Indexes for the Work of Enterprises], *ibid.*, No. 3, 1965, p. 139. Among those agreeing with this formulation were L. M. Gatovskii, A. D. Kurskii, and V. I. Kantor. Leontev's position is typical of the group: although he favors the strengthening of economic tools, the role of profit, and material incentives for workers, he emphasizes that "in a socialist planned economy, the efficient work of an enterprise depends on fulfillment of planned goals for volume of output, assortment, quality, and delivery schedules, and in some cases other conditions as well" (L. Leontev, "Leninskie printsypy sotsialisticheskogo khoziaistvovaniia i burzhuaznye vymysly" [Leninist Principles of Management and Bourgeois Slanders], *ibid.*, No. 4, 1965, pp. 108-17).

56. This point was contested by Vaag and Zakharov (*ibid.*, No. 4, 1963) and by A. M. Birman, "Problema rentabelnosti i finansovaia nauka" [Problem of "Profitability" and Financial Science], *ibid.*, No. 9, 1963, pp. 84-85.

57. See Rusanov and Gatovskii, *ibid.*, No. 11, 1962, pp. 129 and 137; also A. Bachurin and A. Pervukhin, "K voprosu o pribyli pri sotsializme" [On the Question of Profits Under Socialism], *ibid.*, No. 9, 1963, p. 66.

58. Bachurin and Pervukhin, *ibid.*, p. 67.

59. A. Kurskii, "Voprosy postroeniia ekonomicheskikh pokazatelei raboty predpriiatii" [Problems of Constructing Economic Indexes for Enterprises], *ibid.*, No. 12, 1964, p. 42.

The practical objections to the use of profit as the sole criterion are just as strong. Profitability may vary without necessarily reflecting any corresponding change in the performance of the enterprise or in the production of goods useful to society. The usefulness of profit as a synthetic index of performance could, to start with, be distorted by the enterprise itself. The management of an enterprise can manipulate the difference between the profitability of its principal and secondary products and realize higher profits on production less useful to society.[60] The same effect could be obtained my manipulating quality[61] or the relation between capital and labor. Using Liberman's index of profitability (the ratio of profit to fixed and working capital), an enterprise could try to increase profit by substituting labor for capital. Such a policy would not only hamper technical progress but also create disparities in market supplies of consumer goods.[62] In general, a saving in expenditures on social labor may be obtained by means of various factors without necessarily resulting in an increase in profit.[63]

Total profits could also vary for reasons completely unconnected with the efforts of an enterprise. A change in the assortment of products imposed from above can turn profits into losses. Changes, even minor ones, in conditions of supply may also deprive the personnel of an enterprise of bonuses. And profit itself is obtained differently in different sectors: in sectors where production is limited by available raw materials, an increase in profit can come only from reduced costs and not from increased

60. M. Maslova, "Sovershenstvovat sistemu pooshchreniia inzhenerno-tekhnicheskikh rabotnikov" [Improve the System of Incentives for Engineers and Technicians], *ibid.*, No. 11, 1962, p. 126.

61. M. Bor, "O povyshenii nauchnogo urovnia planirovaniia narodnogo khoziaistva" [On Raising the Scientific Level of National Economic Planning], *ibid.*, No. 3, 1963, p. 12.

62. See, for instance, Kasitskii, *ibid.*, No. 11, 1962, p. 89; Kosiachenko, *ibid.*, p. 112; B. Kapitonov, "Pribyl ne mozhet sluzhit obobshchaiushchim merilom" [Profit Cannot Serve as a General Criterion], *ibid.*, p. 131; also N. Maslova, "Pribyl i fond predpriiatiia" [Profit and the Enterprise Fund], *ibid.*, No. 7, 1963, p. 44.

63. Bachurin and Pervukhin, *ibid.*, No. 9, 1963, p. 74.

production, a situation that could not fail to affect the conditions under which bonuses are granted to workers.[64]

OBJECTIONS TO THE PROPOSED PRICE SYSTEM

The fact that profit is tied to prices is not questioned. Liberman himself estimates that long-range profitability norms should be maintained as long as wholesale prices are constant. However, he strongly criticizes those who want improvement of the price system to be a prerequisite of reform:

"We do not yet know how to regulate prices. . . . Some people think that everything would be perfect if prices were ideal. However, we have often changed prices without being satisfied with the results. Why? Because [wholesale] prices are not very important to the economy. The buyer has to have the goods delivered in time no matter what the price. He has no difficulty including any price in his investment estimate or in his planned costs, no matter how high it may be raised by the supplier."[65]

For Liberman, price reform is not a precondition but rather a consequence of the direct links that would be established between enterprises.[66] This position is challenged by Sukharevskii, who believes that the present price system does not take into account either productive conditions or outlays of socially necessary labor. Instead, it promotes the existing structure of consumption.[67]

64. These problems have often been cited. At the meeting of the Academy of Sciences they were emphasized by F. Veselkov, "Materialnye stimuly vysokikh planovykh zadanii" [Material Incentives of High Planned Goals], *ibid.*, No. 10, 1962, p. 14; Sukharevskii, *ibid.*, No. 11, 1962, p. 23; D. Onika, "Plan i materialnoe stimulirovanie" [The Plan and Material Incentives], *ibid.*, pp. 32-33; E. Kapustin, "Kak pooshchriat predpriiatiia" [How to Stimulate Enterprises], *ibid.*, p. 98; Rotshtein, *ibid.*, p. 120; Maslova, *ibid.*, p. 126; Kapitonov, *ibid.*, p. 131; and Gatovskii, *ibid.*, p. 137. See also Bor, *ibid.*, No. 3, 1963, p. 12, and Bachurin and Pervukhin, *ibid.*, No. 9, 1963, p. 73.

65. *Ekonomicheskaia gazeta*, November 10, 1962, p. 11.

66. Liberman's radio address in Moscow on October 19, 1964, cited by Basile Kerblay, "Les propositions de Liberman pour un projet de réforme de l'entreprise en U.R.S.S.," *Cahiers du Monde Russe et Soviétique*, No. 3, 1963, p. 308.

67. Sukharevskii, *Voprosy ekonomiki*, No. 11, 1962, p. 23. See also Kapustin, *ibid.*, p. 98.

A critical issue is whether Liberman's proposals would lead to more economical use of resources. According to Liberman, Atlas, Vaag, and Nemchinov, establishment of rental charges for fixed capital would constitute a decisive move in that direction. Bachurin and Pervukhin disagree, contending that an enterprise needing machinery or equipment to fulfill its plan will buy it at any price. The rental charge on fixed capital would simply be an additional budgetary levy on the enterprises' revenue. To introduce individual rental charges for each enterprise would make no sense as the present tax on profits already takes into account the special conditions of every enterprise.[68] The enterprise would not be interested in lowering prices or in producing what is most useful for society, but in selecting the most convenient production from the point of view of prices.[69]

Another objection to the proposed system bears on the implied constant fluctuation of prices. In effect, the proposed system would try to equalize profit per unit of productive capital. However, profitability would vary for different reasons, especially because of varying evolution of costs. Hence constant price revision would become necessary, a condition that Kosiachenko considers unthinkable in a planned economy.[70] Other authors believe that in the Soviet economy price fluctuations are unavoidable.[71]

PRACTICAL DIFFICULTIES IN INTRODUCING THE PROPOSED SYSTEM

Soviet authors have no trouble proving that introduction of the Liberman system would entail great complications. As to long-range profitability norms, they point out that it would not be easy to classify enterprises by similarity of technical and natural

68. Bachurin and Pervukhin, *ibid.*, No. 9, 1963, p. 71.

69. Kapustin, *ibid.*, No. 11, 1962, p. 98, and Plotnikov, *ibid.*, p. 113. This view is challenged by Liberman, who argues that enterprises will not choose the most profitable production, but rather one for which there is sufficient demand (see Liberman, *Ekonomicheskaia gazeta*, November 10, 1962, p. 11).

70. Kosiachenko, *Voprosy ekonomiki*, No. 5, 1963, p. 92. See also Bachurin and Pervukhin, *ibid.*, No. 9, 1963, p. 73.

71. *Izvestia*, October 8, 1962.

conditions and to work out a large number of valid scales.[72] According to some economists, special scales would have to be drawn up for almost every enterprise.[73]

Another defect of the profitability norms would be their instability. Soviet planning experience indicates that it has been impossible to plan profitability for a long period: serious discrepancies in such projections are apparent, for instance, between those in the 1959-65 Seven-Year Plan and the corresponding annual plans. The instability results from new production techniques, changes that require rational use of available resources,[74] reconstruction of enterprises charged to state funds, and changes imposed on the production and assortment plans.[75]

The practical problems raised by revision of profitability norms would not be easy to solve. Special agencies would have to be given that job, but they would soon find themselves in conflict with other managerial agencies. Enterprises that could not meet their planned profitability would immediately pose a problem; enterprises that had a higher profitability would be in no hurry to ask for a revision of norms, *i.e.*, an increase in goals.[76]

It might also be difficult to explain to workers why there are differences in the bases for awarding bonuses. Workers in heavy industry, where profitability is low because of lower prices, would be in a generally unfavorable position.[77] The defects of the system prior to 1959, which favored engineers and technicians at the expense of workers, would reappear.[78] Incentive funds

72. Veselkov, *Voprosy ekonomiki*, No. 10, 1962, p. 14.
73. Onika and Kapustin, *ibid.*, No. 11, 1962, pp. 31 and 98.
74. Rotshtein, *ibid.*, p. 121.
75. Kapustin, *ibid.*, p. 98.
76. Zverev, *ibid.*, p. 97.
77. Rusanov, *ibid.*, p. 130.
78. Under the old system, engineers and technicians received bonuses as high as 50 or even 100 per cent of their salaries, whereas the workers' bonuses never exceeded 30 or 40 per cent of their wages (Onika, *ibid.*, p. 33). After the 1959 reform, total bonuses for engineers and technicians could not exceed 60 per cent of their monthly salaries in the following industries: mining, iron and steel, oil, coal, and chemicals. For other industries, agriculture, and transportation, the limit was set at 40 per cent. Other restrictive conditions on granting bonuses were also imposed on that

and bonuses would tend to increase in an exaggerated fashion, so that government would have to revise profitability norms. The result would be a general reduction of bonus payments, which would be justified only by the fact that they were too high.[79]

ECONOMIC ARGUMENTS AND POLITICAL POSITIONS IN THE DEBATE

The basic objections to Liberman's proposals are difficult to challenge. He preserves the sacred nature of the plan as far as several important performance indexes for enterprises are concerned, and in doing so provides forces that would distort the rationality of his economic calculus. Actions of enterprise management and external influences could take away from profit its role as the yardstick of economic efficiency. The long-range profitability norms might become unstable or inequitable and in any case would provoke constant complaints. They would be a poor substitute for price reform, which might have to be imposed too frequently anyhow.

Moreover, it is difficult to see how the amendments proposed by Nemchinov could "save" the new system. A system of decentralized funds such as he visualizes would require greater flexibility in economic legislation than one can anticipate, and without such flexibility the schedules for the funds could produce undesirable results.

It is also evident that the freedom of the central planner in setting production targets for the enterprise would be considerably curtailed. Total wages and the volume of investment would determine to a large extent the assortment of goods to be produced. In short, to make the new system more coherent, other concessions would probably have to be made to the enterprise making it more autonomous in formulating its own plan and in setting prices. Soviet leaders have felt that one decentralization measure would lead to another, the result being a general slippage toward a market economy with free play of supply and demand.

---

occasion (see V. Maier, *Zarabotnaia plata v period perekhoda k kommunizmu*, p. 164).

79. Onika, *Voprosy ekonomiki*, No. 11, 1962, p. 33.

These apprehensions are the basis for the contention of opponents of reform that unrestricted exchange is incompatible with economic planning and that profit cannot be the goal of socialist production.

If one wished to take the first part of this contention literally, it would be difficult to argue against it. How is it possible to plan centrally and also maintain the conditions of perfect competition? However, the objection is not valid against a system of flexible planning that retains collective ownership of the means of production, such as Liberman and Nemchinov propose. One has the impression that words like free trade, automaticity in the working of economic laws, or free play of supply and demand are used simply to emphasize the incompatibility of the proposed reforms and the existing political regime. Adoption of these reforms would displace the center for economic decisions and would create undesirable consequences for those in power. This consideration is implicitly taken into account by virtually all parties to the discussion, and the Soviet economist Chakhurin expresses it quite openly:

"Some of those engaged in the discussion are obstinately trying to produce a system that would work automatically and be managed by engineers, technicians, and economic leaders."[80]

The second part of the contention—that profit cannot be the goal of socialist production—is also politically inspired. Vaag and Zakharov easily show that, for society, profit represents a net revenue serving to motivate growth in material production and improvement in the standard of living of workers. They even quote Lenin to support their thesis that profit satisfies social needs in a society where power is in the hands of the proletariat.[81]

80. *Ibid.*, p. 107.

81. *Ibid.*, No. 4, 1963, p. 99. According to Bukharin "under capitalism, production would aim at surplus value, at profit. In a state where power is in the hands of the proletariat, production is carried out with a view to satisfying social needs." Lenin criticized that argument in writing: "Not well put. Profit also satisfies 'social' needs. It should have been put this way: the surplus value is appropriated not by the class of property owners but by all workers and only by them." Cited from *Leninskii Sbornik* [Collection of Lenin's Writings], Vol. XI, pp. 381-82 (publication data unavailable).

These practical and political reservations lead opponents of reform to insist on preservation of centralized planning in essentially its present form. Since Liberman's system cannot work and since radical reforms would gravely jeopardize the socialist regime, the only solution remaining is to retain all the basic tools of a centralized planning system. Only a few minor revisions in that system are, in their view, required. It is this last course that seems originally to have received the backing of Soviet authorities.

CHAPTER 6. Experiments with Flexible Administrative Controls

Having rejected the course of fundamental reform, Soviet leaders have tried instead to cope with growing economic problems by introducing tentative and piecemeal changes in the administrative mechanism. The most notable experiment has been with the so-called method of "direct links" (*priamye sviazi*) between seller and buyer, or production to order rather than to plan. Other devices for more flexible administrative control are also being tried on an experimental basis.

It is too early to make a final judgment on the success of these experiments, but one can already see that islands of quasi-autonomy will have great difficulty surviving in a sea of centralized planning. Ultimately, the experiments must be either extended or discontinued. The course likely to be taken is not yet clear.

THE INITIAL EXPERIMENT WITH "DIRECT LINKS"

Use of "direct links" was first decreed by U.S.S.R. Sovnarkhoz on July 1, 1964, for two clothing factories: the Bolshevichka Factory in Moscow and the Maiak Factory in Gorky.[1] Their plans were from then on to be based on contracts made with retail stores, which would replace the former procedure whereby relations between seller and buyer were fixed by the Retail Clothing Trade Organization (Rostorgodezhdo). Plans are to set delivery

1. Among the most important articles describing this experiment are: E. Fedorova (General Manager of Maiak), "Po zakazam potrebitelei" [Following the Consumers' Orders], *Ekonomicheskaia gazeta*, November 11, 1964, p. 10; N. Kozlov, "Fabrika-magazin" [Factory-Store], *ibid.*, June 27, 1964, pp. 6-7; V. Sokolov, M. Nazarov, and N. Kozlov, "Firma i pokupatel" [The Firm and the Buyer], *ibid.*, January 6, 1965, pp. 21-22, 27-28; N. Kozlov, "Nevidimyi barier" [The Invisible Barrier], *ibid.*, February 8, 1965; and E. Narbekova, "Zakazy pokupatelei–osnova planirovaniia proizvodstva tovarov narodnogo potrebleniia" [Orders of Buyers as the Basis of Planning Production of Consumer Goods], *Planovoe khoziaistvo*, No. 5, 1965, pp. 34-40.

schedules and quantity and quality of goods according to fashion, model, and color. Direct contracts are to specify prices for the entire assortment of goods (on the basis of prevailing price lists, the seller taking account of packing and handling costs not included there) as well as conditions of packing, shipping, storing to protect goods from deterioration, and branding. The firms themselves determine the necessary inventories, those in excess of their working capital being credited by Gosbank. They also determine—on the basis of the volume of production and sales—the productivity, costs, wage fund, and needed materials. Payments into the enterprise fund are fixed at 4 per cent of profits—calculated as the difference between selling price and cost excluding capital charges (*sebestoimost*)—and are made conditional only on exact fulfillment of orders.[2] The Bolshevichka and Maiak factories also have the right to select suppliers of fabrics from the entire territory of the Soviet Union.

Many limitations on the enterprises' freedom of action have been retained. Although delivery contracts may be freely made, all stores are not free to come in contact with the pilot enterprises; in fact, only twenty-eight stores (twenty-two according to other sources)[3] have the right to enter into contracts with Maiak and twenty-two with Bolshevichka, as compared with the 228 and 230 stores they used to deal with. The new contracting stores were chosen from among the large ones in Moscow and Gorky. No stores in other cities and no individuals are allowed to take part in this experiment with direct links between producers and consumers.[4] Moreover, the stores with which Maiak and Bolshevichka enter into contractual agreement are, in most cases, not

2. Payments into the fund are to be made every quarter, but engineers, employees, and supervisory personnel may collect half their bonuses each month, the balance being paid at the end of the quarter. Credits for the workers' incentive fund can be provided directly out of profits under conditions specified by regulations. See Sokolov, *et al.*, *Ekonomicheskaia gazeta*, January 6, 1965, p. 22; and "Sovershenstvovanie pokazatelei planirovaniia raboty predpriiatii" [Improvement of Planning Indexes of the Enterprises], *Voprosy ekonomiki*, No. 3, 1965, p. 139.

3. "Priamye sviazi" [Direct Links], *Ekonomicheskaia gazeta*, October 28, 1964, p. 4; and Narbekova, *Planovoe khoziaistvo*, No. 5, 1965, p. 36.

4. Kozlov, *Ekonomicheskaia gazeta*, February 8, 1965, p. 35.

legal entities but rather subsidiaries of a Torg (an agency under the Ministry of Domestic Trade); thus problems arise when the Torg is in financial difficulty.[5] Finally, investment does not seem to be under the control of Bolshevichka and Maiak.

Officially, these two enterprises are bound by only two success indicators: the volume of marketed production and total profits. These indexes are confirmed (according to some sources)[6] or established (according to others)[7] by the Sovnarkhoz or its counterpart, which may modify them for the account of specially constituted reserves. In general, the actual limits to the managerial powers of Maiak and Bolshevichka are not very well known since the relevant regulations have not been published. Soviet authors complain of invisible barriers that, in the form of all sorts of instructions, circumscribe the enterprises' freedom of action.[8]

The results of the experiment with these two enterprises have been judged as encouraging, with emphasis on claims that demand has been definitely better satisfied, assortment expanded, quality improved, and the plan made considerably more realistic from the viewpoint of disposal of merchandise.[9] In the course of the year, the pilot enterprises succeeded in reducing prices by about 10 per cent, raising average monthly wages from 104 to 122 rubles, and increasing profits.[10]

5. *Ibid.*, p. 35.

6. Fedorova, *ibid.*, November 11, 1964, p. 10.

7. S. Nesterova, "Priamye sviazi promyshlennosti i torgovli i sovershenstvovanie form khoziaistvovaniia" [Direct Links Between Industry and Trade and Improvement of Forms of Economic Management], *Planovoe khoziaistvo*, No. 5, 1964, pp. 54-55.

8. Kozlov, *Ekonomicheskaia gazeta*, February 8, 1965, p. 35.

9. Whereas elsewhere unsold stocks amounted to 270 million rubles in the textile industry (see Henri Pierre in *Le Monde*, June 20-21, 1965, p. 11), in the second half of 1964 production of Bolshevichka exceeded contractual orders by only 5.3 per cent (17.7 per cent in December) and of Maiak by only 9.3 per cent (18 per cent in December). In the first half of 1964, their production exceeded contractual obligations by only 0.9 and 0.7 per cent, respectively. See Narbekova, *Planovoe khoziaistvo*, No. 5, 1965, p. 37.

10. Henri Pierre, *Le Monde*, June 20-21, 1965, p. 11. In the second half of 1964, only Bolshevichka increased its profits (from 5.4 per cent of costs in the first half to 6.5 per cent in the second). Maiak's profits dropped

Some difficulties arose because of the need to produce a larger assortment of goods. It is thought by some that too many stores had contracted with Maiak and Bolshevichka and that no more than five should do so in each case.[11] Other troubles were caused when local economic administrations failed to observe the new regulations. For example, Glikin, head of the garment section of the Volga-Viatsk Sovnarkhoz, by invoking directives of local Party agencies and threatening Maiak's manager with administrative sanctions, forced that factory to accept a large order for winter clothing. The Maiak factory had to switch its production three times and suffered losses by virtue of a 50 per cent increase in labor input; it also failed to deliver on time 3,500 coats that had been ordered by the regular procedure.

Administrative imposition of targets for volume of production and profits continues to raise serious problems for textile enterprises placed under the new regime in the first quarter of 1965. The prices of fabrics displayed at the trade fair in January-February, 1965, were reduced, a situation that had to have an unfavorable effect on their plans for production and profits. Yet their plans for the second half of the year were not modified by the Moscow City Sovnarkhoz until April, 1965.[12] Similarly the problem of pricing new products has not been solved satisfactorily.[13]

Success of the experiment is often threatened by the trading sector. The Gorky retail stores selling clothing from the Maiak factory come under several different administrations, place their orders all at the same time in the "assaulting" (*shturmovoi*) fashion, and do not coordinate their work.

The greatest difficulty lies in the supplying of fabrics. Maiak is supplied by forty-nine textile mills and Bolshevichka by thirty-

---

(from 25.8 per cent in the first half to 21.2 per cent in the second). See Narbekova, *Planovoe khoziaistvo*, No. 5, 1965, p. 37.

11. Fedorova, *Ekonomicheskaia gazeta*, November 11, 1964, p. 10; also "Priamye sviazi," *ibid.*, October 28, 1964, p. 4.

12. Nesterova, *Planovoe khoziaistvo*, No. 5, 1964, p. 55.

13. The same is true of supplements to current wholesale prices for packing and handling expenses not covered in price lists. See Narbekova, *ibid.*, No. 5, 1965, p. 39.

nine. They do not always succeed in making contracts with suppliers of fabrics in time, and the contracts are not carried out satisfactorily.[14] Hence promised delivery of goods by Maiak and Bolshevichka has been jeopardized.[15]

EXTENSION OF THE DIRECT LINKS EXPERIMENT

Khrushchev's resignation did not stop the experiment. Shortly before his downfall, this procedure was extended to some enterprises in heavy industry, such as the Perm machine-building plant and the iron mines under the Lvov Sovnarkhoz; these extensions have continued in force. At a meeting of the Collegium of U.S.S.R. Sovnarkhoz,[16] it was proposed that the experiment be extended to 31 per cent of the garment factories, 17 per cent of the textile mills, 33 per cent of the footwear factories, and 10 per cent of the leather plants in Moscow, Leningrad, Gorky, and "other cities."

In his speech presenting the annual plan for 1965, Kosygin emphasized the need to establish direct links between industrial enterprises and trade agencies. According to him, planning based on direct links should not be limited to the consumer goods industry but should be extended to other branches of the economy.[17] The extension program was adopted by U.S.S.R. Sov-

14. In 1964 Maiak placed its order for fabrics at the spring Interrepublic Fair, *i.e.*, before concluding delivery contracts for clothing, whereas the reverse procedure would have been correct. In November, 1964, some of these orders were still unfilled (see Fedorova, *Ekonomicheskaia gazeta*, November 11, 1964, p. 10). The Peter Alekseev factory supplied in October, 1964, only 298 meters of fabric out of 2,000 meters ordered; the Arzhensk factories and the Minsk combine also failed to deliver in full (see "Priamye sviazi," *ibid.*, October 28, 1964, p. 4).

15. See Sokolov, *et al.*, *ibid.*, January 6, 1965, p. 28. Narbekova, *Planovoe khoziaistvo*, No. 5, 1965, p. 39, points out that, in August, 1964, Moscow's garment industry did not receive 22 ordered fabrics and that as a result 33,000 garments were not delivered to trade organizations that had ordered them. In the course of the third quarter of 1964, Bolshevichka failed to fulfill its plan for assortment and did not deliver 15,500 suits according to specified models.

16. Reported in *Ekonomicheskaia gazeta*, October 28, 1964, p. 4.

17. A. Kosygin, *Izvestia*, December 10, 1964, p. 3.

narkhoz early in 1965.[18] It was decided that by the beginning of the second quarter of 1965, the following enterprises were to be added to the direct links system: 19 enterprises in the cotton industry, 49 in the wool industry, 8 in the linen industry, 25 in the leather industry, 6 in the artificial leather industry, 10 in the furniture industry, and 4 in the fur industry.

Starting with the third quarter of 1965, this system was to be extended to the entire garment industry under the Moscow City Sovnarkhoz and in the cities of Leningrad, Kiev, Odessa, Kharkov, Lvov, Minsk, Vilnius, Riga, and Tallin. Certain enterprises under the Sovnarkhozes of Moscow Province, Belorussia, Alma-Ata, Georgia, Moldavia, Armenia, Uzbekistan, Tadzhikistan, Kirghizia, and Turkmenia were also to be transferred to this system. In 1965 the direct links policy was to cover 25 per cent of the garment factories, 28 per cent of the footwear factories, 18 per cent of the textile mills, and 30 per cent of the leather factories.

In March or April of 1965 the government decided to switch over to the direct links system several trade organizations for which only two indexes were to be fixed—turnover and profit; the remaining indexes were to be fixed independently by the interested parties.[19] The experiment was supposed to be extended in the second half of 1965 to Estonia, Moldavia, the city of Moscow, and more provinces of the Russian and Ukrainian Republics. It was also to be applied to foodstuffs in the same areas, and the number of compulsory indexes was to be reduced to three (turnover, sales, and profits) or even to two (sales and profits).[20]

18. "Priamye sviazi rasshiriaiutsia" [The Direct Links Expand], *Ekonomicheskaia gazeta*, January 20, 1965, pp. 33-34.

19. There were complaints on this occasion that managers of stores were not ordinarily invited to participate in drawing up the plans that were imposed on them from above and later modified several times. For example, the Kiev Trade Administration changed the turnover targets for Store 113 three or four times a month during 1963 (see "Nazrevshie voprosy torgovli" [The Current Problems of Trade], *ibid.*, April 14, 1965, p. 2).

The unions of Consumer Cooperatives were allowed to conclude contracts directly with industrial enterprises as of January 1, 1965, provided those enterprises were located in the same republic or—in the case of Uzbekistan, Kirghizia, Tadzhikistan, and Turkmenia—came under the same Sovnarkhoz, namely, that of Central Asia (*ibid.*, November 11, 1964, p. 37).

20. I. Khrekin, "Po dvum pokazateliam" [With Two Indexes], *ibid.*, June 23, 1965, p. 32.

The starting point of July 1, 1965, seems to have been adhered to, and several enterprises were transferred to the direct links system on that date. Vladimir Dzhakov, Vice Chairman of the Russian Republic Council of Ministers, confirmed at the opening session of the Council that the program had been extended at that time to retail trade and food products.[21] This declaration was given official endorsement by the presence of Brezhnev, Kosygin, and Mikoyan at that session. But in a speech a few days later, Brezhnev warned against excessive haste in embarking on this path.[22]

Nevertheless, extension of the direct links system seemed imminent for several enterprises operating at different stages of production and even for machine-building plants, as preparation to this effect had been made by the U.S.S.R. Sovnarkhoz.[23] A special meeting of the Party Central Committee was to be held on this problem in June or July of 1965, but it was delayed until September 27-29, most likely because of continuing official deliberations. Meanwhile, the Soviet press mentioned Yugoslav experience with interest.[24]

In the end, Kosygin did not extend the direct links experiment further, but instead instituted a much more modest reform, generalized and graduated in nature, as we have already seen and shall see further in the next chapter.

The future of the direct links experiment was beclouded by the new reform. While Kosygin had a few kind words to say for direct links in his speech of September 27 (they had, he said, prepared the ground for greater autonomy of enterprises), their relation to the new reform was not specified.

In practice, the reform has amounted to superimposing new regulations onto old ones governing Soviet enterprises. "Experimental" enterprises are in principle not subject to the regulation of October 4, 1965, continuing to operate instead in accordance

21. *Le Figaro*, July 9, 1965, p. 15; Henri Pierre, *Le Monde*, July 10, 1965, p. 5; and *Ekonomicheskaia gazeta*, September 8, 1965, p. 2.

22. Vero Roberti, *Corriere Della Sera*, July 11, 1965, p. 16.

23. See *Trud*, as cited in *Le Figaro*, July 9, 1965, p. 15.

24. *Izvestia*, June 5 and 16, 1965.

with the various temporary regulations decreed at the time the experiments were initiated. The October reform, which has had the primary immediate effect of imposing a charge for use of capital (Soviet authorities avoid uttering the term "interest rate"), could, however, be applied to experimental as well as regular enterprises. The statutes for experimental enterprises have simply been modified to encompass the provisions in the "Kosygin reform" announced on September 27, 1965. For this reason, the Bolshevichka factory becomes listed among the first forty-three enterprises subsumed under the "Kosygin reform" after January 1, 1966. Such accommodation seems to have been prepared by the straining and stretching of original regulation under pressure from the direct links enterprises (see pp. 138-40 of this chapter).

PARALLEL EXPERIMENTS IN ADMINISTRATIVE FLEXIBILITY

Efforts to render the administrative system more flexible have taken other forms in addition to direct links. One of the most interesting experiments was at the Nevsky Machine-Building Plant in Leningrad.[25] Studied and approved by committees of specialists from the U.S.S.R. Academy of Sciences, it follows Liberman's proposals rather closely.

The plan of the enterprise is based on a list of products approved by higher agencies and revised by contracts. Delivery schedules are specified by the contracts. The quarterly plan is divided into monthly plans only if the month of delivery is specified. Production stipulated in contracts later cancelled is deleted from the plan and that of new contracts incorporated into it. Production not fulfilled within the scheduled period is re-entered in the plan for the following period.

Profits are determined from the production program and planned costs, the latter being calculated independently by the

25. V. Kantor, L. Levinson, B. Tabachnikov, "Nomenklatura, pribyl, rentabelnost" [Nomenclature, Profit, Profitability], *Planovoe khoziaistvo*, No. 5, 1965, pp. 47-53; A. Sokolovskii and S. Anufrienko, "Na proverke—novye pokazateli" [Being Tested—New Indexes], *Ekonomicheskaia gazeta*, December 16, 1964, p. 7; *Voprosy ekonomiki*, No. 3, 1965, p. 141.

enterprise.[26] Total profits, broken down by quarters, are to be communicated to higher authority. The profitability level is calculated as the ratio of total profits to the value of fixed productive capital (including equipment not yet installed) and working capital. Regulations governing this experiment also provide for a new bonus system for engineers, supervisory personnel, and rank and file workers. In contrast to the Liberman system, the incentive fund is based on wages (relative to the annual profitability norm) instead of total fixed capital. However, Liberman's essential idea of profitability rates was preserved.

Investments in the factory as provided by the national plan are centrally financed. For some projects designed to improve production, a special fund exists in the enterprise financed by levies on fixed capital that are inversely proportional to the level of profitability.

Transfer prices within the factory are to be calculated from the costs and profits of internal shops. Profits are prorated among shops according to basic wages, the factory's planned profitability being taken into account. The performances of shop and factory are thereby directly linked and the effort of shops stimulated.

Another experiment, dealing with five trucking enterprises (three in Moscow and two in Leningrad), has been in progress since May, 1965. The Soviet government seems to be watching it closely. In September the experiment was discussed by the Presidium of the Council of Ministers, which found the results satisfactory. Chairman Kosygin offered it as an example to follow in his important speech on September 27, 1965.[27] According to Kosygin, the increase in autonomy of these enterprises consists in a reduction in the number of planned indexes imposed from above, and in the greater flexibility of regulations on the use of

26. Kantor, *et al.*, *Planovoe khoziaistvo*, No. 5, 1965, pp. 47-53, state: "Planned profits *must be determined* [my emphasis—E.Z.] on the basis of programs of production and cost calculated independently." It therefore remains uncertain who, in the final analysis, determines planned profits—the enterprise or higher authority.

27. Kosygin, *Pravda*, September 28, 1965, p. 3. See also Garbuzov, "Finansy i ekonomicheskie stimuly" [Finance and Economic Incentives], *Ekonomicheskaia gazeta*, October 13, 1965, p. 4.

profits in excess of plan and of savings in the wage fund. That is to say, these enterprises are given more freedom in disposing of funds that can be used for material stimulation of workers, improvement of social and cultural conditions, and modernization of equipment.[28] In practice, the enterprises can themselves determine the types of material incentive, the wage fund, and employment. The government determines whose goods are to be hauled and what rates are to be charged as well as the taxes on profits to be paid into the budget. The enterprises may, however, accept additional customers and offer them services at lower rates.[29]

Another parallel experiment is taking place in the lumber enterprises formerly under the Central Urals Sovnarkhoz. In the case of one of these enterprises, Krasnaia Ufima, formerly more than thirty groups of planned indexes were imposed from above. In 1964 this number was reduced to six: volume of gross production, volume of marketed production, list of products, wage fund, utilization of fixed capital, and total profits. All remaining indexes are established directly by the enterprise itself. The result of this experiment was deemed conclusive in 1964: all planned objectives, both those set by the Sovnarkhoz and those fixed independently by the enterprise, were achieved. The same was true for the lumber enterprise of Nizhnii-Serginsk. However, at Avangard, a furniture factory, the results were less satisfactory, in part because of a reorganization of enterprises into firms—each firm being a group of enterprises.[30]

Among the efforts to render the planning system more flexible, one may also mention Velikomistovskaia Mine of the Chervonogradugol Trust in the Lvov-Volynie coal basin. The special

28. Kosygin, *Pravda*, September 28, 1965.

29. Iu. Konstantinov, "Na polnoi samookupaemosti" [Toward Costs Fully Covered], *Ekonomicheskaia gazeta*, June 16, 1965, p. 12. Although Konstantinov claims that a single planned index is imposed on the enterprise (the tax on profits to be paid into the budget), it is evident from his own article, as well as from Kosygin's speech, that this is either a misstatement or use of "colorful" language.

30. S. Rudinsky and I. Tungusova, "Po ogranichennomu chislu pokazatelei" [With a Reduced Number of Indexes], *ibid.*, December 2, 1964, p. 8.

interest of this experiment lies in the fact that it is run by the coal industry, which is working at a loss and is supported by budgetary subsidies. In this case, profit has been replaced by "conventional profit," or reduction of losses. Before the experiment, the mine had about thirty indexes imposed on it by higher agencies.[31] Since January 1, 1965, the mine has been given only three indexes: amount of coal to be mined annually broken down by quarters; amount of subsidy per ton of coal mined; and quality of coal (ash content). In addition, the chronological plan for development of mines has been centrally determined, and the present procedure of investment planning and capital repairs has been maintained. The principal reliefs from centralized planning consist in autonomous planning of costs, employment, and the wage fund, and in a new set of regulations for bonuses, which are now granted on the basis of two indexes: fulfillment of the production plan and realization of "conventional profitability."

The results of the first six months of this experiment were deemed satisfactory, and two more mines of the Lvov-Volynie coal basin were switched over to the new planning system starting July 1, 1965: Novovolynskaia No. 3 and Chervonogradskaia No. 1.[32] In the spring and summer of 1965, continuation and extension of the experiments seemed likely.[33] Various proposals on this subject appeared in the specialized press.

Some discussants would like to go further in reforming the system. They suggest, for instance, extending the experiments, not by sector, but by groups of enterprises—no matter what stage of production they represent—and advocate even greater autonomy for the enterprise. Nesterova believes, for example, that the assortment plan of a textile mill as based on consumers' orders should be its only mandatory plan, the remaining indexes being used solely as guideposts.[34] Some economists wonder whether

31. One is tempted to believe that these were forms to be filled out rather than indexes.

32. Iu. Spektorov, "Tri pokazatelia vmesto tridtsati" [Three Indexes Instead of Thirty], *ibid.*, June 16, 1965, p. 14; "Eksperiment rasshiriaetsia" [The Experiment Expands], *ibid.*, July 21, p. 16.

33. *Voprosy ekonomiki*, No. 3, 1965, p. 143.

34. Nesterova, *Planovoe khoziaistvo*, No. 5, 1964, p. 54.

the experiment should be extended to producer goods, but on this point opinion is divided.[35]

Among detailed issues discussed, one may mention stockpiling of seasonal articles, recruitment of new supervisory personnel,[36] investments, studies of consumer demand, and reform of regulations for retail stores so that they would have accounting autonomy. Reform of the bonus system has also been suggested, and some authors advocate doubling the payments to the enterprise fund as specified by present regulations,[37] as well as removing the present limit on total bonuses imposed by basic wage payments.[38]

RESULTS OF THE DIRECT LINKS EXPERIMENT

Since the direct links experiment is still in progress, we cannot pass final judgment. The most complete report published so far is for light industry,[39] covering mainly the second and third quarters of 1965 for the Russian Republic only. It shows that between 1964 and 1965 the value of marketed production rose by 4.5 per cent in the clothing industry and 8.9 per cent in the rayon industry, but fell by 0.9 per cent in the cotton industry, 8.5

35. V. Naidenov, for instance, believes that centralized planning must be maintained for producer goods at the same time as more independence is conferred on enterprises, primarily by extending the terms of contracts over several years. See *Ekonomicheskaia gazeta*, May 19, 1965, p. 10.

36. During the October, 1964 meeting of the Collegium of U.S.S.R. Sovnarkhoz, there were proposals to create the new positions of chief model designer, trade director, and various supervisory officials for sales and economic and commercial services. These proposals were accepted in principle by U.S.S.R. Sovnarkhoz when the "direct links" experiment was decided upon for 1965. See "Priamye sviazi," *ibid.*, October 28, 1964, p. 4; and "Priamye sviazi rasshiriaiutsia," *ibid.*, January 20, 1965, p. 34.

37. Nesterova, *Planovoe khoziaistvo*, No. 5, 1964, p. 56. It is interesting that, according to the Minister of Finance, V. Garbuzov, the Material Incentive Funds and the Social, Cultural, and Housing Funds of enterprises were almost to double between 1965 and 1966 according to an estimate of the effects of new provisions introduced during 1966 (see Garbuzov, *Ekonomicheskaia gazeta*, October 13, 1965, p. 4).

38. Nesterova, *Planovoe khoziaistvo*, No. 5, 1964, p. 56.

39. N. Volkov, V. Chebotaev, V. Aleksandrova, and M. Nazarov, "Predpriiatie, magazin, pokupatel" [Enterprise, Store, Buyer], *Ekonomicheskaia gazeta*, No. 11, 1966, pp. 26-28.

per cent in the woolen industry, and 2.5 per cent in the footwear industry. Since these declines occurred while plans were being overfulfilled in all sectors, the experimental enterprises in question must have planned a lower value of output for 1965 than for 1964. The reduction can be explained in part by lack of pressure to draw up taut plans, in part by a reduction in prices brought about by substituting synthetic for natural fibers, and in part by restrictions on the supply of cotton and leather.

The same report states that profits exceeded their planned level by 4 per cent in the second quarter of 1965 and by 11.4 per cent in the third. At the same time, profits were lower than for 1964. This decline was caused by the fall in both marketed production and the profitability of various products. In fact, planning based on orders from trading enterprises led to an assortment of products with reduced profitability. Differences in profitability did not reflect the efficiency of enterprises—the return on capital or on labor—but simply the actual structure of prices. For example, children's clothing, which the government wants to sell at low prices for social reasons, remained quite unprofitable, while fashionable women's clothing was expensive and profitable.[40] Hence the distinction has not been eliminated between "convenient" and "inconvenient" goods from the point of view of producing enterprises.[41]

Utilization of fixed capital did not improve, and output per ruble of fixed capital was actually lower in the second and third quarters of 1965 than in the same period for 1964, by 24 per cent in the silk and rayon industry and 36 per cent in the linen industry. These results, which surpassed planned targets, were brought about because important technological improvements made a change in product assortment necessary. Here too the change in assortment and production of low-priced goods had much to do with the decline, affecting output-capital ratios in this case. Soviet authors have become aware of the fact that there is

40. Imogene Erro, "Economic Reform in the Soviet Consumer Industries," in *New Directions in the Soviet Economy*, Joint Economic Committee, 89th Congress, 2nd Session (Washington, 1966), Part II-B, p. 562.

41. Volkov, *et al.*, *Ekonomicheskaia gazeta*, No. 11, 1966, p. 27.

presently no scientific method for adjusting indexes of the efficiency of capital so that they reflect improvements in quality.[42]

The enterprises operating in the direct links system also experienced a sizable increase in the volume of working capital, in part because of the change in product assortment and the large number of small orders (Maiak later fixed 500 articles as the minimum order it would handle, and Bolshevichka fixed 400 suits).[43] But inventories rose primarily because of the way in which supply of material and equipment was organized. Enterprises were still being mechanically supplied with materials ordered back in 1964, when there were shortages in materials needed for the new product assortment. The increase in inventories was attributable also to the higher norms authorized in March, 1964.

Despite the poor performance shown by official indexes, the funds earmarked for workers' bonuses during the second and third quarters rose from 1964 to 1965 as follows: from 391,000 to 458,000 rubles in the silk and rayon industry; from 1,269,000 to 1,477,000 rubles in the cotton industry; and from 266,000 to 638,000 rubles in the woolen industry. In the case of industries producing footwear, leather, and clothing, the funds earmarked during the third quarter rose between 1964 and 1965 by 50, 100, and 40 per cent, respectively. Such increases were made possible by the new regulations for financing the Enterprise Fund that substitute a flat 4 per cent levy on actual profits for the previous variable levy of 1 to 6 per cent on planned profits and 30 to 60 per cent on profits in excess of plan.

More generally, the direct links experiment has been endangered by a persisting failure to appreciate the importance of enforcing contractual obligations. As pointed out in the preceding chapter, the general system of fines is inadequate: 3 per cent for failure to deliver in the case of producer goods and 2 per cent in the case of consumer goods. In 1965 the fines collected in the Russian Republic for breach of contract amounted

42. *Ibid.*

43. *Sovetskaia torgovlia*, August 26, 1965, as cited by Erro in *New Directions in the Soviet Economy*, p. 563.

to only 2.44 per cent of profits in the footwear industry, 2.12 per cent in the leather industry, 1.62 per cent in the woolen industry, and 1.33 per cent in the silk and rayon industry.[44] Moreover, fines paid out are treated as costs by an enterprise and hence have only an indirect bearing on its financial results. If fines received exceed those paid out (as may be the case primarily for trading enterprises), the excess is appropriated by the government.

When the four hundred enterprises were transferred to the direct links system in 1965, it was stipulated that the size of fines would be raised between five- and sevenfold. But such an across-the-board increase has not provided for coverage of actual losses. The major difficulty arises from the fact that fines levied for failure to meet a scheduled delivery are based on wholesale prices in the case of producer goods and on retail prices in the case of consumer goods, allowances being made in both cases for authorized delays. As a result, enterprises bearing a heavy burden of turnover taxes—for instance, those in the woolen industry where the turnover tax represents about half the retail price—may suffer uncompensated losses from delayed or missed deliveries amounting in effect to an arbitrary levy on their profits.[45] Efforts to get reimbursement for such losses are likely to be ineffective since the enterprises both paying and receiving the fines in question are often subordinate to the same agency (central administration, etc.), and it is concerned with reducing the total amount of fines paid by the branch of industry under its control. The only solution that Soviet commentators now visualize is to link the size of fines for an enterprise to the average rate of turnover tax for the branch to which it belongs.[46]

The record strikes a somewhat more optimistic note in the case of the experiment with more flexible planning that has been applied since July 1, 1965, to seventy thousand retail stores and restaurants. These enterprises account for 13 per cent of total

44. D. Manzheev and V. Dvoretskii, "Razmyshleniia o shtrafakh" [Observations on Fines], *Ekonomicheskaia gazeta*, No. 38, 1966, p. 12.

45. *Ibid.*

46. *Ibid.*

turnover in this sector, and their turnover exceeded plan in both the second half of 1965 and the first half of 1966. Their profits for the second half of the year were 12.1 per cent higher in 1965 than in 1964, while those for comparable enterprises within the normal planning regime were only 3.2 per cent higher. Profits for experimental enterprises exceeded plan by 5.8 per cent. Under the new system commercial costs have declined, the assortment of goods offered for sale has grown, sales of goods in ample supply have expanded, and facilities have been more efficiently utilized. Suspension of the normal sanctions designed to prevent an enterprise from exceeding its plan for wages and commercial costs has stimulated initiative and raised sales and profits. At the same time, it should be noted that inauguration of the experimental system coincided with a raising of average wages by 22 per cent for workers in the trade sector.[47]

The primary defects of the new system have been its failure to grant accounting autonomy (*khozraschet*) to enterprises and to provide adequately financed Funds for Material Incentives. With establishment of centralized accounting authority, three-quarters of the trading enterprises have been deprived of accounting autonomy in the Russian Republic, and the situation has been similar in other republics. The small commissions authorized for enterprises have caused the profitability rate to drop to a very low level: 1.32 per cent of turnover in 1965 as compared with 2.56 per cent in 1958. In 1965 one retail store out of seventeen and one restaurant out of five operated at a loss. Hence budgetary subsidies have become indispensable.

Such low profitability has not facilitated accumulation in the Enterprise Fund, financed by a 3 per cent levy on profits in the case of retail stores and a 6 per cent levy in the case of restaurants. Nor has it contributed to better utilization of the Fund for Material Incentives, financed by 10 per cent of planned wages, an additional 3 per cent for each percentage point by which planned turnover is surpassed, and 3 per cent of actual profits. Use of

47. K. Skovoroda, "Tovarooborot i pribyl" [Turnover and Profit], *ibid.*, No. 21, 1966, pp. 26-28. This is a report on a conference of workers in trading enterprises organized by the U.S.S.R. Ministry of Trade.

material incentives has remained insignificant, the government relying mainly on appeals to the civic spirit of workers.[48]

RELATION OF THE DIRECT LINKS EXPERIMENT TO THE SYSTEM OF ADMINISTRATIVE PLANNING

Enterprises in the direct links system still function within the framework of administrative planning. Plans continue to be imposed not only for value of output and profits but also for prices, investment, supplies, and budgetary appropriations.

Official Soviet sources emphasize the desirability of extending the system to new enterprises and to new sectors. The considerable extension that took place during the first year of the experiment gave the impression of movement toward more flexible planning. In reality, the extension of direct links was being counterbalanced by a nibbling away of the powers granted to experimental enterprises as continual restrictions and changes in the rules of the game were imposed.

The direct links in the system were intended to be those between producers and retail outlets. For Bolshevichka and Maiak, the number of stores authorized to enter into direct contracts was reduced in order not to overload the enterprises with distributional burdens. As the experiment has expanded, it has become increasingly difficult to bypass wholesale trade and to introduce direct contracts with tens of thousands of stores. From the middle of 1965 onward, therefore, experimental enterprises have been forced to make contracts with wholesale depots of the Ministry of Trade or with commercial unions (Torgs).[49] Instead of leaving the enterprises free to choose whether to make use of the wholesale network, the administrative system has required recourse to these intermediaries, even if large orders make direct shipments to the retailer more efficient. The wholesale trade depots soon began "filtering" orders from stores and struggling to retain vested rights in order to keep their turnover and wage funds from falling.[50] They also occasionally intercepted

48. *Ibid.*, p. 28.
49. Erro in *New Directions in the Soviet Economy*, p. 561.
50. B. Zubovich and Iu. Khokhriakov, "Chto meshaet priamym sviaziam"

deliveries made within the direct links system.[51] Orders (*nariady*) of the wholesale trade depots, moreover, have often conflicted with contractual agreements under direct links.[52]

The setting of prices for new products is another important area in which the powers of experimental enterprises have been restricted. Maiak and Bolshevichka had been entitled to raise prices to cover costs attributable to improvements in quality and changes in fashions and assortments. When the experiment was extended in 1965, they were required to get permission from higher authority (at first the Sovnarkhoz and later the Ministry) before increasing prices.[53]

The freedom to accumulate inventories granted in the original statute has also been restrained. Although the decree of the U.S.S.R. Sovnarkhoz on direct links stipulated that enterprise managers could set their own inventory norms, this right was not respected in practice by the Volga Sovnarkhoz.[54]

For lack of more precise documentation, it is impossible to assess the magnitude of restrictions on initial powers of experimental enterprises. Many restrictive practices have arisen, such as imposition of geographical limits on parties to contracts.[55] Sovnarkhoz officials often simply refused to heed the special statute on direct links and continued to hand down instructions and plans as before.[56] The statute itself has also been amended in such a way as to alter the spirit of the experiment. For example, the primary criterion of success has been changed from fulfillment of planned profits to fulfillment of planned sales.[57]

[What Interferes with the Direct Links], *Ekonomicheskaia gazeta*, No. 32, 1966, p. 28.

51. Rush V. Greenslade, "The Soviet Economic System in Transition," in *New Directions in the Soviet Economy*, Part I, p. 14, points out an instance of such an interception of a Maiak delivery.

52. Volkov, *et al.*, *Ekonomicheskaia gazeta*, No. 11, 1966, p. 28.

53. Erro in *New Directions in the Soviet Economy*, pp. 558 and 561; and Morris Bornstein, "Soviet Price Theory and Policy," in *New Directions in the Soviet Economy*, Part I, p. 93.

54. A. Myzhin, "Dogovor, iarmaka" [Contract, Fair], *Ekonomicheskaia gazeta*, August 18, 1965, p. 31.

55. Erro in *New Directions in the Soviet Economy*, p. 561.

56. *Ibid.*, p. 563.

57. *Ibid.*, p. 561.

This nibbling away of original concessions granted to Maiak and Bolshevichka can be explained in large part by the way in which the Soviet planning system operates. The first experimental enterprises were able to benefit from privileges so special that they were sometimes referred to as artificial or "plush" conditions.[58] Priorities relating to these enterprises were changed along with the planning system. As the experiment expanded, this privileged position and the accompanying priorities were not accorded to other enterprises. Hence there followed a nibbling away of concessions to the original participants.

Watering down of the experiment would seem to be an unavoidable consequence of its extension, and many Soviet commentators probably realized that such a development would take place. This realization may explain some of the quite violent criticisms of the very principle of the economic experimentation. For example, I. S. Malyshev, a well-known Soviet economist, has contended that recourse to such experimentation represents a flight from theoretical analysis and a clear manifestation of the poverty of Soviet economic science. Soviet economic theory is, he says, incapable of finding answers to the great problems of the day, such as price formation, plan indexes, and optimal sizes for individual enterprises. In the absence of a guiding and scientifically established conception, experiments are doomed to failure, in his view, because they must be based on contrived assumptions.[59]

The evolution of the direct links experiment has fully confirmed Malyshev's predictions of 1964. A new reform, this time generalized, seems to have been put in force in September, 1965, as we shall discuss further in the next chapter.

58. Editorial in *Ekonomicheskaia gazeta*, November 11, 1964.

59. I. S. Malyshev, *Science économique et pratique des affaires* (Moscow, 1964), pp. 9-10, cited by Marie-Louise Lavigne, "Les experiences économiques en URSS," in *Annuaire de l'U.R.S.S., Droit, Economie, Sociologie, Politique, Culture* (Paris, 1965), p. 308.

CHAPTER 7. The Reforms of October, 1965

The principal texts on the reforms of October, 1965,[1] contain numerous declarations of intentions to promote liberalization. The following proposals were made: to abolish useless regulation; to leave more funds at the disposal of an enterprise; to introduce legal guarantees of the rights of an enterprise; to reduce the number of products included in the plans imposed on enterprises; to present goals in the form of aggregative indexes; to prepare stable plans; to base plans on calculations and standards that are scientifically justifiable and differentiated by sector; to pass gradually from centralized allocation of resources to wholesale trade; to extend the "direct links" system among

1. A. Kosygin, "Ob uluchshenii upravleniia promyshlennostiu, sovershenstvovanii planirovaniia i usileniia ekonomicheskogo stimulirovanii promyshlennogo proizvodstva" [On Improving Industrial Management, Perfecting Planning, and Increasing Economic Incentives for Industrial Production], *Pravda*, September 28, 1965, pp. 1-14. The resolution of the Party Central Committee on the same subject was adopted at the Plenary Session of September 29, 1965. See *Izvestia*, October 1, 1965, p. 1; K. I. Mazurov, "Ob uluchshenii upravleniia promyshlennostiu" [On Improving Industrial Management], *ibid.*, October 2, 1965, pp. 2-3; "V Tsentralnom Komitete KPSS i Sovete Ministrov SSSR" [At the Central Committee of the Communist Party of the Soviet Union and at the U.S.S.R. Council of Ministers], *Pravda*, October 10, 1965, p. 1; V. Garbuzov, "Finansy i ekonomicheskie stimuly" [Finances and Economic Incentives], *Ekonomicheskaia gazeta*, October 13, 1965, pp. 4-5; A. Poskonov, "Khoziaistvennaia reforma i kredit" [Economic Reform and Credit], *Pravda*, November 19, 1965, p. 3.

During the first half of 1966, the Soviet government made a serious effort to specify the legal conditions of the new reform. The provisional instructions of December 6, 1965, were replaced on January 24, 1966, by "Metodicheskie ukazaniia po perevodu otdelnykh promyshlennykh predpriiatii na novuiu sistemu planirovaniia i ekonomicheskogo stimulirovaniia v 1966 godu" [Instructions on the Methods of Transferring Individual Industrial Enterprises to the New System of Planning and Economic Incentive in 1966], *Ekonomicheskaia gazeta*, No. 6, 1966, pp. 31-35. These instructions were later completed by provisional instructions on bonuses, funds for material incentives, long-term credits, funds for social and cultural purposes, funds for the development of production, conditions for levying charges for use of fixed and working capital, and budgetary appropriations from profits that were not earmarked for other funds or purposes specified by the regulations.

producing and consuming enterprises; to give greater prominence to economic contracts; and to increase the role of economic incentives.

These declarations of intentions all give the impression of a continuous—and perhaps even an accelerated—movement toward a system of flexible planning. It is by comparing the declared intentions with actual reforms that one can form an opinion on whether such a trend exists.

The reforms actually adopted cover three aspects of administration:[2] (1) the enterprises' finances and their relations to the budget; (2) profit sharing by personnel of the enterprise; and (3) the planning autonomy of the enterprise.

THE ENTERPRISE'S FINANCES

At the present time, enterprises do not pay any interest on capital, and their payments of taxes on profits do not depend on the volume of productive capital. This state of affairs leads enterprises to request as much as possible in the way of investment funds. During recent years, a decline in the rate of return on capital has been observed.[3] Recent decisions provide for introduction of taxes based on fixed and working capital. Long-range profitability norms are to be established to enable enterprises to retain a share of the profits to meet planned expenses and to finance the incentive fund.

Payment of interest or rental charges for use of fixed and working capital will be made only at the end of the planning period during which the capital has been utilized. Enterprises will be exempt from these levies for two years when investments are financed from their own resources. Different profitability rates will be drawn up for each group of enterprises, taking into account the present level of profitability.[4] Certain regulations about these levies still need further elucidation: it has not yet

2. For a discussion of the new regulation on enterprises, see Chapter 4.

3. Kosygin, *Pravda*, September 28, 1965, p. 1.

4. O. Nekrasov, "Otraslevoi printsip upravleniia promyshlennostiu i tekhnicheskii progress" [The Sector Principle of Managing Industry and Technical Progress], *Voprosy ekonomiki*, No. 11, 1965, p. 11.

been decided how present profitability should be calculated for different enterprises. There is also some question about whether to take into account initial cost or to include interest, etc.[5]

Levies on productive capital are not supposed to be a new burden on enterprises, but rather a different form of taxation for the budget. With the present structure of wholesale prices, rental charges for use of productive capital may, in the immediate future, be collected only in industries now paying a turnover tax. Once the reform of wholesale prices announced by Kosygin for 1967 or 1968 has been carried out, rental charges for use of productive capital and the tax on profits will become the main source of budgetary income.

According to the new provisions, the rental or interest charges on capital are fixed individually for each enterprise by its ministry. The instructions of January 24, 1966, stipulate that in 1966 this charge is to be fixed in general at 6 per cent.[6] Only in those exceptional cases in which profitability is lower than 10 per cent is the interest charge to be set at 3 per cent.[7] It should be noted that, according to the instructions of January 24, 1966, the charges on capital were levied on gross profits as they appeared in enterprises' accounts and were not to be counted as part of cost.[8]

The new regulations also provide for gradual replacement of

5. B. Sukharevskii, "Ekonomicheskoe stimulirovanie proizvodstva na novuiu, vysshuiu stupen" [The New Higher Stage of Economic Incentives of Production], *ibid.*, No. 10, 1965, p. 26.

6. See also "Vremennaia instruktsiia o poriadke vznimaniia v biudzhet platy za proizvodstvennye fondy i oborotnye sredstva s predpriiatii, perevedennykh na novuiu sistemu planirovaniia i ekonomicheskogo stimulirovaniia promyshlennogo proizvodstva" [Provisional Instructions on the Budgetary Procedure for Levying Rental Charges on Productive and Working Capital of the Enterprises Operating on the New System of Planning and Economic Incentives], *Ekonomicheskaia gazeta*, No. 17, 1966, p. 32.

7. V. Bocharov, 'O differentsii norm platy za fondy" [On Setting Different Norms for Charges on Capital], *Planovoe khoziaistvo*, No. 5, 1966, pp. 63-66.

8. It should be noted that some economists from the Eastern Bloc countries do not agree with this solution and consider that the charges on capital (interest charges) ought to be part of costs. See Henryk Fiszel, "Oprocentowanie" [Interest Charges], *Zycie Gospodarcze*, No. 1, 1966, p. 6.

budgetary subsidies of investments with long-term credits. The system of credits will be used, first of all, to finance investments made in already existing enterprises. For new construction projects, long-term credits will be advanced to sectors in which the time necessary to recover the investment is relatively short. According to Poskonov, President of Gosbank, that time should not exceed five years.[9] A slightly longer time—six years—is allowed when credits are used to finance introduction of new technology.[10]

At present, the share of credit in financing investments is very low. In 1965, credit was used to finance only 5.3 billion rubles of investment out of an aggregate of 48.3 billion rubles (including private and collective farm investments).[11] According to Garbuzov, Minister of Finance, more than half the present investment in fixed capital, *i.e.*, some 20 to 25 billion rubles, could be financed by means of credits.[12] As to working capital, 40 per cent has already been provided in the form of credit.[13] An increase in this percentage is expected, along with a reduction of reimbursable advances. By 1968, about 80 per cent of investment in fixed productive capital of industry is supposed to be financed from the enterprises' own sources and from long-term credits from the State Bank. Credit is supposed to play a particularly important role in new construction and to account for 70 to 75 per cent of its value.[14] It should be noted that budgetary subsidies

9. *Pravda*, November 19, 1965, p. 3.

10. *Ibid.*, p. 3.

11. P. Podshivalenko, "Khoziaistvennaia reforma i kapitalnye vylozheniia" [Economic Reform and Investments], *Ekonomicheskaia gazeta*, No. 32, 1966, p. 13.

12. See Garbuzov, *ibid.*, October 13, 1965, p. 5. This provision seems to apply only to 1967 at the earliest. Out of a total of 40.6 billion rubles of centrally planned investment, the budget for 1966 provides for budgetary subsidies of 22.8 billion, 16.8 billion being financed by the enterprises' own resources. Decentralized nonplanned investments of 12 billion were also provided for. These proportions correspond to those of other years. See Garbuzov, *Pravda*, December 8, 1965, p. 5.

13. Garbuzov, *Ekonomicheskaia gazeta*, October 13, 1965, p. 5. We may note that Poskonov, *Pravda*, November 19, 1965, p. 3, estimates this share at 44 per cent for industrial enterprises.

14. Podshivalenko, *Ekonomicheskaia gazeta*, No. 32, 1966, p. 13.

granted when the plan for profits has not been fulfilled or when unforeseen losses have been incurred must, by law, be replaced by credits.[15]

Interest rates will differ according to the use of credit. The lowest rates will apply to financing inventories in seasonal industries. Medium rates will apply in the case of loans for fixed and working capital and for inventories that exceed norms. When planned profits are not realized or when unforeseen losses are suffered, credits for working capital will be granted at a higher interest rate. The same will be true for credits granted as an exception for inventories exceeding norms and in the case of delays in payment of bills. Neither interest on bills nor penalties for delays can be included in costs but must have a direct effect on the financial results of an enterprise's operations. In general, the primary criterion for receiving credit will be the degree of implementation of plans for marketed production and profit. Enterprises showing the best results will obtain the better credit conditions. The agencies of Gosbank will have more say in the granting of credits.[16]

In seasonal industries Gosbank can now make an agreement with the buyer to pay the seller directly; the buyer thus becomes indebted to the bank instead of the seller, as is now the case. In addition, all industrial and construction enterprises may receive thirty days credit in case of financial difficulties in paying for deliveries, and credits are to be made available if the Fund for Development of the Enterprise is not sufficient to finance introduction of new technology. In the case of enterprises producing consumer goods, the latter loans may be repaid by recourse to as much as half the turnover taxes applicable to sales of supplementary production. Loans that can be refunded in less than five years may be used not only for capital improvements but also for construction of new enterprises. Finally, Gosbank may grant credits to finance inventories in excess of the norms needed to produce new or improved commodities, provided these loans

15. Garbuzov, *ibid.*, October 13, 1965, p. 5.
16. Poskonov, *Pravda*, November 19, 1965, p. 3.

can be repaid within a year out of profits from sales of the products involved.[17]

The rules for self-financing of enterprises have also been changed. Up to now self-financing has been based on profits after payments to the budget and to superior agencies as compensation for losses suffered by other enterprises in the same sector. In 1962, for instance, profits of industrial enterprises were distributed as follows (in per cent):[18]

Payments to the budget	*ca.*	64
Payments to superior agencies	*ca.*	5
Total		70
Financing of investments in fixed capital		14
Financing of investments in working capital		11.5
Payment to the enterprise fund and to other workers' incentive funds[19]		4.5
GRAND TOTAL		100

The new rules for self-financing provide for every enterprise to create a fund for the development of production, to be fed from three sources: (1) levies on profits of the enterprise; (2) part of the amortization allowance for replacement of capital (today that part is distributed centrally for the financing of investments in general); and (3) proceeds from the sales of equipment unused by the enterprise (these proceeds are at present paid into the state budget).

It is hoped that funds at the disposal of enterprises for self-financing will be considerably increased. In this connection, Kosygin cites some figures, but they refer only to expenses connected with introduction of new industrial technology and with

17. Z. V. Atlas, *Khozraschet, rentabelnost i kredit* [Economic Accounting, Profitability, and Credit], Moscow, 1966, pp. 35-37.

18. Sukharevskii, *Voprosy ekonomiki*, No. 10, 1965, p. 24. The figures do not sum to the total presumably because of rounding.

19. At least 20 per cent of the enterprise fund was earmarked for introduction of new technology, modernization of equipment, and so on.

the development of production and not to total investments financed by the enterprises' own funds. Moreover, they cover expenses financed from the enterprise fund of industry only, excluding other sectors.[20] Kosygin's figures are as follows (million rubles):

1964	
Expenses of industry paid from enterprise fund	120.0
Expenses of industry paid from bank credit	600.0
TOTAL	720.0
1967 (estimates)	
Total expenses of industry (from enterprise fund and bank credit)	4,000
Less deduction for amortization	2,700
TOTAL	1,300

The financial planning of an enterprise is also to be strengthened through some easing of bank controls. For example, the necessity to register bills for administrative and managerial expenses with financial agencies has been eliminated.[21]

PROFIT SHARING

Before the October, 1965, reforms, incentive payments came from different sources: (1) the enterprise fund; (2) the consumer goods fund (separately for improvements in quality and for production from waste, *otkhody proizvodstva*); (3) the socialist competition fund; (4) bonuses for introduction of new techniques; and (5) bonuses for export deliveries. The first was the principal source, representing more than half the incentive fund. One to 6 per cent of planned profits and 30 to 60 per cent of profits in excess of plan were paid into the enterprise fund.[22] In

20. Kosygin, *Pravda*, September 28, 1965, p. 3.
21. Garbuzov, *Ekonomicheskaia gazeta*, October 13, 1965, p. 4.
22. A. I. Denisov, *et al.* (eds.), *Trudovoe pravo–Entsiklopedicheskii slovar* [Labor Legislation–Encyclopedic Dictionary], Moscow, 1963, p. 533.

1962 that fund could not exceed 5.5 per cent of the wage fund, but lately the limiting percentage seems to have risen to 7 per cent.[23] The rules for use of the enterprise fund contained the following provisions: at least 40 per cent of the fund had to be spent on housing construction and repairs and on communal construction; no more than 40 per cent could be spent on bonuses, improvement of workers' living conditions, workers' vacations and visits to rest homes, and special personal assistance when necessary; at least 20 per cent had to be spent on introduction of new technology, modernization of machinery, and extension of production.[24]

The rules for utilization and formation of the enterprise fund do not, in fact, encourage bonus payments to workers. In 1960 and 1961, for instance, the aggregate of enterprise funds available per worker amounted to 1.71 and 1.70 rubles a month, respectively; expenditures per worker out of these funds on bonuses, housing, and welfare needs came to 0.725 and 0.671 rubles a month.[25] If these figures are compared with average monthly wages in industry (91.3 rubles in 1960 and 94.1 rubles in 1961),[26] it is apparent that bonuses of this order (less than 1 per cent) could hardly be much of an incentive to workers. For engineers and technicians, the bonuses were higher (8 per cent of their total wage fund in 1965), but these too were considered insufficient.[27]

Many reforms of the bonus system have been proposed in recent years. Some authors, like Sukharevskii, proposed differ-

23. Zbigniew Lewandowicz, "Radziecka reforma" [Soviet Reforms], *Zycie Gospodarcze*, October, 1965, p. 7.

24. Denisov, *et al.* (eds.), *Trudovoe pravo*, p. 533.

25. L. Pekarskii, "Pooshchritelnye fondy predpriiatii i pribyl" [Incentive Funds of Enterprises and Profit], *Planovoe khoziaistvo*, No. 10, 1963, p. 11.

26. For 1960, *Narodnoe khoziaistvo SSSR v 1964 godu* [The Soviet Economy in 1964], Moscow, 1965, p. 555. For 1961, calculated as an increase of 3.1 per cent over 1960, see V. Garbuzov, "Reshitelno povysit uroven ekonomicheskoi i kontrolnoi raboty—vazhneishaia zadacha finansovykh organov" [To Raise Decisively the Level of Economic and Control Work Is the Most Important Task of Financial Agencies], *Finansy SSSR*, No. 10, 1962, p. 7.

27. S. Shkurko, "Materialnoe pooshchrenie rabotnikov" [Material Incentives for Workers], *Ekonomicheskaia gazeta*, No. 8, 1966, p. 21.

entiating criteria for financing the incentive fund according to economic sector: the level of production and its growth would be used for sectors not dependent on raw materials (*e.g.*, mining) and having extensive market outlets; the level of profitability and its growth, for sectors with uniform production; and reduction of costs, for other sectors.[28] Veselkov has proposed that eight or ten indexes be prepared, the supervisory agency applying two to four to each enterprise designed to meet its particular circumstances.[29] It has also been suggested that the supervisory agency be authorized to "purify" the profitability index by adjusting it for imperfections of the other planned indexes and for factors beyond the control of an enterprise.[30] Another proposal was to retain existing incentive funds (the enterprise fund, the fund for production of consumer goods, and the fund for socialist competition) and add such new ones as a fund for development of production.[31] Still another proposal was to differentiate the incentive funds, establishing one specialized for workers and another specialized for engineers, technicians, and salaried employees, and adding another for stimulation of new techniques.[32]

There was considerable discussion about reforming the bonus system during 1962-65, but the government has not yet taken any decisive action, except for the regulation on experimental enterprises. Incentive payments out of enterprise funds have remained quite insignificant. In September, 1965, Kosygin pointed out that about half the industrial enterprises do not have a fund based on profits and that the other half have one of insignificant size.[33] Hence most bonuses are paid, not out of profits, but out of the wage fund.

The new system proposed in October, 1965, reforms replaces

28. B. Sukharevskii, "O sovershenstvovanii form i metodov materialnogo stimulirovaniia" [On Improving the Forms and Methods of Material Incentives], *Voprosy ekonomiki*, No. 11, 1962, pp. 24-27.

29. F. Veselkov, "Materialnye stimuly vysokikh planovykh zadanii" [Material Incentives of High Planned Goals], *ibid.*, No. 10, 1962, p. 8.

30. *Ibid.*, No. 3, 1963, p. 142.

31. Pekarskii, *Planovoe khoziaistvo*, No. 10, 1963, pp. 8-14; Veselkov, *Voprosy ekonomiki*, No. 10, 1962, p. 21.

32. Sukharevskii, *ibid.*, No. 11, 1962, p. 26.

33. Kosygin, *Pravda*, September 28, 1965, p. 3.

the enterprise fund with three separate funds: the first for the development of production; the second for material incentives; and the third for cultural and social welfare and housing. The other sources of incentive payments have not been affected by the reforms.

The funds for material incentives and for cultural and social welfare and housing are financed by levies on profits, the norms being fixed by the ministry supervising the enterprise, in agreement with the State Committee on Employment and Wages, Gosplan, and the Central Association of Trade Unions.[34] Bonuses paid to workers from the wage fund are also part of the fund for material incentives in its broader sense.

Norms for levies on profits are to be set for several years at a time and for groups of enterprises with similar profitability and working conditions. Individually set norms are to be the exception. Norms related to increases in marketed production (or profit) and to annually planned levels of profitability are to be set independently as a percentage of the wage fund for production personnel. That is to say, for each percentage point of increase in

34. "Metodicheskie ukazaniia," *Ekonomicheskaia gazeta*, No. 6, 1966, pp. 31-33.

A. Volkov and V. Grishin, "Metodicheskie ukazaniia po razrabotke polozhenii o premirovanii rabotnikov otdelnykh promyshlennykh predpriiatii, perevodimykh na novuiu sistemu planirovaniia i ekonomicheskogo stimulirovaniia promyshlennogo proizvodstva v 1966 godu" [Instructions on the Methods of Awarding Bonuses to Workers in Individual Industrial Enterprises Operating on the New System of Planning and Economic Incentives for Industrial Production in 1966], *ibid.*, No. 7, 1966, pp. 31-32. (Volkov is Chairman of the State Committee on Labor and Wage Problems; Grishin is Chairman of the Central Council of Trade Unions.)

"Vremennye ukazaniia ob obrazovanii i raskhodovanii fonda materialnogo pooshchreniia dlia otdelnykh predpriiatii perevodimykh na novuiu sistemu planirovaniia i stimulirovaniia v 1966 godu" [Provisional Instructions on the Formation and Utilization of the Fund for Material Incentive for Individual Enterprises Operating Within the New System of Planning and Incentives in 1966], *ibid.*, No. 11, 1966, p. 23.

"Vremennye ukazaniia ob obrazovanii i raskhodovanii fonda sotsialno-kulturnykh meropriiatii i zhilishchnogo stroitelstva dlia otdelnykh predpriiatii, perevodimykh na novuiu sistemu planirovaniia i stimulirovaniia v 1966 godu" [Provisional Instructions on the Formation and Utilization of the Fund for Cultural and Social Welfare and Housing for Individual Enterprises Operating Within the New System of Planning and Incentives in 1966], *ibid.*, No. 12, 1966, p. 36.

marketed production (or profit) and for each percentage point of profitability (calculated as the ratio of profits to fixed and working capital), the enterprise will be authorized to transfer from its profits a sum corresponding to a specified fraction of its planned wage fund.[35] The new provisions envisage a possible increase of up to 50 per cent in the funds for material incentives and for cultural and social welfare and housing as the share of new products rises.

The levies on profits for the cited funds are to be made quarterly, once payments into the budget for rental charges on fixed and working capital and for interest on bank credit are under way. They will depend on fulfillment of plans for marketed production and profit in the preceding quarters of the year. Another precondition is fulfillment of the planned assortment of major products as set by the ministry.

If the plan for marketed production or profits is not fulfilled, authorized levies are reduced below the norms. The reductions are fixed by the ministry but cannot be less than 3 per cent for each percentage point by which the plan is not fulfilled, provided that the amount collected for material incentives or for cultural and social welfare and housing is no less than 40 per cent of the goal set in the annual plan. The last provision represents an important change from present practice.

The practice to be followed in case of overfulfillment of the plan has also been changed significantly. The traditional policy of raising the authorized levies has been replaced by one of

35. A simple calculation cited by F. Gorin, "Fond materialnogo pooshchreniia" [The Fund for Material Incentive], *ibid.*, No. 27, 1966, p. 14, enables one to understand the method used: for each percentage point of increase in profits, profits amounting to 0.5 per cent of the planned wage fund may be transferred into the incentive fund; for each percentage point of increase in profitability, profits amounting to 0.25 per cent may be transferred. If planned and actual profits increase by 8 per cent and profitability by 20 per cent, $(0.5 \times 8) + (0.25 \times 20)$, or 9 per cent, of the planned wage fund for production personnel is to be deducted from profits and placed in the Fund for Material Incentives. If bonuses for workers paid out of the wage fund are added, the sum represents the fund for material incentives in its broader sense. It should be noted that the latter bonuses are not treated as deductions from profits in applying the norms for levies on profits.

reducing them by 30 to 40 per cent for each percentage point by which the plan is exceeded, the purpose being to encourage enterprises not to underestimate their potential.

The fund for material incentives is to finance bonuses, *ad hoc* compensation, special rewards for annual performance (an innovation), and various benefits to workers. Limitations on aggregate bonuses based on the wage fund or other relationships have been eliminated,[36] and accumulated sums not used during the year can be carried forward to the following year instead of reverting to the state budget.

Enterprise managers, in consultation with trade union representatives, have been granted greater latitude in choosing procedures for awarding bonuses, in selecting those entitled to them, and in setting their size.[37] Nevertheless, different rules are envisaged for bonuses to workers, on the one hand, and to engineers, technicians, and salaried employees, on the other. In the case of workers, bonuses for improvements in quality of work and productivity and for economizing on raw materials are to be paid from both the fund for material incentives and the wage fund, payments from the latter being part of the fund for material incentives in its broader sense. In the case of engineers, technicians, and salaried employees, bonuses are to be paid solely out of the fund for material incentives and only for fulfillment or overfulfillment of plans for marketed production and profits, subject to conditions laid down by the agency supervising the enterprise. The general regulations on bonuses set forth certain conditions that must be met before bonuses can be paid (such as fulfillment of the assortment plan and of specified tasks in the areas of production, costs, and so on) and other conditions that, if not met, reduce bonuses by up to 50 per cent. The general regulation also provides that, in the event that an enterprise's wage payments exceed the planned wage fund, aggregate bonuses must be reduced in the same proportion, provided they do not fall below 50 per cent of the otherwise authorized level.[38]

36. *Ibid.*
37. Volkov and Grishin, *ibid.*, No. 7, 1966, p. 32.
38. *Ibid.*, No. 38, 1966, pp. 18-19, gives an example of such regulations

On the whole, the new provisions for material incentives are more flexible than preceding ones, but they will be put into practice gradually along with other aspects of the October, 1965, reforms. Even so, expenditures by enterprises for material incentives, cultural purposes, and housing are expected to be twice as high in 1966 as in 1965.[39]

THE PLANNING AUTONOMY OF THE ENTERPRISES

In Kosygin's speech of September 27, 1965, and in the Instructions on Procedures for 1966 of January 24, 1966, the following were listed as indicators that would continue to be imposed on the enterprises: (1) volume of marketed production; (2) classification of essential products defined in physical terms, with specification of goods to be exported and details on quality; (3) aggregate wage fund; (4) aggregate profits and profitability relative to basic productive capital and working capital; (5) budgetary levies and subsidies; (6) volume of centralized investment, with specification of construction and assembly work; (7) installation of fixed capital and new productive capacity financed by centralized investment; (8) targets for assimilation of new products and technology and for mechanization and automation of production affecting industry as a whole; and (9) supply of raw materials, materials, and equipment by superior agencies to the enterprise.

It seems that the planning autonomy of an enterprise will increase in the case of control over employment, costs, and the number of planned indicators. The freedom in planning employment seems to be the major concession. The freedom to determine productivity indexes and average wages is only apparent since marketed output and the wage fund, both centrally planned, predetermine these values. Even the freedom in planning employment seems quite limited since the recently reactivated ministries will control employment and wage policies. Wage schedules and rates will be fixed, and regional differences

as set by the Kirov Watch Works in Moscow separately for (1) engineers, technicians, and employees, (2) workers, and (3) aggregate annual performance.

39. Garbuzov, *ibid.*, October 13, 1965, p. 4.

in employee compensation will be centrally regulated. It is anticipated that wage scales for each sector will be more strictly applied, the various inter- and intra-sector wage rates being applied not only to workers paid by piecework but also to those paid by time. A similar policy will be followed for salaried personnel like engineers and technicians.[40] Although employment is officially under the jurisdiction of the enterprise, work norms and wages will, in fact, be fixed centrally. Therefore, this freedom may be an illusion inasmuch as the structure of production imposed from above will determine the structure of employment.

In general, it is expected that the number of products centrally planned will be considerably reduced. However, no precise information on this subject is available at this time. Reduction of the list of products will probably be insignificant in the case of producer goods but somewhat more substantial in the light and food industries. The reduction is to be progressive, depending on the capacity of industries to satisfy needs. The same policy is planned for the transition from centralized allocation of resources to wholesale trade.[41]

It must not be forgotten that the distinction between compulsory and noncompulsory indexes may sometimes be very vague since superior agencies, which can issue any order they please to the enterprise, often take into account the so-called "accounting" indexes that are not compulsory. Higher authorities now impose upon the enterprise a financial plan, which is a detailed statement of income and expenditures. According to the October, 1965, reforms, only budgetary levies and subsidies, profits, and profitability can be imposed upon the enterprise.[42] The plan for costs will, therefore, be prepared by the enterprise itself.[43] In reality, one wonders what this new freedom will amount to. Kosygin em-

40. Sukharevskii, *Voprosy ekonomiki*, No. 10, 1965, pp. 30-31.

41. A. Bachurin (Vice Chairman of Gosplan), "Sovershenstvovanie planirovaniia" [Planning Improvement], *Ekonomicheskaia gazeta*, No. 47, 1965, p. 10, speech made at the conference on "Economic Laws and the Management of the National Economy" and "Economic Propaganda Under the New Conditions" (held in Moscow, November 22-24, 1965).

42. *Ibid.*

43. Sukharevskii, *Voprosy ekonomiki*, No. 10, 1965, p. 20.

phasized the need to include reduction of costs in the plans of enterprises. The higher authorities that determine the structure of production, aggregate marketed production, and profits cannot fail to be interested in the plans for costs.

Since supply of materials and equipment will continue to be regulated from above, enterprises operating within the system established by the October, 1965, reforms are not free to choose suppliers and customers, as the direct links enterprises are in principle. However, as we have already noted, the government seems to envisage increased flexibility in the authoritarian allocation of resources and at least partial substitution of contractual relations. Such contracts are not always visualized as agreements freely entered into by the parties concerned. For example, some are conceived as being imposed on enterprises within the framework of the plan in order to link supplier and customer enterprises for periods longer than the current plan. Such a proposal was advanced by a decision of the Party Central Committee and the Council of Ministers on October 13, 1961, and confirmed by Khrushchev in his speech to the Seventh Session of the Supreme Soviet on December 6-8, 1961.[44] Some commentators advocate that such contracts should cover a period of fifteen months to provide continuity during the first quarter of the year while adjustments are made in accord with the definitive version of the annual plan.[45] The commentators state: "The frequent adjustments made in the annual production goals while they are being executed are usually accompanied by corresponding changes in the plan for supply of materials and equipment. It is then indispensable to change certain suppliers and to choose new ones, which in turn entails new adjustments and a long correspondence with superior agencies that have jurisdiction over planning of supply of materials and equipment."[46]

These commentators emphasize that adjustments in the plan

44. I. Maievskii and A. Fomin, "Nekotorye voprosy sovershenstvovaniia planirovaniia narodnogo khoziaistva" [Some Questions on Improving National Economic Planning], *ibid.*, No. 12, 1962, pp. 44-45.

45. *Ibid.*, p. 44.

46. *Ibid.*, p. 40.

are made inside a vast pyramid of superior planning agencies without keeping the enterprise informed. As a result, discordances are created that appear only in the process of executing the plan. Under this state of affairs, it has not been possible to introduce a general system of such long-term contracts. There has been some exploration of the possibility of direct links between large enterprises, such as the Gorky Automobile Works, the Volgograd (formerly Stalingrad) Tractor Factory, or the Likhachev Automobile Plant in Moscow.[47]

Nevertheless, the idea of directly linking supplier and customer enterprises is still under discussion. It was supported in the resolutions of a conference organized in April or May of 1966 by the Ministry of Light Industry and *Ekonomicheskaia gazeta.* Agreement was reached on the need for introducing direct links between enterprises and their immediate suppliers of raw materials, chemical products, dyes, and (in the case of light industry) transportation services. At present, the consuming and supplying enterprises are officially tied (*prikleplat*) to each other by the Republic Ministries of Trade and by the industrial Central Administrations (Glavks).[48] Freedom of contract does not seem to be among the concessions now being granted to enterprises benefiting from the less rigid system established by the October, 1965, reforms.

REGROUPING OF ENTERPRISES

Discussions on the autonomy of enterprises has brought to light another closely related problem, namely, the appropriate size of enterprise. A solution to this problem has been sought by cre-

47. N. Razumov, "O polozhenii i pravakh promyshlennogo predpriiatiia" [On the Situation and Rights of the Industrial Enterprise], *ibid.*, No. 7, 1963, p. 131.

48. "Rekomendatsii ekonomicheskoi konferentsii: Opyt raboty predpriiatii v novykh usloviiakh i zadachi rabotnikov legkoi promyshlennosti k perekhodu no novuiu sistemu planirovaniia i ekonomicheskogo stimulirovaniia" [Recommendations of the Economic Conference on the Experiment of Enterprises Working Under New Conditions and the Tasks of Workers in Light Industry in Transferring to the New System of Planning and Economic Incentive], *Ekonomicheskaia gazeta*, No. 25, 1966, pp. 26-27.

ation of "producers' unions" (*proizvodstvennye obedineniia*), also called "firms."[49] A producers' union or firm is created by consolidation within a geographic area (an *oblast*, or administrative region) of several enterprises in the same sector. The largest of these enterprises is usually given the status of "parent enterprise" and the others of subsidiary enterprises.

There are three types of firms: (1) the type in which subsidiary enterprises preserve their legal entity and keep independent accounts (*khozraschet*) (*e.g.*, the Lvov-Dniester Union of Liqueurs and Vodka); (2) the type in which some of the enterprises preserve their legal entity and accounting autonomy while others lose it (*e.g.*, the Riga's Garment Union *Rigas Apgerbs*); and (3) the type in which all subsidiary enterprises lose their legal entity and accounting autonomy (*e.g.*, the Lvov Footwear Union *Progress* and the Moscow Footwear Union *Zaria*).[50]

Creation of firms was strongly encouraged after the November, 1962, session of the Party Central Committee. In the second half of 1963, there were already 112 firms in the Russian Republic, including 637 enterprises, covering more than 400,000 workers, and accounting for an estimated annual production of three billion rubles.[51] In 1964, there were firms in 80 per cent of the Sovnarkhozes employing a total of 820,000 people.[52] During the first quarter of 1965, the number of firms passed the 500 mark.[53]

The principal advantages usually ascribed to the firm are those of large-scale production and the accompanying greater

49. On this subject, see: Ia. Chadaev, "Sovershenstvovat planovoe rukovodstvo narodnym khoziaistvom" [Improve the Planned Management of the National Economy], *Planovoe khoziaistvo*, No. 11, 1963, p. 7; E. Utkin, "K voprosu o firmakh" [On the Problem of Firms], *Voprosy ekonomiki*, No. 10, 1963, pp. 27-37; A. Vilkov, "Nekotorye voprosy khoziaistvennogo rascheta proizvodstvennykh obedinenii" [Some Problems of Accounting Autonomy in the Producers' Unions], *ibid.*, No. 2, 1965, pp. 29-38; V. Rutgaizer, "Obobshchenie opyta raboty sovetskikh firm" [Examining the Experiment of Soviet Firms], *ibid.*, No. 4, 1965, pp. 151-54.

50. Vilkov, *ibid.*, No. 2, 1965, p. 29.

51. Chadaev, *Planovoe khoziaistvo*, No. 11, 1963, p. 7.

52. Marie-Louise Lavigne, "Les experiences économiques en URSS," in *Annuaire de l'U.R.S.S., Droit, Economie, Sociologie, Politique, Culture* (Paris, 1965), p. 304.

53. Rutgaizer, *Voprosy ekonomiki*, No. 4, 1965, p. 151.

maneuverability in the use of resources. Specialized shops servicing subsidiary enterprises can be established, mass production instituted, and products standardized. Many small enterprises, formerly backward, have managed in this way to raise their productivity. Their output has risen relatively more than that of larger enterprises. It has also been possible to utilize the skills of engineers, technicians, and managerial personnel more efficiently in firms. Centralized supplying of materials and equipment to the enterprises has become easier thanks to concentration of resources, reduction of inventories, simplification of nomenclature, and accelerated turnover of working capital. It has also become possible to apply modern calculating techniques.

Rapid expansion in the number of firms has, at the same time, had its shortcomings. The haste with which consolidation was carried out has not always encouraged specialization, and enterprises without organic links have often been merged together.[54] Nor has it been possible to formulate uniform procedures applying to every firm: in some cases, planned indexes are handed down directly to subsidiary enterprises, while in others they are passed through the management of the firm.[55] The number of compulsory indexes varies from one supervisory agency to another. Rules on the constitution and use of the enterprise fund vary. Allotment by subsidiary enterprises of general expenses leaves much to be desired. Procedures for setting transfer prices within the firm are not uniform: sometimes planned accounting prices are used, and sometimes planned factory costs or costs of the preceding month.

Hired personnel have not always benefited from creation of firms. Engineers, technicians, and managerial personnel of parent enterprises have greater responsibilities and duties but receive the same salaries as before. As to the managers of subsidiary enterprises, their salaries have actually been cut by 10 per cent.

54. *Ibid.*, p. 152, cites the case of the food firm Krasnyi Vostok of the Middle Volga Sovnarkhoz. Its twenty-one enterprises specialize in alcohol, liqueurs, vodka, vinegar, and fish breeding (the last enterprise being under construction), among other things.

55. Vilkov, *ibid.*, No. 2, 1965, p. 30.

As early as January, 1965, it was pointed out that, in several cases, firms were exercising the functions of sectoral supervisory agencies (then the Sovnarkhozes).[56] In his speech of September 27, 1965, Kosygin cited the firm as an example of the natural tendency toward management by economic sectors.[57] Such a system having been instituted with re-establishment of industrial ministries, some changes in regulations applying to firms may now be necessary.

During the year following the October, 1965, reforms, industrial ministries have had second thoughts on the subject of firms. Officials of the Sverdlov Producers' Union for Construction of Machine Tools and the Karl Marx Producers' Union for Machine-Building (both in Leningrad) have expressed in the press their fears that these firms faced eventual liquidation.[58] There was a note of reproach toward the ministry concerned for having prematurely combined, into the Karl Marx Union, factories that should have been subordinated to different central administrations. In another case (the firm Tempo of Penza) the ministry and its Central Administration for the Production of Textile Machinery have virtually ignored the existence of a firm since the 1965 reform, while doing nothing to establish a new one.[59] Despite such problems, some Soviet economists still strongly recommend formation of firms as a means of providing the component enterprises with a satisfactory legal status and autonomy. Others, such as Cherniavskii, argue for a more flexible attitude and skepticism toward uniform solutions.[60]

After several studies of the question, a draft charter for firms

56. Rutgaizer, *ibid.*, No. 4, 1965, p. 151.

57. *Pravda*, September 28, 1965, p. 3.

58. G. Kulagin, "Tsentralizovannoe upravlenie i samostoiatelnost predpriiatii" [Centralized Administration and the Autonomy of the Enterprises], *Ekonomicheskaia gazeta*, No. 48, 1965, p. 8. (Kulagin is the manager of the Sverdlov Producers' Union for the Construction of Machine Tools in Leningrad.) S. Balbekov, "Ministerstvo i zavody" [Ministry and Factories], *Pravda*, July 29, 1966, p. 2.

59. *Ibid.*, p. 2.

60. V. Cherniavskii, "Voprosy sovershenstvovaniia planirovaniia i upravleniia proizvodstvom" [Problems of Improving the Planning and Management of Production], *Voprosy ekonomiki*, No. 6, 1966, p. 26.

was prepared in early 1965 by the Research Institute of U.S.S.R. Sovnarkhoz, with the assistance of more than eighty other agencies.[61] The Central Laboratory for the Economy and for the Organization of Production (U.S.S.R. Sovnarkhoz) also made some suggestions on the structure, organization, and technological and economic aspects of firms. It has been argued that the process of concentrating production must be made orderly through long-range plans for the amalgamation of enterprises. A study has been suggested to look into the question of firms made up of enterprises from more than one ministry.[62]

Experience so far shows that spectacular results should not be expected from regrouping of enterprises.[63] Although yielding many favorable results, amalgamation and concentration of enterprises—implemented uniformly and hastily—are likely to introduce more problems than they solve. In any case, such a measure would eliminate none of the defects inherent in an authoritarian and administrative planning system. The same applies, of course, to other partial managerial reforms and such "innovations" as the "Chief Economists," or the "Production Committees" representing workers in the management of an enterprise.[64]

REACTIONS OF SOVIET ECONOMISTS

The New Framework of Discussion. It is very difficult to discern the true opinions of Soviet economists about a reform whose implications are as much political as economic. The press and all channels of public expression are controlled by the government and Party, and decisions of the Central Committee and political

61. Rutgaizer, *ibid.*, No. 4, 1965, p. 152. The author reports on the meeting held in Moscow on January 28-30, 1965, to examine the experiment with producers' unions.

62. *Ibid.*, p. 154.

63. It has been reported that, since the industrial ministries were reestablished, there has been a tendency for firms to be liquidated and for their enterprises to be placed under Glavks (Central Administrations) of ministries. See Kulagin, *Ekonomicheskaia gazeta*, No. 48, 1965, p. 8.

64. See Chadaev, *Planovoe khoziaistvo*, No. 11, 1963, p. 8; and G. Kosiachenko, "Stoimostnye pokazateli plana i povyshenie effektivnosti materialnogo stimulirovaniia" [Cost Indexes in the Plan and the Increase in Efficiency of Material Incentives], *Voprosy ekonomiki*, No. 5, 1963, p. 101.

instructions are formally binding on all those who wish to publish their views. Hence it is out of the question to find open criticism of the reform as such. Differences of opinion may be expressed only on specifics.

An organized press campaign in favor of the official reform has been in progress since October, 1965, demonstrating that the government is sticking to its policy. Soviet commentators are not blind to the organized nature of these expressions of opinion. For instance, the former editor-in-chief of *Pravda*, A. M. Rumiantsev, declares "that it is not a secret that many are somewhat tired of reforms and that confidence in innovation has been undermined. Actually they are tired not of reforms per se but of the triumphal parade drums that have always accompanied reforms in the past."[65] Another Soviet author, S. Balbekov, remarks ironically that "all the noise and all the controversies" about the role of profit in a socialist society stopped immediately after the reforms of October, 1965.[66]

The Soviet government applied pressure for enactment of the reform program throughout the year following the meeting of the Party Central Committee on September 27-29, 1965. There was some hesitation and some dragging of feet on the part of the administrative apparatus, but the policy associated with Kosygin was pursued relentlessly.[67] Until October, 1966, there was no general debate on the subject in the Central Committee or the Supreme Soviet. The debates of the Twenty-third Party Congress (March 29-April 6, 1966) on the state of the domestic economy were concerned with prospects of the five-year plan for 1966-70. Aside from a few favorable references by Kosygin and Brezhnev, the reforms of October, 1965, passed almost unnoticed in the many speeches made by the delegates. Nor were the economic

65. A. M. Rumiantsev, *Iunost*, No. 1, 1966, p. 67, as cited by John P. Hardt, D. M. Gallik, and Vladimir G. Treml, "Institutional Stagnation and Changing Economic Strategy in the Soviet Union," in *New Directions in the Soviet Economy*, Joint Economic Committee (Washington, 1966), p. 60.

66. *Pravda*, May 27, 1966, p. 2.

67. "Union Soviétique—Réflexions sur la 'crise de l'été,'" *Le Courrier des Pays de l'Est*, No. 62, 1966, pp. 37-39.

reforms on the agenda of the brief constitutive session of the Supreme Soviet of August 2-3, 1966 (First Session of the Seventh Legislature), although in his speech Kosygin mentioned technical aspects such as wholesale prices, norms for levies on profits, regulations in preparation, and the role of ministries.[68]

On the whole, the discussion of reforms has been conducted in a new atmosphere since September, 1965, but it has remained restricted and channelized. Soviet commentators are bent above all on criticizing the concepts and practices condemned by the Central Committee on September 27-29. For instance, L. A. Leontev condemns the thesis that market production and the law of value merely represent vestiges of capitalism in a planned economy; I. S. Malyshev and S. P. Pervushin insist on the importance of financial criteria and planning in value terms; and D. Allakhverdian recognizes the importance of research on the laws that regulate the flow of financial resources.[69] Under attack are criticisms of profit as an economic regulator, the practice of calculating profitability relative to costs that exclude charges for capital, the practice of providing capital free of charge, undervaluation of prices of producer goods, and the many, often contradictory, success criteria for an enterprise.[70] Some economists

68. Kosygin, *Pravda*, August 4, 1966, pp. 1 and 3-4.

69. S. P. Pervushin, *Neobkhodimost i sushchnost khoziaistvennoi reformy* [The Necessity and the Essence of the Economic Reform], Moscow, 1966; L. A. Leontev, *Khoziaistvennaia reforma i nekotorye voprosy ekonomicheskoi teorii* [The Economic Reform and Some Problems of Economic Theory], Moscow, 1966; I. S. Malyshev, *Ekonomicheskie zakony sotsializma i planirovanie* [The Economic Laws of Socialism and Planning], Moscow, 1966. These three pamphlets are part of a series entitled *Ekonomisty o novoi khoziaistvennoi reforme v SSSR* [Economists on the New Economic Reform in the U.S.S.R.], edited by *Ekonomika* in Moscow. See also: S. P. Pervushin, "Plan i tovarnoe proizvodstvo" [The Plan and Market Production], *Ekonomicheskaia gazeta*, No. 10, 1966, pp. 26-27, and D. Allakhverdian, "Finansovoe planirovanie v novykh usloviiakh" [Financial Planning in the New Conditions], *Planovoe khoziaistvo*, No. 9, 1966, pp. 42-50.

70. On this subject, see the pamphlets in the series mentioned in footnote 69. In addition to the one by Malyshev cited above, see also: B. S. Nikolaev, N. A. Petrakov, and S. I. Lushin, *Pribyl, ekonomicheskaia kategoriia sotsializma* [Profit, an Economic Category of Socialism], Moscow, 1966; Atlas, *Khozraschet*; L. A. Vaag, *Plata za proizvodstvennye fondy i effektivnost ikh ispolzovaniia* [Payments for Productive Capital and the

such as Leontev insist on the importance of relaxing restrictions on utilization of raw materials from local resources and ridicule the "traditional" ban on studies of the economic situation (*koniunktura*). A Laboratory for Study of the Economic Situation of the Textile Industry has just been established in the region of Ivanovo.[71]

One does not find anywhere in all this literature any critiques of the reforms as a whole, despite the fact that enacted reforms diverge considerably from proposals of the principal proponents of reform. These men, while praising enacted reforms, try to influence their future course by presenting plans for reforms to come or by advising on corrections that they believe are needed to avoid compromising the reform program.

Reactions of Proponents of Reform. Liberman[72] tries first of all to defend the reforms against the advocates of centralized planning. He argues that the profit criterion is compatible with centralized planning not requiring recourse to administrative methods. Centralization, he says, is guaranteed by collective ownership of means of production. Optimal centralized planning should consist primarily in fixing economic proportions that will ensure maximum growth of national income. These proportions should be calculated with the help of balances so that the ag-

---

Efficiency of Their Use], Moscow, 1966; V. D. Belkin and N. I. Buzova, *Ekonomicheskie metody khoziaistvennogo rukovodstva i peresmotr tsen* [Economic Methods of Managing the Economy and a Review of Prices], Moscow, 1966.

71. L. Leontev, "Plan i khoziaistvennaia initsiativa" [The Plan and Economic Initiative], *Pravda*, April 29, 1965, pp. 2-3.

72. E. Liberman, "Plan, priamye sviazi i rentabelnost" [The Plan, Direct Links, and Profitability], *ibid.*, November 21, 1965, pp. 2-3. See also an interview granted by Liberman in October, 1965, when he declared that "Libermanism is a myth" and "profit is not there to abolish planning but to reinforce it." (Henri Pierre, "Le Libermanisme est un mythe, affirme le Professeur Liberman," *Le Monde*, October 12, 1965, p. 2.) In another interview with Tass on the first anniversary of the reform, Liberman declared that the reform had met with complete success but that it was not quite "broken in" yet because of supply defects and certain meddling methods of the ministries (Liberman, *ibid.*, September 20, 1966, p. 6). Since Liberman's name has a certain ring to it, his statements to the radio and press should be read with caution.

gregative goals, in value terms, may be appropriately subdivided and assigned to enterprises. These goals would be merely advisory control figures, serving as guideposts for independent preparation of plans.

According to Liberman, "vertical" accord between plans made by the central authorities and those made independently by enterprises would be achieved through the "horizontal nexus" of contractual links and purchase orders made autonomously by enterprises. This purpose could be served by groups of orders for basic commodities placed with the wholesale trade network or the depots for material and equipment supplies. The most important orders would be placed for a period of several years and could not be changed without mutual agreement of the contractors.

The number of goals imposed on the enterprises in physical quantities should be reduced, Liberman argues, and limited to the most important products. The promises of liberalization made by Kosygin on September 27 encouraged Liberman to envisage successive stages of the reform: abolition of a mandatory wage fund imposed from above, gradual reduction in the number of products planned by superior agencies, and finally the organization of supplies through the wholesale trade network. "Some excess of supply over demand will cost much less than the complicated system of distributing production and eliminating disproportions," he says.[73] Such an increase in the autonomy of the enterprise should be accompanied by a rise in the share of profits at the disposition of the enterprises.

Liberman has also responded to various objections on the part of those opposed to the reforms. If purchase orders exceed control figures, it is evident, he believes, that the ministry can raise the control figures; if they fall short, the ministry can solicit orders for the affected enterprises that would enable them to utilize their productive capacities more fully. In any case, in the new system there will be no reason for continuing the present practice of forcing enterprises to produce an unprofitable assortment of products. Differences in the objective conditions of

73. Liberman, *Pravda*, November 21, 1965, p. 2.

enterprises can be evened out by redistributing fixed capital, imposing interest charges, and setting shadow prices. Efforts will be made to avoid imposing unprofitable production on enterprises and, in exceptional cases, losses will be compensated for by temporary prices and by subventions from the Reserve Fund of the Council of Ministers. On the whole, the planned assortment will consist of products for which enterprises have freely accepted orders. Whatever is ordered in addition by the ministry should have its profitability assured by special arrangements.

A. M. Birman, one of the most enthusiastic supporters of the October, 1965, reforms, has also commented on the reforms.[74] He considers them, like NEP (New Economic Policy) and the Stalinist reforms of 1929-32, one of the most important events in the history of the Soviet Union. He not only criticizes the past but also indirectly answers Kosygin's criticisms of Soviet economists, not hesitating to put the blame on the government. The weaknesses of economic analysis are due, he says, to inadequacies of statistics and to the scarcity of qualified economists. The number of Soviet economic institutes and economics departments in universities has recently been reduced, and the educational program, while being stiffened through inclusion of mathematics, has been shortened from five years to four. Moreover, Soviet economists are not in a position to discuss controversial questions publicly, since journals and reviews are all organs of various institutions and as such they refuse to publish criticisms of those institutions.

While approving the reforms wholeheartedly, Birman deplores the fact that the new provisions are being applied by many officials who opposed the reforms while they were in the stage of discussion. All this does not prevent him from being optimistic about the outcome, and he manifests this optimism in an article published in *Pravda* on March 9, 1966.

The advocates of "production prices" have had every reason to be satisfied by the October, 1965, reforms since their principle demand—introduction of charges for use of capital—was adopted.

74. A. Birman, "Mysli posle plenuma" [Thoughts After the Plenary Session], *Novyi mir*, No. 12, 1965, pp. 194-213.

Nevertheless, introduction of these charges is in their view but one aspect of price reform, and several members of this school of thought—such as Malyshev, L. A. Vaag, and V. D. Belkin—insist on the need for a general revision of wholesale prices in accord with the principle of "production prices."[75] Belkin and N. I. Buzova declared that the performance of enterprises transferred to the new system must be viewed as provisional until the government decrees a reform of prices.[76]

It is evident from their writings that reforms so far undertaken are only partial in the eyes of the proponents of "production prices." Z. V. Atlas says, for instance: "The only way to get rid of the hypertrophy of centralized economic management is to introduce a system of *complete economic accounting*, in which enterprises, guided by generalized planned goals, prepare their own detailed production plans and retain freedom of maneuver with their resources."[77]

Atlas criticizes the fact that the volume of gross production is used as a criterion for differential grants of credit by Gosbank while profitability is not. He also criticizes the present policy of Gosbank that links disbursement of funds for wage payments to the percentage of plan fulfillment in the case of gross production. This policy has been only slightly revised under the new system, control by the bank being differentiated according to economic branch and monthly accounts being replaced by quarterly ones.[78]

Vaag's comments are in the same vein. He restates his earlier position that profit should be the synthetic criterion of performance and argues that price reform should affect enterprises in the same productive activity equally. Fines for breaking contracts should be set so that they reimburse for actual losses, and the size of an enterprise's wage fund should not be fixed by superior authorities.[79]

75. See footnotes 69 and 70.
76. Belkin and Buzova, *Ekonomicheskie metody*, p. 11.
77. Atlas, *Khozraschet*, p. 11.
78. *Ibid.*, pp. 38-41.
79. Vaag, *Plata za proizvodstvennye fondy*, pp. 21-23 and 30.

Vaag and Cherniavskii[80] also criticize the practice of differentiating charges for use of productive capital by economic sector or enterprise group. They feel that such differential charges have neither a theoretical foundation nor a practical value and that they pave the way for arbitrary decisions. Cherniavskii considers, moreover, that all enterprises, even those operating at a loss, should have to meet these charges, an opinion shared by some fellow economists in Eastern Europe. For instance, the Polish economist Henryk Fiszel, in discussing Polish reforms, favors a uniform rate of interest for determining capital charges, and inclusion of those charges in costs.[81] Cherniavskii feels that the appropriate interest rate should be between 4 and 6 per cent; Belkin and Buzova, between 5 and 6 per cent. For Poland, Fiszel considers the proper rate of interest to be at least 10 per cent.

Cherniavskii goes on to criticize the retention of eight groups of mandatory indexes for the enterprise. He has no difficulty in demonstrating that each index can be fulfilled at the expense of another, so that it is possible, for example, to reduce costs of production and wage payments by sacrificing quality and underutilizing productive capital. Preserving all these indexes does not, he argues, guarantee a combined fulfillment of them that is optimal from the viewpoint of the interests of the state.[82]

The proponents of "production prices" directed all these criticisms against the system existing before the October, 1965, reforms, and they continue to direct them against the new system. In their view, the October reforms represent no more than a first step toward the system of flexible planning that they advocate.

Reactions of Enterprise Managers. From the viewpoint of enterprises, reforms have largely consisted in changes in relations with superior agencies—Glavks (central administrations), or ministries.

80. *Ibid.*, pp. 14-15; and Cherniavskii, *Voprosy ekonomiki*, No. 6, 1966, p. 21.

81. Fiszel, *Zycie Gospodarcze*, No. 1, 1966, p. 2.

82. Cherniavskii, *Voprosy ekonomiki*, No. 6, 1966, pp. 16-17.

Complaints about the supervision of ministries have mounted, as evidenced during the special meeting organized by Gosplan's Interdepartmental Committee in May, 1966.[83] The participants agreed that ministries continue in many cases to exercise "excessive supervision" over enterprises. They modify plans arbitrarily, issue directives altering contractual ties against the interest of enterprises, stifle their autonomy, and meddle in their productive relations.

The continual interference by higher agencies results, according to G. Kulagin, from a mistaken concept of planning and the illusion that electronic computers and cybernetics make possible perfect solutions to problems. "Our economy is too big," he says, "too much in flux, to permit us to freeze plans for a long period of time and use them to regulate all relations of enterprises with superior agencies. Drought, floods, discoveries of new deposits, valuable inventions—all these inevitably lead to interference in the life of enterprises. Such unforeseen events will always exist, under the most ideal planning. Life is life and it does not stand still."[84]

According to Kulagin, the statute of October 4, 1965, does not include any provision guaranteeing the sole responsibility of an enterprise to its superior agency. Any organization with administrative jurisdiction can impose any kind of measure on an enterprise that has legally defined obligations. Kulagin adds: "In our system the chief foreman can give any order he wants to the foreman, the manager to the chief foreman, and the Sovnarkhoz to the manager; each person in a higher position considers himself more competent. But this is manifestly not so. . . ."[85]

Examples of excessive supervision and arbitrary behavior on the part of higher agencies abound in the Soviet press. According to Balbekov, ministries continue to demand daily reports on gross production and other matters, such reports being in addi-

83. "Vnedriat novuiu sistemu, sovershenstvovat pokazateli planirovaniia" [Introduce the New System, Improve the Planning Indexes], *Planovoe khoziaistvo*, No. 7, 1966, pp. 31-41.

84. Kulagin, *Ekonomicheskaia gazeta*, No. 48, 1965, p. 8.

85. *Ibid.*

tion to those that an enterprise is required to submit to statistical agencies. They also continue to redistribute resources and funds among enterprises. They take from one enterprise to help another, in order to achieve an "average" result. The Ministry of Machine-Building for the Light and Food Industries managed to surpass its plan for gross production by a wide margin in the first half of 1966, but its enterprises did not realize planned profits because of an increase in both unsold inventories and unfinished production. Yet the ministry refused to correct plans calling for production that could not be sold.[86] In the case of the Kranolutsk Meat Combine of the Lugan region, planned profits for the first quarter of 1966 were set at 248,000 rubles on February 7, but were revised to 306,000 rubles on April 8 after the quarter had ended.[87] In some cases, enterprises have been refused the right to benefit from the general statute of October 4, 1965, on the pretext that they had not been brought into the new system announced by Kosygin on September 27 and gradually put into operation after January 1, 1966.[88]

Enterprise managers believe that absence of material interest on the part of superior agencies is responsible for all these defects. The new system of management has been introduced only in enterprises, while the material incentives of superior agencies remain unchanged. Hence there is no link between the interests of an enterprise and those of the agency that supervises it.[89]

Enterprise managers have therefore been induced to request introduction of autonomous economic accounting (*khozraschet*) into superior agencies—first of all, into the Glavks of ministries. Kulagin has been reiterating this suggestion since December,

86. S. Balbekov, "Ministerstvo i zavody—A kak idet plan?" [Ministry and Factories—How Is the Plan Progressing?], *Pravda*, July 27, 1966, p. 3.

87. V. Laptev, "Protiv pravovogo 'nigilizma' " [Against Nihilism in Law], *Ekonomicheskaia gazeta*, No. 21, 1966, p. 20.

88. G. Izakson (Deputy Director of the Kemerovo Chemical Combine), "Instruktsii i khoziaistvennyi raschet" [Instructions and Economic Accounting], *ibid.*, No. 28, 1966, p. 30.

89. *Planovoe khoziaistvo*, No. 7, 1966, p. 40.

1965,[90] and the meeting in May, 1966, organized by Gosplan took notice of it. The Soviet government is now studying the question, perhaps with the intention of codifying regulations on the new system as suggested by V. Laptev, a member of the Institute of State and Law in the Academy of Sciences. Laptev insists that the rights and obligations of enterprises and superior agencies be defined and goes so far as to request the issuance of a regulation fixing the rights and obligations of ministries, which would henceforward be considered as agencies for economic direction rather than for administration.[91] Many of these suggestions seem to have been accepted by Kosygin, for he indicated in his speech of August 3, 1966, that regulations were then being drawn up specifying the responsibilities of ministries and that preparations were being made to draft legal norms regulating activities and reciprocal relations for various agencies of economic administration on the basis of economic methods of management.[92]

Reactions of Those Supporting the Traditional System. The arguments of those supporting the present system were expressed in detail in the fall of 1962, and there is no point in repeating them.[93] Nevertheless, it is of interest to cite a few points made during the first months after the October, 1965, decisions, since the Soviet leadership attached importance to them. These arguments were essentially concerned with (1) the relationship between plan and market; (2) the role of profit as a means of reconciling the interests of individuals, enterprises, and society; and (3) the respective roles of administrative and economic instruments in the plan.

Supporters of the prevailing system argue that commercial relations are not the only form of economic relations.[94] Commercial relations contain contradictions resulting from the discrepancy between value and costs that may cause disproportions.

90. *Ekonomicheskaia gazeta*, No. 48, 1965, p. 8.
91. Laptev, *ibid.*, No. 21, 1966, p. 20.
92. Kosygin, *Pravda*, August 4, 1966, p. 3.
93. See Chapter 5.
94. G. Kozlov, "Ekonomicheskie i administrativnye rychagi" [Administrative and Economic Tools], *Ekonomicheskaia gazeta*, No. 51, 1965, pp. 4-5.

For this reason, commercial relations can be only one element in a planned economy and cannot be subordinated to the market.[95] Planning, they believe, is a conscious effort of men to realize the exigencies of the law of planned proportional development of the national economy and other economic laws of socialism.[96] To allow spontaneity in commercial relations in a system of collective ownership may cause anarchy in price formation, unjustifiable differentials in income, and a disequilibrium in the development of different sectors and regions. It would be false, on the other hand, to pretend that there is no economic mechanism in the Soviet Union that acts as a lever for growth. In any society, this mechanism is represented by the concrete forms of economic relations.[97]

Defenders of the present system also reject the thesis that the interests of the state and of the enterprise stand in opposition to each other. In the Soviet regime, they argue, the interests of the state encompass the profound interests of workers, and hence every individual should be interested in developing social production.[98] It is also wrong, they say, to assert that this alleged disharmony of individual and social interests can be resolved only by introduction of "free" market relations.[99] For this reason they reject profit as the sole or essential criterion of the performance of enterprises.[100] The goal of socialist production is the satisfaction

95. *Ibid.*, p. 5.

96. Bachurin, *ibid.*, No. 47, 1965, p. 8. On the economic laws in the Soviet Union, see Alec Nove, E. Zaleski, *et al.*, "Le leggi dell' economia e la pianificazione sovietica," in *Problemi attuali della pianificazione sovietica*, CESES, Milan, 1965, pp. 19-74 (reports and discussions of the Conference of Rome held November 12-13, 1965, and organized by the Centro Studi e Ricerche su Problemi Economico-Sociali de Milano).

97. Kozlov, *Ekonomicheskaia gazeta*, No. 51, 1965, p. 5.

98. V. Filippov, "Nekotorye voprosy osushchestvleniia khoziaistvennoi reformy" [Some Problems of Carrying Out the Economic Reform], *ibid.*, p. 8.

99. Kozlov, *ibid.*, p. 5.

100. According to Filippov, *ibid.*, p. 8, setting a single index (profit) for enterprises in a socialist economy is the same as intentionally enlarging the scope of the law of value and reducing correspondingly the scope of the law of planned proportional development. Such a move could, in his opinion, only reduce the efficiency of social production. It should be noted that some supporters of profit as the "essential criterion" are quite vague

of needs, and the use of such a criterion could only compromise the planned proportions of investment and consumption.[101]

To defenders of the present system, maintenance of administrative instruments follows directly from supremacy of the plan over the market. In order to defend these instruments against widespread criticism, they distinguish administrative methods of planning, which are only a manifestation of bureaucratic tendencies, and the administrative instruments of the plan, which correspond to the exigencies of the economic laws of socialism.[102] These administrative instruments or direct orders are the only things that make it possible to establish desired proportions among economic sectors, geographical location of production, shares of investment and consumption, and so on.

According to defenders of the system, the role of economic instruments must be subordinated to the principal aim, which is efficiency of the economy as a whole. For this reason, the decision to apply one economic tool or another should not be left to the enterprise but should be the responsibility of central planning agencies.[103] Centralized establishment of norms for utilization of materials and equipment should also not be relinquished when the application of the economic tools of planning is extended.[104]

On the whole, it is evident that, despite the government campaign for reforms, there are quite important divergences of opinion among economists and among those who manage and administer the economy. These divergences will not be resolved

---

on this subject. For instance, Nikolaev, Petrakov, and Lushin, *Pribyl, ekonomicheskaia kategoriia sotsializma*, p. 9, believe that the "essential index" should not be considered as one that replaces all others. Profit "would be the 'essential index' not because it covers the whole work of the enterprise but because it reflects best the economic interrelations in social production." But Nikolaev, Petrakov, and Lushin do not always explain what solutions they would suggest in case of divergencies between the profit criterion and other indexes imposed on the enterprise. They are much more eager to justify the government's decisions than to preserve the coherence of their arguments.

101. Kozlov, *Ekonomicheskaia gazeta*, No. 51, 1965, p. 5.

102. *Ibid.*, p. 4.

103. *Ibid.*, p. 5.

104. Bachurin, *ibid.*, No. 47, 1965, p. 9.

by a "round table" discussion. They can be affected only by the concrete results of reform. For this reason, all parties to the controversy watch with interest the practical application of provisions of the October, 1965, reforms.

THE TIME SCHEDULE

The October, 1965, reforms are to be introduced gradually over several years.[105] The new arrangements do not appear in the 1966 plan or budget, both having been prepared within the framework of the old administrative system. In December, 1965, when the 1966 plan and budget were being drawn up, the program for implementation of reforms was also being drafted by Gosplan, the Ministry of Finance, the State Committee for Employment and Wages, the Central Association of Trade Unions, Gosbank, and the Bank for Financing Investments, with the cooperation of interested ministries.[106] A committee composed primarily of representatives of the same agencies[107] was established to examine the ministries' proposals for transfer of certain enterprises to the new system of planning and incentives. The criteria for such transfer would be adequate profitability, a stable financial situation, and normal conditions of supplies and sales.[108]

After this committee had finished its work, the first group of enterprises was transferred to the new system as of January, 1966. It covered only forty-three enterprises with 300,000 employees and a total value of production of 732 million rubles in the first quarter of 1966. On April 1, 1966, two hundred more enterprises with about 700,000 employees were to enter the new system.

105. The new industrial ministries were, however, to assume the former powers of Sovnarkhozes at the beginning of December 1965. The new ministries were to present reports accompanied by a working program on December 15. See Ia. Chadaev, Chairman of the R.S.F.S.R. Gosplan, as cited by Henryk Chadzynski, "ZSSR–Rachunek, bodźce, gospodarność" [U.S.S.R.–Calculations, Incentives, Savings], *Zycie Gospodarcze*, November 7, 1965.

106. Garbuzov, *Pravda*, December 8, 1965, p. 4.

107. The Central Association of Trade Unions was omitted and the State Committee on Prices (under Gosplan) and the Central Statistical Administration were added. See Garbuzov, *ibid.*, p. 2.

108. *Ibid.*, p. 4.

After this second group had been designated, further extension of the new system was entrusted to the Union ministries and to the federal republic councils of ministers, which must submit their proposals to the ministries concerned and to Gosplan for approval. The government also drew up a time schedule for the transfer of enterprises into the new system within the third and fourth quarters of 1966.

The resulting third group, that of July 1, 1966, comprises four hundred more enterprises employing a million persons and encompassing entire branches of the tobacco, tea, and soda industries and specially designated enterprises producing metals (the Nizhnyi Tagil Combine, Zaporozhstal), chemicals (Makeevka and Lisinsk Combines, synthetic rubber factories of Omsk and Sterlitamaks), and machinery. This third group, like the two previous ones, has been assigned new plans calling for a substantial increase in marketed production and profits.

Although transfer of a fourth group of enterprises to the new system was to take place on October 1, 1966, Gosplan's Interdepartmental Committee (the agency charged with handling the transfer of industrial enterprises to the new system) decided—in accord with requests by several ministries—that this move would be premature and recommended that it be delayed until January 1, 1967. When this transfer is completed, it is expected that enterprises from such entire branches of industry as textiles and sugar and from other areas including machine-building, together accounting for a third of total industrial employment, will be operating within the new system.[109]

109. On the application of the new reforms, see: "Itogi raboty 43 predpriiatii—tsifry i fakty" [Results of the Work of 43 Enterprises—Facts and Figures], *Ekonomicheskaia gazeta*, No. 19, 1966, p. 19; *ibid.*, No. 6, 1966, p. 31; N. Drogichinskii, "Eshche dvesti" [Two Hundred More], *ibid.*, No. 18, 1966, p. 8; "Khoziaistvennaia reforma i ekonomicheskaia rabota na predpriiatiiakh" [The Economic Reform and the Work of the Enterprises], *ibid.*, No. 33, 1966, p. 13; "V Mezhduvedomstvennoi komissii pri Gosplane SSSR po voprosam perevoda promyshlennykh predpriiatii na novuiu sistemu planirovaniia i ekonomicheskogo stimulirovaniia" [In Gosplan's Interdepartmental Committee on the Transfer of Industrial Enterprises to the New System of Planning and Incentives], *ibid.*, No. 35, 1966, p. 19; V. F. Garbuzov, "Biudzhet pervogo goda novoi piatiletki"

The Soviet government considered 1966 a preparatory year, making a concerted effort to lay the legal groundwork for the reforms and to inform enterprise directors on the new provisions. Many conferences were organized for this purpose within ministries, planning agencies, and factories, including the following: one at Uralmash in Sverdlovsk on January 26-27; one organized by Gosplan's Interdepartmental Committee in May; those organized by the Ministries of Light Industry and Trade in May and June; one organized jointly by the State Committee on Supplying Materials and Equipment and the editorial offices of *Ekonomicheskaia gazeta* on July 5; and one organized jointly by *Ekonomicheskaia gazeta* and the local Party agencies in Novosibirsk on July 25-26 with one thousand participants.[110] Additional meetings are certainly to be foreseen. The initial results for factories operating within the new system have received considerable publicity, and innumerable articles have appeared in the press on this subject.

Of course, such preparation on legal, educational, and informative levels is not enough to ensure success of the reforms. Success will hinge at least as much on fulfillment of three preconditions: (1) reform of wholesale prices; (2) introduction of long-range profitability rates for capital owned by enterprises or loaned to them; and (3) introduction of long-range rates for the

[Budget for the First Year of the New Five-Year Plan], *Finansy SSSR*, No. 1, 1966, pp. 8-9; Kosygin, speech at the 23rd Party Congress, *Pravda*, April 6, 1966, p. 4; "Novaia sistema vkhodit v zhizn" [The New System Is Going into Effect], *ibid.*, July 19, 1966, p. 1; Kosygin, *ibid.*, August 4, 1966, p. 3.

Instructions on methods and provisional regulations on the reform were published in *Ekonomicheskaia gazeta*, Nos. 6, 7, 11, 12, 13, 17, and 21, 1966.

110. "Khoziaistvennaia reforma i ekonomika predpriiatiia—Konferentsiia na Uralmashzavode" [The Economic Reform and the Economy of the Enterprises—Conference at the Uralmash Factory], *ibid.*, Nos. 5, 6, 7, and 8, 1966; *Planovoe khoziaistvo*, No. 7, 1966, pp. 31-41; "Predpriiatiia v novykh usloviiakh" [Enterprises in the New Conditions], *Ekonomicheskaia gazeta*, No. 25, 1966, pp. 26-31; "Tovarooborot i pribyl" [Turnover and Profit], *ibid.*, No. 23, 1966, pp. 26-28; "Ekonomicheskaia reforma i khoziaistvennyi dogovor" [The Economic Reform and the Contract], *ibid.*, No. 30, 1966, pp. 18-20; and *ibid.*, No. 33, 1966, pp. 13-17.

levies on profits to be used to finance the various funds managed by the enterprise. The most important prerequisite is reform of wholesale prices. For the time being, the rental charge on capital can be applied only in sectors liable to the turnover tax (essentially consumer goods and petroleum). In order to extend the rental charge, prices of producer goods will have to be raised, an action that poses a delicate problem.

According to V. Sitnin, chairman of Gosplan's Committee on Prices, work on revising prices was barely under way in November, 1965.[111] In extractive industries (coal, petroleum, iron mining) there will have to be "token prices" to ensure normal profitability for every enterprise. That is to say, a system of subsidies is in effect proposed for that sector. In the case of processing industries, prices are expected to be based on average costs in each industry so that each enterprise will have an incentive to make the best possible use of its resources. Sitnin insists on the need for uniform prices throughout the whole country. For new products, he advocates fixing provisional prices that would be revised automatically after serial production gets under way. Partial revisions of prices are also expected for industries put onto the new planning system before 1967-68.

The basic outline of the prospective price reform was revealed in October, 1966.[112] While foreseeing maintenance of retail prices at their present level, Gosplan's Committee on Prices envisages the following rises in wholesale prices (in per cent): heavy industry, 11-12; coal, 75; gas, 55; crude petroleum, 100; fuel oil, 10; gasoline and kerosene, no change; and ferrous and nonferrous metals, 35-40. Railroad tariffs are expected to be increased for short hauls and lowered for long hauls.

Such increases are to be made feasible by setting the follow-

111. V. Sitnin, "Tsena—vazhnyi instrument khoziaistvovaniia" [Price—An Important Instrument of Economic Management], *Pravda*, November 12, 1965, p. 2.

112. Sitnin, *Kommunist*, No. 14, 1966 (reproduced entirely in translation in *Documentazione sui Paisi dell' Est*, October 15, 1966, pp. 1561-76). A. Komin, "Problemy sovershenstvovaniia optovykh tsen promyshlennosti" [Problems of Improving Wholesale Prices in Industry], *Planovoe khoziaistvo*, No. 10, 1966, pp. 10-16.

ing new levels of profitability in relation to fixed and working capital (in per cent): total industry, 15 (also 13-16 per cent of costs as compared with about 10 per cent at present); electricity, 10; coal, 7.5; ferrous metals, 8-15; machine-building industry, 15; chemical industry, 15 (compared with 20 at present); lumber, 20 (compared with 8 at present); textiles, 15 (except 3 for cotton and woolen textiles); and light industry, 30-35 (except 6-8 in certain cases).

The new prices and profitability norms do not seem to have met with unanimous approval in the Soviet Union, especially among the partisans of "prices of production." Several associates of the Institute of Electronic Computers for Management (A. S. Kronrod, L. M. Voronina, Iu. F. Nazarov, V. D. Belkin, I. N. Buzova, and others) prepared a model of the national economy for 1964 and for 1959-64 in which "economically valid" prices were based on the ratio of profit to wages, with some account being taken of differential rents. These calculations, which yielded an aggregate profitability rate of 14.2 per cent, were considered by those who made them to form the necessary basis for introducing economic methods of management in the national economy.[113] Quite large increases in wholesale prices and railroad tariffs resulted from these calculations: 53 per cent for ferrous and nonferrous metals, 27 per cent for machine-building, 83 per cent for coal, 64 per cent for electric power, 30 per cent for chemicals, 29 per cent for lumber, 48 per cent for construction materials, 24 per cent for construction and assembly work, and 42 per cent for merchandising.

The general increase in prices of producer goods called for under these proposals would certainly be much greater than the 11 to 12 per cent suggested by Sitnin. He was probably referring to these calculations when he criticized certain economists for proposing that prices of producer goods be raised by 40 to 45 per cent. The arguments made by Sitnin against so large an increase clearly demonstrate the practical difficulties confronted in trying to fix prices that are "economically valid" or that are based on "socially necessary cost."

113. Belkin and Buzova, *Ekonomicheskie metody*, pp. 14-15.

Sitnin argues that price increases should not play a major economic role and that they must be introduced with caution. Care must be taken in his view to prevent a rise in retail prices and to maintain the present economic relationship between industry and agriculture. The recent price reductions decreed by the government for agricultural machinery, spare parts, and tires should be maintained; and increases in the prices of basic products, such as coal, must be restrained to prevent a consequent rise in the industrial price level as a whole. Sitnin speaks out against theoretical proposals for a uniform pricing policy, denying in the first place that there are now separate pricing policies for producer and consumer goods. He cites existence of high profits in production of producer goods, like petroleum, gas, and several types of machinery, and existence of losses in production of some consumer goods and services. He believes that the proposed levels of wholesale prices and profitability are consistent in general with present consumption, investment, and distribution of income. In other words, Sitnin fears that a rise in wholesale prices sufficiently large to make them "economically valid" would create new political problems in the area of distribution of income. This fear of compromising established governmental policy no doubt leads Sitnin to defend present authoritarian methods of price formation and to deny the need for improving them.

A timetable set up early in 1966[114] called for revisions in the wholesale prices for light industry after October 1 to facilitate adjustment to the new system on the part of enterprises that were to be incorporated into it on that date. For some machinery enterprises to be incorporated at the same time, a minor reform in wholesale prices was to be introduced on July 1. Since the date for transfer of these enterprises into the new system has been postponed from October 1 to January 1, 1967, it is not clear at the moment whether these price reforms have actually occurred. In any case, general introduction of new wholesale prices was

114. A. Bachurin, "Etapy vnedreniia novoi sistemy" [Stages of Introducing the New System], speech at the conference of the Uralmash Machine-Building Plant in Sverdlovsk on January 26-27, 1966, *Ekonomicheskaia gazeta*, No. 7, 1966, p. 4.

fixed for July 1, 1967, and a recent article by Sitnin[115] confirms that this date still holds.

The experience of past years shows that it is difficult to predict exactly when a general price reform will be introduced. The last general reform of wholesale prices dates back to 1949. Since then, there have been partial reforms, the one of 1955 being more far-reaching than the others. In July, 1960, the Soviet government decided that a general revision of prices for equipment and machinery should be carried out in the course of 1961 and 1962. That revision, which was soon extended to all wholesale prices, was at first to be enforced early in 1963. It has since been postponed from year to year, the last deadline being January 1, 1966. The scope and difficulty of work involved in such a revision of wholesale prices is indicated by the fact that final drafts of price lists have come to 38,400 printed pages.[116]

Adoption of the principle of interest or rental charges on capital makes all this work futile. Preparation of new wholesale prices will be even more difficult than in the past for several reasons. According to Belkin and Buzova, revisions should be made in accordance with new principles of price formation, they should be completed more rapidly (within a year and a half instead of four years), they should be most significant for critical prices, and they should have the net effect of enhancing the role of prices in organizing the economy.[117] Hence it is evident that the new price reform may give rise to a number of controversies postponing the effective date of the October reforms beyond 1968.

The other reform, which consists in establishing profitability rates for capital and levies on profits to be paid into the different funds managed by the enterprise, is a prerequisite equally hard to carry out.

When the first group of enterprises was introduced into the new system, each was assigned its own norms for levies on prof-

115. Sitnin, *Kommunist*, No. 14, 1966.

116. Marie-Louise Lavigne, "La réforme des prix de gros dans biens d'équipement en URSS," *Le Courrier des Pays de l'Est*, November 4, 1964, p. 35.

117. Belkin and Buzova, *Ekonomicheskie metody*, p. 19.

its. Norms were then broadened to cover groups of enterprises on a provisional basis starting in the second or third quarter of 1966. A twofold explanation has officially been given for failure to adhere entirely to the principle of uniform norms: faults in pricing are such that differences in profitability are only temporarily significant, and introduction of the new system was not accompanied by revisions in budgetary relations. Additional profits were simply to be obtained by undertaking production over and above the plan.

The earliest efforts to develop norms for groups of enterprises gave rise to serious difficulties. The first problem was how to group enterprises. If they were to be classified according to state of technology, the backward state of some enterprises might be perpetuated. If, on the other hand, they were to be classified according to achieved level of profitability, the most efficient and profitable enterprises might be penalized. Some commentators such as A. Miliukov proposed grouping on the basis of similar productive activities, but others objected that this criterion was not sufficient in itself. Miliukov suggested also taking account of the structure of assets (the ratio of fixed to working capital, the share composed of plant, etc.) and of special characteristics of each industrial branch (degree of concentration of production, cost of raw materials, etc.). Miliukov argued in addition that "branches" needed to be more clearly defined through new regulations.[118] Economists disagree on the question of uniformity of norms. S. Shkurko, for example, proposes that there be a uniform norm for each group of enterprises in the cases of marketed production and profit but different norms in the case of profitability.[119] The tasks facing economists who are to apply the reforms are not easy.

As pointed out in Chapters 4 and 5, the difficulty was clearly seen during the discussion of Liberman's theses in the fall of 1962. Classification of enterprises into profitability categories

118. A. Miliukov, "Pooshchritelnye fondy i gruppovye normativy" [Incentive Funds and Group Norms], *Ekonomicheskaia gazeta*, No. 24, 1966, p. 17.

119. Shkurko, *ibid.*, No. 8, 1966, p. 21.

poses many serious problems, and it would be a delusion to pretend that norms could be of long duration. In accepting this part of Liberman's proposals, the Soviet government seems to have been willing to accept inconveniences less grave than those caused by the present free use of capital. However, the adopted solution is even more complicated than the one suggested by Liberman in September, 1962. Instead of making the long-range profitability rates a substitute for price reform and postponing the latter, the government is bent on putting through both reforms at the same time. It is obvious that this dual policy, however reasonable it may seem, will not be easy to put into operation within such a short period as two or three years.

The reforms of October, 1965, as they stand do not confer any material advantages directly on the enterprises. The advantages are to be felt only indirectly as a result of more economical management.[120] They will depend to a great extent on how three problems connected with practical application of reforms are solved: first, how rental charges on capital are to be paid; second, what rental rates are set; and third, how the problem of making plans coherent is solved.

Under the present system, charges are made for capital only indirectly in the form of tax payments on profits. In principle, these taxes are designed to make up for unjustified differences in profitability. The logic of the new system requires that rental rates on capital be fixed every year to take into account the structure of production and the cooperation between enterprises at various stages of production. If such a procedure is followed, it is difficult to see how rental rates on capital and levies on profits for benefit of funds managed by enterprises could be of long duration. There would be a return to the current practice of penalizing enterprises for performance this year by raising objectives for next year.

Some Soviet economists have noted this problem. For example, V. Filippov believes that, in order to avoid encouraging

120. The enterprise stands to benefit directly from higher rates of payments into funds managed by it. However, these rates are still to be fixed.

production advantageous to the enterprise but useless to the state, it would be necessary to single out instances of good and bad results attributable solely to changes in the structure of production and to make proper allowance for such cases in evaluating an enterprise's performance. Either the changes in profits reflecting only modifications in the structure of output as imposed by the annual plan should be deducted from profit, or marketed production should be used to determine incentive funds or the long-term rates at which levies are made on profits for the benefit of incentive funds. The first solution, which would not jeopardize the stability of levies on profits, is preferred by Filippov. Changes in the structure of production that reflect trends in value desirable to both enterprise and consumer should not be subject to corrective adjustment. As for the practical possibilities of introducing such correctives, Filippov cites practices in the machine-tool industry (1955-56), the Moscow region Sovnarkhoz (1957-62), and the Moscow City Sovnarkhoz (1962-64), whereby the sums to go into the enterprise fund and the deductions from them for housing needs were determined.[121]

It seems doubtful that such alterations would remedy the defects of a system of long-term rates. Their effect would be to make matters impossibly complicated by raising additional controversies. Generally speaking, the envisaged system of capital charges and incentive payments could function satisfactorily only under flexible planning, allowing every enterprise to choose that structure of production most advantageous to it. Trying to introduce such flexibility into a framework of administrative planning would have as much effect as adding a fifth wheel to an automobile.

The advantages a Soviet enterprise might derive from the present reforms depend heavily on the interest rates (rental charges) to be imposed on capital. If the government fixes the rates too high, it may force enterprises to suffer losses, leading to explicit or implicit subsidies. If the interest rate is too low, capital will not be efficiently utilized. And if the government

121. Filippov, *ibid.*, No. 51, 1965, p. 9.

pushes differentiation of rates in accord with profitability too far, controversies will arise and limit the economic advantages of the operation.

The government's solution to the problem of making plans coherent will also be of major importance. In order to ensure success of the reform, the government will have to reduce the tautness of plans to avoid the wide-spreading consequences of unforeseen disturbances. The past gives little reason to expect such a policy.

Finally, the success of reforms will surely depend on how they are applied. Unless solutions are found that are satisfactory to enterprises, they will not wish to ask for higher targets. Bargaining with higher agencies (now the ministries) will continue, and there is no reason to assume that the interests of enterprise and government will always coincide.

CHAPTER 8. Permanence and Change in Soviet Planning

It is certainly too early to draw up a balance sheet for planning reforms undertaken since Stalin's death. It may, however, be of interest to single out some permanent features inherent in the system that seem to resist the reforming trend, elements that can be attributed neither to Stalin nor to the level of maturity of the Soviet economy in the 1930's.

CENTRALIZATION OF AUTHORITY

The principle of centralized authority in planning does not seem to have been shaken in recent reforms. While claiming to liberate the enterprise from the supervision of higher agencies, the Soviet leadership still imposes all the essential elements making up an enterprise's plan: quantity and quality of output, suppliers and customers, employment, wages, costs, profits, and investments.

At higher echelons, stability of political power is matched by instability of central planning and managerial agencies. Administrative reorganization and shifts in positions of responsibility are the typical reactions of the Party when confronted with economic difficulties.

The old idea still thrives: that the plan, as an expression of the Party's will, is intangible and that real life moves according to it. As Khrushchev put it at the Plenary Session of the Party Central Committee on November 19, 1962: "Comrades! In a socialist country, the national economy evolves strictly according to the plan."[1] One should not be surprised, then, when a Soviet author exclaims: "The plan is law!"[2]

Because of the confusion between compulsory and accounting

1. N. S. Khrushchev, *Stroitelstvo kommunizma v SSSR i razvitie selskogo khoziaistva* [Building of Communism in the U.S.S.R. and the Development of Agriculture], Moscow, 1963, VII, p. 358.

2. D. Onika, "Plan i materialnoe stimulirovanie" [The Plan and Material Incentives], *Voprosy ekonomiki*, No. 11, 1962, p. 29.

indexes, what is plan for a higher agency becomes command for a lower one. Such odd but current expressions as "planning *for* the enterprise" or "*bringing* the plan *to* the enterprise" mean in common parlance nothing more than "preparing directives" or "handing down commands."

All this was well known in the Stalinist system of planning. It is important to note that recent reforms have brought virtually no change as far as decentralization in economic control is concerned. In agriculture, the planning powers of Party and government have actually been enhanced recently, so that collective and state farms are far removed from control over their own plans.[3]

3. One can hardly fail to notice the inconsistencies in Khrushchev's approach to agricultural planning. On the one hand, he vigorously condemned the practice (contrary to the decree of March 9, 1955) of imposing sowing and production plans on collective and state farms, and protested against the bureaucratic approach of controlling agencies (speech of February 28, 1964). On the other hand, two months later (speech of April 13) he denounced what he described as anarchy and haphazard production on collective farms, declaring that "agricultural production must be controlled." In the same speech he added, however, that control should be in the form of recommendations rather than directives and that bureaucratic interference and direct administrative orders should be avoided.

The spirit of control characterized all decisions on agriculture made by the Soviet government after 1961. On February 25, 1961, the Committee of State Procurements was formed (under Chairman N. G. Ignatev); on March 22, 1962, the Collective and State Farm Territorial Administrations were created. The latter had jurisdiction over planning and "guiding" production and procurements, examining financial plans, and supervising implementation of plans. Another reform, introduced in November, 1962, created special Party bureaus for agriculture and tightened control even further. All that, however, did not satisfy Khrushchev: on April 19, 1964, he created a special commission, headed by N. V. Podgorny and composed of top Party leaders (L. I. Brezhnev, G. I. Voronov, A. N. Kosygin, A. I. Mikoyan, D. S. Polianskii, P. F. Lomako, V. E. Dymshits, V. N. Novikov, etc.), to make further recommendations on how to organize production of certain commodities (eggs, meat, poultry) and to "improve the work of Collective and State Farm Territorial Administrations."

See *Pravda*, March 7 and April 24, 1964; the March 22, 1962, decree in K. I. Orliankin (ed.), *Sbornik reshenii po selskomu khoziaistvu* [Collection of Decisions on Agriculture], Moscow, 1963, pp. 577-88; Howard R. Swearer, "Agricultural Administration under Khrushchev," in *Soviet Agricultural and Peasant Affairs*, edited by Roy D. Laird (Lawrence, Kansas, 1963), pp. 9-40.

Some Western specialists believe that the over-all effect of reforms enacted between 1956 and 1962 was to centralize even more the planning, administration, and management of the Soviet economy.[4]

ARBITRARY GOALS AND INTERNAL INCONSISTENCY OF PLANS

The arbitrary fixing of goals that prevailed under Stalin was recently denounced again by Khrushchev in the following terms:

"In the practices of planning agencies, we have not yet overcome the legacy of the cult of personality, which led to plans without adequate economic foundations and without assurance of success or necessary resources . . . [Such plans] are not always based on economic analysis or conscientious calculations: growth rates for the various industries and economic regions are fixed in accord with existing trends and sometimes entirely by rule of thumb."[5]

The practice of summing up individual goals instead of selecting among them on the basis of available resources, the manipulation of consumption coefficients for materials, and the revision of already accepted norms are often responsible for lack of coherence in the plan at the central level.[6] At lower levels and particularly at the enterprise, haggling often replaces study of real capacities. The authority that "hands down the plan" puts on pressure for a raising of targets, while the economic unit that "receives the plan" tries to minimize its capacities and conceal its resources. Bargaining begins in this way, and a variety of subterfuges is used by the enterprise to obtain maximum resources from the budget for investments.[7]

On the defects in Soviet agricultural planning after Khrushchev's fall, see Brezhnev's speech of March 24, 1965, *Pravda*, March 27, 1965, pp. 2-4.

4. See, *e.g.*, Gregory Grossman, "The Soviet Economy," *Problems of Communism*, March-April, 1963, p. 39.

5. Khrushchev, *Stroitelstvo kommunizma v SSSR*, VII, pp. 358 and 359.

6. *Ibid.*, p. 365; also A. Kochubei, "Nazrevshie voprosy sovershenstvovaniia planirovaniia" [Current Questions of Improving Planning], *Planovoe khoziaistvo*, No. 11, 1962, p. 10.

7. See "Stroitelstvo kommunizma i planirovanie" [The Building of Communism and Planning], *Planovoe khoziaistvo*, No. 10, 1962, p. 5.

It is hard to see how reforms under way could improve this state of affairs. Argumentation about the plan in the Council of Ministers, which is responsible in large part for lack of coherence in the plan, will certainly not be eliminated by the new structure of planning and managerial agencies. And there is just as little chance that haggling at the enterprise level will disappear. As long as the plan maintains its mystical character, overfulfillment will remain the primary success criterion, and enterprises will prefer to minimize targets rather than to compromise in the hope of gaining hypothetical bonuses.

Some improvement in coordination of the plan might be achieved through continuous planning. Experience shows, however, that it has not been possible to put annual revision of long-range plans into practice, and so far the elaboration of two-year plans and general application of long-term contracts between enterprises have been advanced only to an experimental stage.

As long as the Soviet government persists in maintaining its centralized and authoritarian system of planning, improvement in the internal consistency of plans can come only from changes in economic policy that slow down the pace of growth, build up reserves, or give higher priority to consumption. Such options were available before the reform movement began.

THE PLAN AS CRITERION OF PERFORMANCE

Use of the plan as the criterion of performance is one of the basic characteristics of Stalinist administrative planning. This practice,

---

Reductions in imaginary costs written into the plan have a real effect because they can be used to justify certain investments. In the Ukrainian Republic the 1962 plan included 74,000,000 rubles of alleged reduction in the cost of machines that became financial resources for investment. It was obvious, however, from results for 1961 and calculations for 1962 that equipment supplied to shops in the Ukraine had not become any cheaper. See Kochubei, *ibid.*, No. 11, 1962, p. 11.

It seems quite improbable that the rental charges for capital and the interest rates for investment credits provided by the October, 1965, reforms could eliminate bargaining. Inasmuch as the enterprise must obey an order to produce and to sell its output at fixed prices, it will always try to prove that plans less advantageous to it cannot be fulfilled and that plans most advantageous should be accepted by the authorities.

never without flaws, has lost much of its propaganda value in the country at large over the course of recent years. The Soviet government has shifted to emphasis on economic competition with the United States, Soviet performance being measured by growth rates and valuations compared with American experience. Although Soviet statistics are generally considered unreliable in the West,[8] such measures of performance are based on hard facts that cannot be manipulated at will like planned targets.

At the enterprise level, the plan imposed from above still remains the criterion of performance. The defects of that

8. According to recent Western calculations, the Soviet indexes of national income, industrial output, and agricultural production remain overstated. See Abram Bergson and Simon Kuznets (eds.), *Economic Trends in the Soviet Union* (Cambridge, Mass., 1963); *Dimensions of Soviet Economic Power* (Washington, 1962); G. Warren Nutter, "The Effect of Economic Growth on Sino-Soviet Strategy," in David M. Abshire and Richard V. Allen (eds.), *National Security: Political, Military and Economic Strategies in the Decade Ahead* (New York, 1963), pp. 149-68.

As to agriculture, harvests have been reported the last several years at bunker weight, *i.e.*, before cleaning and drying. The shortage of adequately constructed storage facilities makes that estimate much higher than one for stored crops. For the year 1960, the official figure is 134.4 million tons of grain, while the U.S. Department of Agriculture estimates only 100 million tons of stored grain, and Naum Jasny ("The Soviet Statistical Yearbooks for 1955 through 1960," *Slavic Review*, March, 1962, p. 129), 115 million tons. Slightly different estimates exist for grain, excluding corn: 112.9 million tons according to A. Kahan; between 93.1 and 93.6 million tons according to the U.S. Department of Agriculture, as cited by Mrs. L. Richter (see *Soviet Agricultural and Peasant Affairs*, p. 166).

According to official statistics, both national income and industrial production in the Soviet Union were roughly 60 per cent of the U.S. level in 1960 (see *Narodnoe khoziaistvo SSSR v 1961 godu* [U.S.S.R. National Economy in 1961], Moscow, 1962, p. 139). According to estimates made by Western economists, Soviet gross national product amounted to the following percentages of the U.S. level in 1960: 24 to 31 per cent, according to Nutter (in *National Security*, p. 160); 46.7 per cent, according to Stanley Cohn (in *Dimensions of Soviet Economic Power*, p. 76); and 48 per cent, according to Abram Bergson (in *Challenge*, March, 1963, p. 5). Soviet industrial production in 1960 was estimated as 29 per cent of the U.S. level by Nutter (in *National Security*, p. 160), and as 75.0 to 76.4 per cent by A. Tarn and R. W. Campbell (in "A Comparison of U.S. and Soviet Industrial Output," *American Economic Review*, September, 1962, p. 718). It should be noted that the Tarn-Campbell estimate was described even by V. N. Starovskii, head of the Central Statistical Administration, as "somewhat exaggerated" (see "Nauchnaia konferentsiia po voprosam metodologii

criterion, long stressed, are still there. The plan, incapable of providing a synthesized view of an enterprise's activities, is unstable and difficult to control. In most cases, it is also inequitable because it penalizes good performance in one year by imposing more difficult targets in the following year.

Everything done so far that bears on the plan's role as the criterion of success has amounted to nothing more than rearrangement of the existing system. Use of profit as the sole and synthetic measure of performance—as suggested by Liberman, Vaag, or Nemchinov—has been rejected. Instead, the criteria for fulfillment of the plan are being multiplied and diversified. In recent years, gross production has sometimes been replaced with marketed production or experimentally with "standard processing cost."[9] The reforms of October, 1965, emphasize marketed production or sold shipments, profits, and fulfillment of the plan for compulsory deliveries as criteria to be used jointly.[10] Supplementary noncompulsory or so-called accounting indexes have

---

sopostavleniia osnovnykh ekonomicheskikh pokazatelei SSSR i SShA" [Scientific Conference on Methodological Questions in Comparing the Basic Indexes of the U.S.S.R. and the United States], *Voprosy ekonomiki*, No. 10, 1963, p. 123).

9. *Normativnaia stoimost obrabotki.* This evaluation of production covers wages (including social insurance), amortization, and overhead factory and shop costs. In other words, it is gross value of production minus profits and cost of materials (excluding overhead costs). See L. Vaag and S. Zakharov, "Platnost proizvodstvennykh fondov i pribyl predpriiatiia" [Payments for Use of Productive Capital and Profits of the Enterprise], *Voprosy ekonomiki*, No. 4, 1963, p. 90.

In his *Pravda* article of September 9, 1962, Liberman criticized this index, used mainly in the garment industry, contending that it stimulated production of garments for which there was not sufficient demand.

On extending use of the index, see V. Lagutkin, "Planovye pokazateli—stimuly povysheniia ekonomichnosti proizvodstva" [Planning Indexes—an Incentive to Increase Saving in Production], *Kommunist*, No. 5, 1964, pp. 88-96; N. Ivanov, Iu. Bulynin, and V. Kondakov, "Planirovanie po normativnoi stoimosti obrabotki" [Planning Based on Standard Processing Costs], *Planovoe khoziaistvo*, No. 10, 1964, pp. 25-39. The last article was summarized and commented on in *L'URSS et les Pays de l'Est: Revue des Revues*, Strasbourg University, No. 4, 1965, pp. 849-52. For a criticism of "standard processing cost," see I. S. Malyshev, *Science économique et pratique des affaires*, Moscow, 1964, pp. 9-10.

10. *Pravda*, October 10, 1965, p. 1.

multiplied. The distinction of compulsory and noncompulsory indexes is, however, purely formal, so that the result is a body of haphazard and often contradictory directives which make it impossible to evaluate the real cost of executing the plan.[11]

PROSPECTS FOR FURTHER REFORMS

The salient feature of recent reforms is their subordination to the framework of administrative planning. The system implied by these reforms is much less flexible than what was proposed by advocates of fundamental reform, dashing even the hopes raised by prospects of general application of the "direct links" experiment. What has happened is nothing more than yet another timid adjustment of the existing system of administrative planning.

Will this adjustment favor more rational economic decisions in the enterprise? Will the hopes placed in charges for use of capital be justified? In principle, such charges should encourage more economical use of capital. However, several obstacles are inherent in the administrative planning system. First, the charges may not correspond to the actual return of capital. Second, the enterprise may not be allowed to make its own decisions on the use of capital, in part because of a fear that its interests will clash with those of the state. In other words, it may be advantageous (*i.e.*, "rational") for the enterprise to ignore the long-term macroeconomic objectives (*i.e.*, "rationality") of central agencies. Third, gains for the enterprise from the promised autonomy may be quite insignificant, leaving it only with the additional burden of charges for capital.

Despite the cautious nature of recent reforms, their survival is precarious because of numerous circumscribing conditions and contradictions brought about by trying to introduce flexibility into the administrative system while simultaneously establishing the vast bureaucratic apparatus of industrial ministries. These ministries have to implement planning, supervise production, and resolve problems of supplying materials and equipment,

11. Vaag and Zakharov, *Voprosy ekonomiki*, No. 4, 1963, p. 89.

finance, employment, and wages. If there had been a real desire to liberalize the economy, it would have been more logical to adopt a different course: gradual transfer of the power of Sovnarkhozes to enterprises and to producers' unions (firms), thus promoting flexible planning.

The fragile nature of recent reforms also stems from the hesitant attitude of government. One gets the impression that the collective leadership in the present Soviet government is subject to a variety of pressures, often from opposing directions, and that reforms staggered over a period of two or three years are, above all, a device to gain time. The tentative character of reforms may soon render them insufficient, and new decisions may have to be made whether to go "forward" or "backward."

To sum up, it looks as though the Soviet Union will, for some time to come, stick to the system of "continuous adjustments" of administrative methods of planning and management, masking its refusal to face radical reforms.

The proliferation of reforms and adjustments raises the question of the future orientation of the Soviet system. Several Western economists—such as Abram Bergson, Alexander Erlich, Rush V. Greenslade, Herbert Levine, and G. Warren Nutter—doubt the possibility of piecemeal conversion to a kind of market socialism.[12] Others, such as Henri Chambre, see the problem in the terms set in 1921 by Lenin: Who whom (*kto kovo*)? Who will win out? According to Chambre, it is not a question of a market economy versus a planned socialist economy, but of an economy managed from the center on the basis of a mathematically calculated central plan versus an economy managed in a decentralized fashion on the basis of a central but nonadministrative plan.[13]

It is difficult to foresee at this time the evolution of the Soviet

12. "A Round Table Discussion. Soviet Economic Performance and Reform: Some Problems of Analysis and Prognosis," *Slavic Review*, June, 1966, pp. 228-30; Rush Greenslade, "The Soviet Economic System in Transition," in *New Directions in the Soviet Economy*, Joint Economic Committee, 89th Congress, 2nd Session (Washington, 1966), Part I, pp. 14-17.

13. Henri Chambre, *L'Economie Planifiée* (Paris, 1966), pp. 125-26.

planning system. It was born in an authoritarian spirit of intolerance and is in a way a by-product of excessive centralization. But erosion of centralism is a problem not only of economic efficiency but also of social relations, and economic studies can say only that the direction in which the standard of living is moving and the complexity of the modern industrial system do not favor such centralism. As for the immediate future, we can observe only that the Soviet Union is slipping into a heterogeneous administrative system more and more complicated by the many experiments imposed one on top of the other. The "coexistence" of enterprises operating on different economic systems wears away ideological prejudices and answers the needs of the moment, but it introduces a certain amount of disorder and confusion and, by arousing new demands, creates a certain stir. The difficulty involved in eliminating authoritarian centralized planning of an administrative type does not really seem so surprising if we remember that ideological premises of the Stalinist system and the immense Party and governmental apparatus have not yet changed very much.

The question remains whether Soviet leaders can long continue ignoring the real criteria of economic and social performance, namely, satisfaction of the citizenry and economic competition with Western countries. It is these criteria that the Soviet government must eventually face in appraising the "profitability" of its administrative, authoritarian, and centralized system and in judging whether the time has come for fundamental reform.

Index of Names

Index of Subjects

M

N

O

P

R

www.ingramcontent.com/pod-product-compliance
Lightning Source LLC
Chambersburg PA
CBHW020351270326
41926CB00007B/394

* 9 7 8 0 8 0 7 8 7 3 8 6 1 *